PERGAMON INTERNATIONAL LIBRARY
of Science, Technology, Engineering and Social Studies

The 1000-volume original paperback library in aid of education, industrial training and the enjoyment of leisure

Publisher: Robert Maxwell, M.C.

THE MIND–BODY PROBLEM

A Psychobiological Approach

THE PERGAMON TEXTBOOK
INSPECTION COPY SERVICE

An inspection copy of any book published in the Pergamon International Library will gladly be sent to academic staff without obligation for their consideration for course adoption or recommendation. Copies may be retained for a period of 60 days from receipt and returned if not suitable. When a particular title is adopted or recommended for adoption for class use and the recommendation results in a sale of 12 or more copies, the inspection copy may be retained with our compliments. The Publishers will be pleased to receive suggestions for revised editions and new titles to be published in this important International Library.

Foundations and Philosophy of Science
and Technology Series

General Editor: MARIO BUNGE

Some Titles in the Series:

THE MIND–BODY PROBLEM

A Psychobiological Approach

by

MARIO BUNGE,

Foundations and Philosophy of Science Unit,
McGill University, Montreal

Epilogue by DONALD O. HEBB
Professor Emeritus of Psychology, McGill University

PERGAMON PRESS

Oxford · New York · Toronto · Sydney · Paris · Frankfurt

U.K.	Pergamon Press Ltd., Headington Hill Hall, Oxford OX3 0BW, England
U.S.A.	Pergamon Press Inc., Maxwell House, Fairview Park, Elmsford, New York 10523, U.S.A.
CANADA	Pergamon of Canada, Suite 104, 150 Consumers Road, Willowdale, Ontario M2J 1P9, Canada
AUSTRALIA	Pergamon Press (Aust.) Pty. Ltd., P.O. Box 544, Potts Point, N.S.W. 2011, Australia
FRANCE	Pergamon Press SARL, 24 rue des Ecoles, 75240 Paris, Cedex 05, France
FEDERAL REPUBLIC OF GERMANY	Pergamon Press GmbH, 6242 Kronberg/Taunus, Pferdstrasse 1, Federal Republic of Germany

First edition 1980

British Library Cataloguing in Publication Data

Bunge, Mario
The mind–body problem.—(Foundations and philosophy of science and technology).—
(Pergamon international library).
1. Mind and body
I. Title II. Series
150   BF161   79–40698

ISBN 0–08–024720–2 Hard cover
ISBN 0–08–024719–9 Flexicover

Printed and bound in Great Britain by
William Clowes (Beccles) Limited, Beccles and London

Contents

Preface

FROM time immemorial people have grown accustomed to accounting for their behavior and their subjective experience in terms of a soul or mind and its putative properties. Thus they say things like 'I have X on my mind', 'I am of two minds about Y', 'May her soul rest in peace', and 'Upon my soul'.

Then, at the beginning of our century, people were told by eminent psychologists and neurophysiologists that all talk of mind was nonscientific—a mere remnant of primitive superstition. They were asked to give up, not only the theological notion of an immaterial and immortal soul, but also the very ideas of mental abilities, dispositions, states, and events. And some of them were successfully trained to speak only of observable facts, whether movements of the whole animal, or of some of their parts.

This ban on the concept of mind paralyzed some philosophers, particularly those with positivistic leanings—since, after all, they had inspired the behaviorist movement. But others went on writing about minds, intentions, mental images, and the like. This was to be expected, for most philosophers do not listen to scientists.

In the meantime the eminent Jean Piaget, oblivious of behaviorist prohibitions, went on investigating the emergence and growth of mental abilities in children and adolescents. Two decades later another equally influential rebellion spread: Donald Hebb stated that neuron assemblies may not only detect and process external stimuli but may also ideate. And he said loudly that human psychology is about the mind. Shortly thereafter the linguist Noam Chomsky launched a direct attack on mindless psychology—without, unfortunately, rescuing the nervous system. This signaled the beginning of the end of the long and boring behaviorist night.

The concept of mind is now back and probably for good. Not only psychologists and philosophers but also some neurophysiologists dare now write about it. Even ethologists are discovering that animals other than men can become aware of what they do, and try to explain some of their behavior on the assumption that they have mental abilities.

Is this comeback of the concept of mind a mere return of the old theological idea of an immaterial and possibly endurable entity hovering above the brain and surviving the dissolution of the latter? In some cases it is. To be sure, such a resurrection is of no great help to science: even though we do need the idea of an idea, that idea need not be idealistic, nay it cannot be if it is to harmonize with science. Because science deals with concrete entities only, because it acknowledges only properties of such entities rather than properties in themselves, it has no use for properties and changes thereof that fail to be properties or changes of some concrete entity or other, be it atom or neuron, brain or galaxy. There is no harm in speaking of mental states or events provided we do not assign them to an immaterial, unchangeable, and inscrutable entity, but identify them instead with states or events of the brain.

This hypothesis, that mind is a collection of brain functions, is as old as it is half-baked. It has inspired philosophers, physiological psychologists, and neurophysiologists, but it has not yet been formulated as a well-organized theory. Unless it be developed into a theory proper it is but a poor substitute for the myth of the soul. It is certainly more fruitful than the latter—which is actually barren at its best—yet so far it has been only an embryonic conjecture.

The main goal of this book is to try to transform that view—i.e. that mind is a set of brain activities—into a theoretical framework, and moreover one compatible with the latest results obtained by neurophysiologists and psychologists, and capable of inspiring further advances in their research. (Neurophysiology is necessary but not sufficient, for it tends to discard psychological categories such as those of purpose and thought. And psychology, though equally necessary, is insufficient as well—unless it is physiological—for it tends to forget about the nervous system.) That is the constructive part of this book.

This work has also a polemical side. Indeed, it intends to show that the idea of a separate mental entity is not only unwarranted by the available data and the existing psychological models, but collides head-on with the most fundamental ideas of all modern science and is thus a stumbling block to progress.

Data gatherers may care little for either aspect of this book, the theoretical or the critical. But data gathering, though a part of scientific research, is not all of it. As Henri Poincaré noted long ago, science is not a heap of facts but an edifice built of facts and hypotheses; and criticism, far from being alien to science, is the salt of science. This holds particularly with regard to problems, such as that of the nature of mind, which are not only scientific but also philosophical and ideological.

In writing this book I have benefited from exchanges with a number of gifted students as well as with Professors Dalbir Bindra (Psychology, McGill), Theodore H. Bullock (Neurosciences, California, SD), Victor H. Denenberg (Biobehavioral Sciences, Connecticut), José Luis Díaz (Investigaciones Biomédicas, UNAM), Bernardo Dubrovsky (Psychiatry, McGill), Augusto Fernández Guardiola (Instituto Nacional de Neurología y Neurocirugía, México, DF), Rodolfo Llinás (Physiology and Bio-physics, NYU Medical Center), Michel Paradis (Linguistics, McGill), Rodolfo Pérez Pascual (Instituto de Física, UNAM), Harold Pinsker (University of Texas Medical Branch), Pablo Rudomín (Centro de Estudios Avanzados del IPN), Paul Weingartner (Institut für Philosophie, Universität Salzburg), and F. Eugene Yates (Biomedical Engineering, University of Southern California). I am also grateful to my father, Augusto Bunge, MD (1877–1943), for having instilled in me a naturalistic, evolutionary, and science-oriented world view. Last, but not least, I am indebted to my childhood playmates the dachshund Dacki, the Belgian shepherd Rip, and the monkey Titi, for having taught me that man is not alone in having a mind.

MARIO BUNGE

Introduction

THIS book deals with one of the oldest, most intriguing, and most difficult of all the problems belonging in the intersection of science and philosophy, namely the so-called *mind–body problem*. This is the system of ancient questions about the nature of the mental and its relations to the bodily.

Here are some of the problems belonging to the mind–body problem circle. Are mind and body two separate entities? If so, how are they held together in the living organism? How do they get in touch in the beginning, how do they fly asunder at the end, and what becomes of the mind after the breakdown of the body? How do the two entities manage to function synchronically: what does it mean to say that mental states have neural correlates? Do these entities interact, and if so how? And which if any has the upper hand?

If, on the other hand, mind and body are not different entities, is the mind corporeal? Or is it the other way around, namely is the body a form of the mind? Or is each a manifestation of a single (neutral) underlying inaccessible substance? In either case: what is mind? A thing, a collection of states of a thing, a set of events in the thing—or nothing at all? And whatever it is, is it just physical or is it something more? And in the latter case—i.e. if mind is emergent relative to the physical level—can it be explained in a scientific manner or can it be described only in ordinary language?

The mind–body problem is notoriously a hard nut to crack—surely even more so than the problem of matter—so much so that some scientists and philosophers despair of it being soluble at all. We submit that the problem, though tough, is soluble, and shall outline a solution to it in this work. But before doing so we shall have to do some philosophical scouting and conceptual cleansing, because part of the problem is that it is usually formulated in inadequate terms—namely in those of ordinary language. These are inadequate not only because ordinary language is imprecise and poor but also because the European languages are loaded with a preconceived solution to the problem, namely psychophysical dualism, or the doctrine that mind and body are separate entities.

To begin with, the very expression 'mind–body problem' suggests that mind and body are two entities on the same footing, like partners in a common enterprise. Yet we do not speak of the motion–body problem in mechanics, or of the reaction–substance problem in chemistry, or of the digestion–digestive tract problem in physiology, or of the unemployment–unemployed problem in sociology. We do speak, on the other hand, of the motion of bodies, the digestive function of the digestive tract, and so on. We do not reify properties, states, or events— except when it comes to the properties, states, and events of the nervous system. It is imperative that we close this gap that keeps the study of mind a scientific anomaly. We propose to do so by abandoning ordinary language and adopting instead the state space language, which is mathematically precise and is shared by science and scientific philosophy.

A first difficulty with the so-called mind–body problem is, then, that it is usually couched in ordinary language, to the point that even linguistic philosophers, who do not have the least scientific curiosity, feel free to speculate about it. (Cf. the essays in philosophical psychology by Wittgenstein and his followers, notably Anscombe, Austin, Pears, and Wisdom, none of whom pays any attention to physiological or to mathematical psychology.) A second difficulty is the extreme youth of neuroscience: recall that Ramón y Cajal's neuronal hypothesis of the brain is less than one century old and was generally ignored until half a century ago.

There were important sporadic discoveries in earlier times, starting with Hippocrates' hypotheses that the brain—rather than the heart or the liver—is the organ of emotion and thought, and that epilepsy is a brain disorder. However, it is only in recent years that a concerted attack at all levels has been launched—in particular through the Neurosciences Research Program. (See, for example, Worden *et al.*, 1975.)

A third difficulty is that, far from being a strictly scientific problem, ours is also a philosophical one. In fact it is a traditional metaphysical problem and one that has aroused the greatest passion—hence also the greatest caution for fear of repression. Moreover, the very formulation of the mind–body problem presupposes a number of ontological notions that are far from clear in traditional metaphysics—in particular those of substance (or matter), property, state, event, emergence, and level of organization. Thus any argument as to whether or not there is a mental substance, or whether or not there are mental states that fail to be brain states, calls for a prior elucidation of the general concepts of substance and state. (For details on these concepts see Bunge, 1977a.)

Fourth and last, another reason for the backward state of research into the brain–mind problem is that it belongs not only to science and philosophy but also to ideology. Indeed, all religions and some political ideologies have a vested interest in the problem and some even claim exclusive ownership. So, far from being interested in the investigation and discussion of the problem they are anxious to have us accept their own ready-made solutions.

In short, there have been many obstacles in the way of a scientific study of mind. Fortunately some of these obstacles are disappearing rather quickly, and the science of mind is making great strides. In fact, three formerly separate currents are converging: neuroscience, psychology, and philosophy. Over the past two decades neurophysiologists have begun to study mental functions of neural systems, physiological psychologists have started to disclose some of the neural mechanisms "mediating" or "subserving" behavior, and philosophers have begun to analyze some of the key concepts involved in the question and to overhaul the ancient doctrine that mental functions are a kind of bodily function. There is still a long way to go before maturity is attained, but the science of mind has finally got off the ground.

This book will offer an examination of rival doctrines of mind as well as a general framework for building specific theories of mental abilities. Our framework will be as exact as possible, for we believe in clarity, particularly when dealing with tricky and controversial matters. Thus we shall not attempt to answer the question whether mind exists, without first defining the concept of mind: there has been enough obscurity on this point for thousands of years, partly because of the unwillingness of philosophers and theologians to state their theses with a minimum of clarity. But of course we shall not attempt to define every one of our terms, for this would result in circularity. We shall borrow some of them from biology and others from exact philosophy, and shall characterize our basic (undefined) concepts by means of postulates (or initial assumptions), the way it is done in the exact sciences. And in postulating (or assuming), as well as in defining, we shall attempt to lay bare the structure of our concepts. Thus brain properties will be represented by mathematical functions, brain states will be construed as values of lists of certain functions, and brain processes as sequences of such states. By proceeding in this way, rather than in the informal manner characteristic of almost the entire literature on the mind–body problem, we shall avoid obscurity and build a vigorous link with both mathematical neurobiology and exact philosophy. However, the mathematics will be kept to a minimum, and the reader uninterested in formalization will be able to skip the formulas—not, however, statements such as "The mind of an animal is not an entity but a set composed of some of its brain processes".

CHAPTER 1

The Mind–Body Problem

1. The problem and its main proposed solutions

Perceiving, feeling, remembering, imagining, willing, and thinking are usually said to be mental states or processes. (We shall ignore for the moment the quaint view that there are no such facts.) Since there are no states or processes in themselves, but only states *of* some entity and processes *in* some entity, we must ask *what* "minds"—i.e. what is the thing that perceives, feels, remembers, imagines, wills, and thinks. This is the very core of the so-called mind–body problem, i.e. the identification of the subject of the mentalistic predicates.

It is possible to take one of three stands with regard to this problem: that it is a pseudoproblem, that it is a genuine but insoluble problem, and that it is both genuine and soluble. The first attitude was taken by behaviorists, reflexologists, and logical positivists, on the strength of the philosophical tenet that only overt behavior can be studied scientifically. This horse has been dead for quite some time. The second attitude, adopted by Hume (1739) and popularized one century ago by the philosopher–psychologist–sociologist Herbert Spencer (1862) and the physiologist Emil Du Bois–Reymond (1872), is that we do not know and shall never know (*ignoramus et ignorabimus*) how brain activities generate mental phenomena. This belief is as unfashionable as it is sterile.

Those who do hope that the mind–body problem can be solved have proposed two main sets of answers. One is that what minds (perceives, desires, thinks, etc.) is the mind (or soul, or spirit); the other, that it is the brain. According to the former, the mind is an immaterial entity wherein all mental states and processes occur: feelings, memories, ideas, and so on, would be in the mind. According to the second batch of answers, the mind is not a thing apart but a set of brain functions or activities:

perceiving, imagining, thinking, etc., would be brain processes.

Occasionally the advocates of the autonomy of mind deny the reality of bodies and, in general, of concrete things: these are the spiritualistic monists ("There are only experiences"). Nowadays most of the believers in the separate status of mind acknowledge the existence of bodies alongside minds: they are called *psychophysical dualists* and they come in various shades. They are united in the conviction that the mind has an existence apart from the brain.

On the other hand, those who hold that the mental is a corporeal (neural) function are called *psychophysical monists* and they, too, come in various kinds. In particular there are leveler monists on the one hand and emergentist monists on the other. The former deny, while the latter affirm, that the brain differs qualitatively from other material systems, in particular computers. (Equivalently: levelers deny the emergentist thesis that the mental functions of the brain are different from its household functions.) But both levelers and emergentists of the kind we are considering hope to be able to understand the mental by studying the brain components and their interactions: i.e. both are reductionists, though of different sorts. The difference will be explained in the next section.

In sum, there are two main genera of solutions to the mind–body problem, to wit, *psychophysical monism* and *psychophysical dualism*. And each of these sets contains at least five different doctrines (see Table 1.1, adapted from Bunge, 1977b). For details on various such doctrines see Armstrong (1968), Borst (1970), Cheng (1975), Feigl (1967), Globus *et al.* (1976), Glover (1976), Hampshire (1966), Margolis (1978), O'Connor (1969), Popper and Eccles (1977), Smythies (1965), and Vesey (1964). We proceed to a cursory examination of all ten doctrines.

2. Preliminary examination of rival views

We need not consider the independence thesis $\mathscr{D}1$, as both introspection and the neurosciences tell us that the bodily and the mental— whatever the latter may be—are interdependent. As for the parallelism or synchronization thesis $\mathscr{D}2$, it begs the question instead of answering it, for what we want to know is precisely what are the peculiarities of the mental and what the mechanisms that bring about the "parallel"

Table 1.1. *Ten views on the mind–body problem*
ϕ stands for *body* (or *the physical*) and ψ for *mind* (or *the mental*)

Psychophysical monism	Psychophysical dualism
$\mathscr{M}$ 1 Everything is ψ: *idealism, panpsychism, phenomenalism.* Berkeley, Fichte, Hegel, Mach, James, Whitehead, Teilhard de Chardin	$\mathscr{D}$ 1 ϕ and ψ are independent. No defenders so far except for L. Wittgenstein.
$\mathscr{M}$ 2 ϕ and ψ are so many aspects or manifestations of a single entity: *neutral monism, double aspect view.* Spinoza, James, Russell, Carnap, Schlick, Feigl	$\mathscr{D}$ 2 ϕ and ψ are parallel or synchronous: *psychophysical parallelism, preestablished harmony.* Leibniz, R. H. Lotze, H. Jackson, some Gestaltists
$\mathscr{M}$ 3 Nothing is ψ: *eliminative materialism, behaviorism.* J. B. Watson, B. F. Skinner, A. Turing, R. Rorty, W. V. Quine	$\mathscr{D}$ 3 ϕ affects or causes (or even secretes) ψ: *epiphenomenalism.* T. H. Huxley, K. Vogt, C. D. Broad, A. J. Ayer, R. Puccetti
$\mathscr{M}$ 4 ψ is physical: *reductive* or *physicalist materialism.* Epicurus, Lucretius, Hobbes, K. S. Lashley, J. J. C. Smart, D. Armstrong, P. K. Feyerabend	$\mathscr{D}$ 4 ψ affects, causes, animates, or controls ϕ: *animism.* Plato, Augustine, Aquinas, S. Freud, R. Sperry, K. R. Popper, S. Toulmin
$\mathscr{M}$ 5 ψ is a set of emergent brain functions (activities): *emergentist materialism.* Diderot, C. Darwin, T. C. Schneirla, D. Hebb, D. Bindra	$\mathscr{D}$ 5 ϕ and ψ interact: *interactionism.* Descartes, W. McDougall, J. C. Eccles, K. R. Popper, J. Margolis

sequences of physiological and mental states. To say that mental events have neural "correlates" is not very informative unless one indicates what a mental state is (in other than ordinary language terms) and explains the nature of its "correlation" with its neural "correlate". For these reasons $\mathscr{D}2$ is vague to the point of being confirmable by all possible data, and of being incapable of suggesting any experiments or theories. Hence $\mathscr{D}2$ is not a scientific hypothesis, ergo we shall discard it.

On the dualist side we are then left with the theses acknowledging one substance's acting upon the other. However, in this case too only the physical is supposed to be knowable, whereas the mental is left in the dark or, at best, in the care of nonscientific philosophers or even theologians. We do indeed understand what it is for a neuron, a neural system, or any other *thing*, to be in such and such a *state*: a state of a thing is the list of properties it possesses at the time concerned. And we understand what is a neural *event* or process, namely a change in the state—hence in some of the properties—of a neural unit (neuron, neuron assembly, or entire nervous system). Consequently we know what it is for one neural unit (neuron or neuron assembly) to act upon another: A acts on B if and only if the states of B when it is connected with A are not the same as those of B when it is not connected. In short, we have a general and precise idea of states and functions (processes) of concrete things such as neurons and neuronal systems. (See Bunge, 1977a, b.)

But these general and precise ideas of state and event, common to all sciences, are not transferable to the mind. (If they are, nobody has shown how.) In particular, mood, memory, and ideation have not been shown to be properties, or changes of properties, of a mental substance (mind, soul, or spirit). In sum, the concepts of mental state, event, and process do not fit within the general framework of contemporary science unless they are construed in neural terms, i.e. as, respectively, a state of the brain or an event or process in a brain. This is one of the reasons for the inability of dualists to go beyond the stage of verbal and metaphorical formulations. This is why there is not a single dualistic model—in particular a mathematical model—in physiological psychology. And this is why dualism is the darling of ordinary language philosophers and philosophical psychologists.

In short, epiphenomenalism ($\mathscr{D}3$), animism ($\mathscr{D}4$), and interactionism ($\mathscr{D}5$) are just as imprecise as parallelism ($\mathscr{D}2$)—which is to be expected of popular, i.e. nonscientific, views. (Recall that ordinary knowledge is largely popular superstition.) And, not being precise hypotheses, they can hardly be put to empirical tests. Moreover, even if parallelism and interactionism were to be formulated in a precise manner, it might not be possible to decide between them on the strength of empirical data. Indeed, it would seem that every psychological experience and every psychophysiological experiment can be interpreted (or misinterpreted) either in parallelist or in interactionist terms, since according to both doctrines neural events are simultaneous with their mental "correlates".

We are led to the conclusion that the two most popular variants of psychoneural dualism, namely parallelism and interactionism, though conceptually different, are equally fuzzy and are empirically equivalent in so far as they accord (much too easily) with the same empirical data. For these reasons—to be examined more closely in the next subsections—dualism is not scientifically viable. Hence it is unacceptable to a science-oriented philosophy. We are then left with psychophysical monism as the only scientifically and philosophically viable alternative.

But, as shown in Table 1.1 (or its equivalent Fig. 1.2), psychophysical monism is a whole class of doctrines, so that we must examine them separately. Idealism ($\mathcal{M}1$) can be written off without further ado because it is incompatible with the sciences, all of which are busy hypothesizing or manipulating concrete entities, many of them unobservable (hence transphenomenal), such as atoms, fields, and societies. Moreover, all science is supposed to adopt the scientific approach, which includes objectivity. In short, the upwards reduction of everything to the mental is incompatible with science.

As for neutral monism ($\mathcal{M}2$), it has yet to be formulated clearly and in agreement with the natural sciences. (Not even Russell, 1921, perhaps the clearest philosopher of all times, succeeded in giving a clear account of neutral monism, which he favored at one time, or in dispelling the suspicion that it is a form of obscurantism for it resorts to a "neutral substance" that must remain unknown except for its manifestations— material and mental.) And energetism (Ostwald, 1902), which is some- what precise, is not exact enough and it refuses to account for the marvellous qualitative variety of the world. (Besides, it rests on the mistaken reification of energy, which is a property of all things, not a thing.) We may therefore dismiss $\mathcal{M}2$ as well and turn our attention to materialism.

We distinguish three main varieties of materialism as regards the mind–body problem, to wit, eliminative, reductive (or leveling), and emergentist. Eliminative materialism ($\mathcal{M}3$) holds that there *is* no such thing as the mental: that everything is material in the strict sense of 'physical'. One version of this doctrine is the Epicurean thesis, elaborated by Lucretius, that the mind is a swarm of subtle corpuscles. (For a contemporary revival, see Culbertson, 1976.) A more refined version of eliminative materialism is behaviorism, which refuses to deal with mental states and events—claiming that there are none—and does not in- vestigate the nervous system but treats the animal as a black box obeying Aristotelian physics. By refusing to face the facts of mentality, eliminative materialism makes a sitting duck for dualists such as Popper and Eccles (1977). By the same token it offers no solution to the mind–body problem: nay, it claims there is no such problem. We can therefore eliminate eliminative materialism or $\mathcal{M}3$.

We are then left with reductive materialism ($\mathcal{M}4$) and emergentist materialism ($\mathcal{M}5$). Both hold that every mental state (or event or process) is a state (or event or process) of the central nervous system (or a part of it). So both acknowledge the existence of the mental while denying that it is a separate entity. Where these doctrines differ is with regard to the nature of the central nervous system—or CNS for short—and therefore as to the proper way to explain mental functions as CNS processes.

According to reductive materialism or physicalism ($\mathcal{M}4$), the CNS is a physical entity differing from other physical systems only in complexity. (Some claim that the brain is a computer.) Hence the explanation of the mental should require only physical concepts and theories in the narrow or technical sense of 'physical'. In philosophical jargon: reductive materialism involves both ontological reduction (i.e. leveling) and epistemological reduction—i.e. the transformation or psychology into a branch of physics. I reject the physicalist ontology because it does not square with the qualitative variety of reality, and the associated epistemology because it is far too naive and quixotic.

Emergentist materialism ($\mathcal{M}5$) holds that the CNS, far from being a physical entity—in particular a machine—is a biosystem, i.e. a complex thing endowed with properties and laws peculiar to living things and, moreover, *very* peculiar ones, i.e. not shared by all bio-systems. (*Example 1*: Spontaneous or self-started activity, conspicuous in nerve cells, is unfrequent elsewhere. *Example 2*: Lateral inhibition, typical of nervous tissue, seems not to occur in physical systems, where every disturbance propagates: Fig. 1.1. Mental functions would thus be CNS functions and, far from being purely physical processes, they would be emergent relative to the physical level.)

The emergence claimed for the mental is double: the mental properties of a CNS are not possessed by its cellular components but are *systemic properties* and, moreover, nonresultant ones; and they have emerged *at some point in time* in the course of a long biotic evolutionary process. (There is prebiotic, e.g. molecular, evolution, but it does not satisfy exactly the same laws.) Consequently, although physics and chemistry

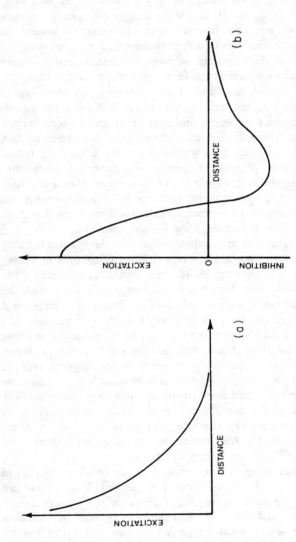

FIG. 1.1. Lateral inhibition as an emergent property of nervous tissue. (a) Propagation of an excitation in a fluid or a field: the excitation spreads out. (b) In nervous tissue there is excitation (positive connectivity) for neighboring neurons and inhibition (negative connectivity) for all others: far from spreading out, the excitation remains confined or localized in the neural system concerned.

are necessary to explain CNS functions, they are insufficient. Nor does general biology suffice: we need to know the *specific emergent* properties and laws of the CNS, not only those it shares with other subsystems of the animal, such as the cardiovascular and the digestive systems.

Emergentist materialism rejects *ontological* reductionism or the bulldozing of qualitative variety: in fact it is ontologically pluralistic with regard to properties and laws. But it embraces *epistemological* reductionism—albeit only moderately, for, while it holds that the mental *can* be explained in scientific terms, and that physics and chemistry are necessary for such explanation, it also claims that new concepts, law statements, and theories, referring specifically to the CNS—though of course compatible with physics, chemistry, and general biology—are necessary to explain the mental in a scientific manner. Hence the rule: Bring together the various approaches to the problem and reduce if you can but do not get stuck in the process: integration is more feasible than, and just as valuable as, reduction. (See Bunge, 1980a.)

Reductive materialism, or physicalism, holds that the brain is nothing but an aggregate of cells, so that knowing the latter is not only necessary but also sufficient for knowing the former and thus explaining the mental. This reductionistic thesis is false. Indeed, to state that the composition of the brain is a set of cells does not imply that the brain is nothing but the latter, any more than to say that the composition of a human society is a bunch of humans is to say that a society is nothing more than the set of its members; and this for the following reasons. First, a thing is not a set; in particular, a system is not identical with the set of its components. Second, a brain is a system, hence something endowed with a structure and an environment, not only a composition. And the structure of the brain includes the connections among its neurons. The result is a system with emergent properties—such as those of being able to perceive, feel, remember, imagine, will, think, and others—which its cellular components lack.

To be sure one can (hope to) understand all such bulk properties in terms of those of the neurons and their interactions. That is, one can (hope to) "reduce" the molar properties of the brain to the properties of its microcomponents and their links. But such an explanation—which is yet to be provided—does not accompany an ontological reduction, i.e. the bulldozing of qualitative variety. Explained vision is still vision, explained imagination is still imagination, and explained consciousness is still consciousness. Therefore ontological reductionism (or leveling) is just as untenable in the matter of mind as it is in the matter of matter. (See Bunge, 1977b, c, 1979a.)

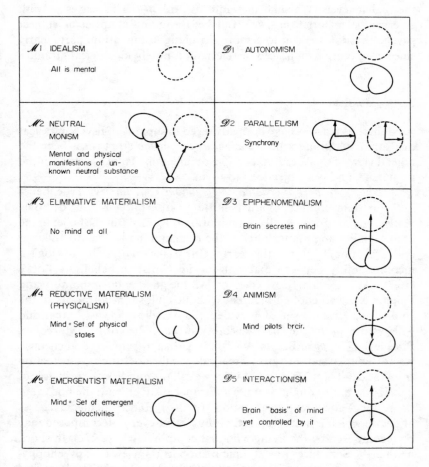

FIG. 1.2. The main views on the mind–body problem in cartoons. Dotted circle: mind; brain-shape: brain.

In short, reductive materialism—or physicalism—is untenable because it fails to account for the specificity of the mental. (As a matter of fact it does not even account for the emergent properties of biosystems.) In particular, it does not allow one to distinguish man from his nearest cousin the chimpanzee, so similar at the cellular level yet so different at the higher levels. We shall therefore discard $\mathcal{M}4$. This leaves us with emergentist materialism ($\mathcal{M}5$). But before taking it up let us subject psychophysical dualism to a more searching examination, particularly since it is so often embraced or rejected on purely ideological grounds.

3. Pro dualism

Numerous reasons have been advanced in support of psychophysical dualism in addition to the *argumentum ad baculum* that it has been the official view of the West for a couple of millennia. Here are some of the arguments and our objections to them.

(i) *Dualism is part of religion, in particular Christianity.* True, belief in the existence of disembodied entities (souls, spirits, ghosts, demons, deities, etc.) is central to all contemporary religions. But the belief in the immateriality and immortality of the human mind is alien to Judaism and was not held by the early Christians. There is no logical incompatibility between materialism and Christian belief. As Locke (1690, Bk. IV, Ch. 3, Sec. 6) wrote: "All the great ends of morality and religion are well enough secured, without philosophical proofs of the soul's immateriality; since it is evident that he who made us . . . can and will restore us to the like sensibility in another world." Moreover, Priestley (1777, *apud* Brown, 1962), the learned theologian and chemist, wrote that materialism "gives a real value to the doctrine of resurrection from the dead" (p. 271). True, "what we call the mind, or the principle of perception and thought, is not a substance distinct from the body, but the result of corporeal organization" (p. 265). Hence the mental ceases at death, which is a decomposition; but "whatever is decomposed may be recomposed by the Being who first composed it" (p. 272). In short, neither the Scriptures nor argument support the view that psychophysical dualism is part and parcel of the Christian religion. The historical truth is that the Christian doctrine of the soul was a latecomer and, moreover, was borrowed from the pagan philosopher Plotinus and the Jewish philosopher Philo.

(ii) *Dualism explains personal survival and ESP.* It certainly does, and this is why it has been defended by believers in survival after death or in the paranormal, such as the nonreligious thinkers Ducasse (1951), Price (1952), Beloff (1962), Broad (1962), and Smythies (1965a, b). In their view, minds outlast their brains, and the mind of the departed dwells in a sort of dream world made up of mental images. This is a spiritualistic version of epiphenomenalism, since it assumes that brains secrete mental entities much as radio transmitters generate radio waves. The troubles with this doctrine are: (a) there is not a shred of evidence for it—unless happenings in séances and old wives tales are counted; (b) it reifies processes such as that of imagining—in fact it detaches images from that which does the imagining; (c) it is inconsistent with basic principles of modern science, as recognized by Broad (1962) himself. (For a defense of dualism from a hylomorphic viewpoint that regards all natural forces and laws as mental entities, see Polten, 1973.)

(iii) *Dualism is enshrined in ordinary language.* In fact, in ordinary parlance we use expressions such as 'I have X in mind', 'I shall keep that in mind', 'He is out of his mind', and 'She spoke her mind'. Even scientists occasionally use phrases redolent of dualism, such as 'the physical basis of mind' and 'the physical control of the mind'. In short, there is no doubt that English and other ordinary languages have dualism built into them. So much the worse for dualism, for that only goes to show that it is a vulgar and obsolete doctrine. Scientific theories, on the other hand, involve technical concepts and statements that call for expressions going beyond, and often against, ordinary language. (Think of any mathematical model in psychobiology.) Ordinary language is the voice of common sense, which in turn is "just a system of myths accepted by a community" (Agassi, 1977, p. 77).

(iv) *Dualism explains everything in the simplest possible way.* True, dualism explains not only man's mental life but everything in the world, either in terms of indwelling spirits (immanent animism) or in terms of some unwordly spiritual beings (transcendent animism). Moreover, it explains everything in simple and familiar, hence intelligible, ways. Thus the dualist may claim that I perceive (or imagine or think up) X because I have X in mind (nativistic dualism) or because my mind lets X

in (empiricist dualism) or because my mind creates X (idealist dualism). All problems about the mental are thus solved with one stroke, namely by labeling: there is no need for any further investigation. But of course these domestic virtues of dualism render it unfit for science, which knows of no panacea and does not regard simplicity as the seal of truth (Bunge, 1963). Dualism explains too much too easily. Science never explains enough and seldom explains easily.

    (v) *Mind must be immaterial because we know it differently from the way we know matter: the former knowledge is private, the latter public.* First of all, our knowing objects of a certain kind—e.g. mental states—does not turn them into entities: those objects might be properties or states of concrete things. Secondly, differences in the manner of knowing do not entail radical differences in the manner of being. Thus our way of knowing atoms is very different from that of knowing sensible bodies, yet both are concrete things. Thirdly, although we do have direct experience of mental events, it is also true that we have direct experience of some of the (other) events in our body even without the help of the external senses. Fourthly, it is not true that all mental events are experienced: we seem to be unaware of most of them. (Routine mental work requires no consciousness unless difficulties arise.) On the other hand, an expert observer equipped with suitable instruments may detect some of the mental events that escape the self-monitoring mechanism. Fifthly, the mind is not as private as is sometimes believed, and this simply because the brain is never fully isolated. In fact the brain is accessible not only from within but also from without and by various means: surgery, electrical stimulation, drugs, and ordinary behavior—from a sweet word to a punch on the nose. Mental states and changes of state (events) are just as private, or public, as the minding brain. Actually our access to them is more expedite than our access to events in an atomic nucleus or in the center of our planet. So much so that, whereas the latter are accessible only to highly specialized scientists, mental states and events can also be guessed by nonscientists endowed with some psychological penetration. Moreover, ordinary people and other animals can empathize, e.g. feel joy or pain when they see somebody exhibiting signs of joy or pain. In sum, there is no iron curtain between the private and the public: only a (philosophical) smoke curtain (Quine, 1953).

(vi) *Phenomenal predicates are irreducible to physical ones, so the mind must be substantially different from the brain.* A standard example is the difference between light (or some other physical stimulus) and the perception of light (e.g. seeing blue). To be sure there is a great difference between the two processes, and also between the predicates employed to describe them. However, this does not establish the existence of a separate mental entity. It only goes to show the qualitative difference between physical and biological processes, particularly when the latter occur in the nervous system. As for the predicates themselves, the difference is this. While all phenomenal predicates (e.g. "blue", "warm", "soft", "sweet") belong to ordinary knowledge (and language), scientific predicates are nonphenomenal. Asserting that the gap between them will never be closed is begging the question and sentencing physiological psychology before hearing its case. Indeed, one of the goals of this discipline is to explain phenomena in deep (nonphenomenal) terms—just as physics and chemistry explain surface and bulk properties in terms of atomic and molecular ones. There is no reason to deny the possibility that one day theoretical neurophysiology may come up with definitions like this one:

Organism b feels pleasure of kind $K =_{df}$ Subcortical system s of organism b, under stimulation by events occurring in c (another neural system, or sense organ, or even electrode implanted in s) fires according to pattern p.

Denying this possibility is sheer obscurantism.

(vii) *Whereas neurons fire digitally, we can have continuous experience, e.g. we can perceive a gapless green surface.* This is the so-called "grain objection" raised by Sellars (1963) and sharpened by Meehl (1966). It is no more troublesome than the analysis of the solid and smooth table into a system of tightly coupled atoms. Indeed, mental events do not occur in single neurons or even in pools of a few dozen neurons, but they are presumably changes of state of neural systems composed of thousands or millions or even billions of neurons. Physicists know that, when large numbers of events summate, a quasi-continuous process ensues, that can usually be modeled as continuous in space and time. (See some field-theoretic models of neural activity in

MacGregor and Lewis, 1977.) After all, the human eye does not perceive any discontinuities in the images projected by a motion picture reel, which is a string of discontinuous frames. So, the argument from the grainy structure of the brain holds no water.

(viii) *There must be a mind animating the brain machinery, for machines are mindless.* Brains are often likened to computers just because the latter are designed to mimic (hence fill in for) certain brain functions, such as memorizing data and performing routine computations. The analogy has some heuristic value—for computer engineering rather than for brain science. The disanalogies between brains and computers are at least as obvious as the analogies. For one thing neurons can fire spontaneously (and can be excited only if they are active before the excitation reaches them). On the other hand, computer elements are not supposed to have any spontaneous activity. For another, inter-neuron connections can be plastic (variable), whereas the connections among elements of a computer, once established by the program, are fixed. Thirdly, whereas computers are idle without programmers, the brain is self-programmed. Fourthly, computers are not alive; so, while they can fake some aspects of ideation, they do not ideate. Fifthly, computers are designed (with some purpose), whereas brains are not. The brain–computer analogy, in short, has been overrated. Worse: it has made some psychologists despair of ever being able to understand the mind unless taking it for granted—which is no explanation at all. If we recall that brains are not machines but extremely complex biosystems engaged in a multitude of functions, and that whereas brains can design machines but not conversely, then we can dispense with the ghost (soul, spirit, mind) animating the machine. (By the way, it is often overlooked that the computer model of mind, with its dichotomy between hardware and software, and its suggestion that computer operations are "embodiments of the mind", is inspired by dualism instead of underwriting materialism. Eighteenth-century machinism, a version of vulgar materialism, has become a subtle version of psychophysical dualism.)

(ix) *There is ample evidence for the power of mind over matter—e.g. voluntary movement and planning.* (Not to speak of psychokinesis, invoked by Eccles (1951) and other interactionist dualists.) Surely not all actions in the central nervous system are of the bottom-up type:

some, particularly in the primate brain, are of the top-down kind. However, neither type of action calls for positing an independent mind, let alone a consciousness hovering above the brain (as, for example, Sperry has done). All such "mind–body interactions" can be accounted for, at least in principle, in terms of interactions among neural systems. My typing this sentence can be explained as a result of the action of certain ideation processes in my cortex on the motor center of the same. (See Hebb, 1966, and Bindra, 1976.) Likewise your turning the page looking for more or closing the book in disgust. From a monistic perspective, the so-called mind–body interactions are interactions among neural systems or among them and other subsystems of the same body (e.g. the endocrine system or the cardiovascular system). Strictly speaking, then, there is neither "upward causation" (or bottom-up action) nor "downward causation" (or top-down action): all causal (and noncausal) actions in the nervous system are "horizontal" in the sense that they occur between neural systems, not between them and some "higher" nonembodied entity. The epistemological advantage of this ontological hypothesis is obvious: it rescues such interactions from the grips of obscurantism and subjects them to scientific investigation.

(x) *Dualism squares with emergentism and the hypothesis of the level structure of reality.* So it does, but compatibility does not ensure deducibility. Psychophysical dualism is the cheapest way to guarantee emergence and levels but not the only one. In other words, *substance pluralism* (in particular dualism) is not necessary to resist the bulldozing of qualitative variety effected by both mechanism and spiritualism. One can adopt *property pluralism* (not just dualism), as Spinoza did. According to this view (a) there are only things (concrete or material objects) but not all things are physical: some are chemical, others biological (in particular some of these can feel, think, etc.), and so on; (b) mental events are certainly emergent relative to nonmental biological events (such as cell division), but they are events in certain biosystems, namely nervous systems. (For details on this system of ontology, see Bunge, 1977a and 1979a.) This kind of pluralism—namely emergentist materialism—takes the wind out of the sails of those psychophysical dualists who are anxious to preserve the variety of the world and the distinctive qualities of the mental.

So much for the reasons in support of psychophysical dualism and our objections to them. Thus far the score is 0 pro and 10 con dualism. Let us now examine some reasons for rejecting that view.

4. Contra dualism

The main objections against psychophysical dualism are these.

(i) *Dualism is fuzzy.* Firstly, it fails to give a precise characterization of the notion of a mind. At best, dualists offer *examples* of mental states (e.g. a happy mood) or mental events (e.g. a perception). But they do not state *what* is in such states or undergoes such changes—unless of course they claim that those are states of and changes in the mind, which is in turn circularly defined as whatever can be in such states or experience such changes. Secondly, dualism does not elucidate the notion of *correlation* occurring in the standard expression 'mental states (or events) have neural correlates' (either parallel to or interacting with the former). Because dualism in either of its main versions—parallelism and interactionism—is imprecise, it can hardly be put to empirical tests. It tells us that whatever we introspect or retrospect is mental, and whatever is mental has some "neural correlate". So, dualism labels instead of explaining, and remains always on the safe side of vagueness. In sum, dualism is a nonhypothesis (Bindra, 1970).

(ii) *Dualism detaches properties and events from things.* To talk of mental activities, such as perceiving and deciding, as being parallel to, or interacting with, but being radically different from, brain events, is like talking of chemical combinations parallel to the combining atoms or molecules, or of social events parallel to the actions of their actors. Modern science started by rejecting the Platonic idea of autonomous forms (properties) and events as being relics of animism. Science construes properties as properties possessed by some thing or other. This construal is reflected in the formalization of the concept of a property as a function whose domain includes (e.g. as a cartesian factor) the set of things possessing the property concerned. (For example, age is conceptualized as a function that maps the set of all concrete things, or perhaps only organisms, into the set of positive real numbers.) Just as electrical conductivity is represented as a function on the set of bodies and blood pressure as a function on the set of cardiovascular systems, so visual acuity is conceptualized as a function on the set of visual systems, and the ability to speak as a function on the set of speech systems. Remove the things occurring as members of the domain of the function, and the function itself will be gone—both mathematically and ontologically. (In the simplest possible case a psychical or mental property or faculty is conceptualizable as a function on the Cartesian product of the set of all plastic central nervous systems by the set of all time instants. No nervous system, no precise concept of a mental function.)

(iii) *Dualism violates conservation of energy.* If immaterial mind could move matter, then it would create energy; and if matter were to act on immaterial mind, then energy would disappear. In either case energy—a property of all—and only concrete things would fail to be conserved. And so physics, chemistry, biology, and economics would collapse. Faced with a choice between these "hard" sciences and primitive superstition, we opt for the former. Should it be rejoined that, after all, the brain is just an information processor, and that information processing takes little or no energy, the proper answer should be: Rubbish! Firstly, every information signal rides on some process that transports energy—e.g. a traveling wave or an electrolytic reaction. (The fact that information *theory* disregards the physical basis of information, and in particular the energetics of information flow, does not annihilate that basis.) Secondly, the human brain happens to be the most expensive system of the body: although it weighs only 2 per cent of the total, its blood supply is 15 per cent and its oxygen intake 20 per cent of the total. In short, the mental functions would seem to consume more energy than any other bodily function.

(iv) *Dualism refuses to acknowledge the evidence for the molecular and cellular roots of mental abilities and disorders.* There is little doubt that the propensity to acquire certain mental skills, as well as certain mental disorders, is inheritable—i.e. transmitted by DNA molecules. (This does not prove that DNA itself is talented or psychotic, but only that those mental properties are anchored to our biochemical, in particular genic, make-up.) Nor is there any doubt that our mental proficiency is very sensitive to metabolic and hormonal changes. All this is consistent with the thesis that the mental is a function of the central nervous system, not with the thesis that the mind is an independent entity. In other words, neurochemistry and psychopharmacology favor materialism, not dualism.

(v) *Dualism is consistent with creationism, not with evolutionism.* Indeed, by regarding mind as supernatural and immutable rather than natural and evolving, dualism collides with evolutionary biology and blocks all research into the prehuman antecedents of mental faculties. Only materialism jibes with the developmental and evolutionary studies of animals. Certainly some dualists do not embrace the thesis of the supernatural character of mind and, moreover, pay lip service to evolutionary biology and even to the hypothesis of the evolution of mental faculties. However, such an acceptance of evolutionism is not consistent: a consistent evolutionist, such as Darwin (in Gruber and Barrett, 1974), need not postulate immaterial minds and will postulate instead that mental functions, no matter how exquisite, are neuro-physiological activities. On the other hand, those who—like Popper and Eccles (1977)—adopt Plato's simile of the pilot (the soul) and the ship (the body), are forced to imagine two different evolutionary mechanisms—one for the pilot that controls or "animates", the other for the ship. And this is inconsistent with the theory of evolution, which is strictly naturalistic. (After all, the theory is aptly called 'the theory of *natural* selection'.)

(vi) *Dualism cannot explain mental disease except as demonic posses-sion or as escape of mind from body.* If the mind were an autonomous immaterial entity, then it should be immune to brain injury, drug action, and the like: it should be either healthy or sick from the start, or else susceptible only to the action of evil spirits. Therefore the consistent dualist, when confronted with mental disease, should resort exclusively to exorcism, prayer, or logotherapy (e.g. psychoanalysis). On the other hand, psychoneural monists feel free to use surgery, drug therapy, or behavior therapy, as the case may be: in each case they will try to act on the brain in order to bring it back to normal, or at least to minimize the overt and covert effects of whatever started the brain disorder. (Sometimes psychiatrists have to go down to the molecular level: this happens when the disorder is cellular rather than systemic. Thus a deficiency in the amino acid tryptophan, common among people who eat almost exclusively corn, produces both psychoses and pellagra. Both symptoms disappear by administration of nicotinic acid, not by questioning about childhood experiences.) The dualist who agrees to try nonmagical treatments, or indulges in drinking coffee or wine, is being inconsistent, for every such stimulant modifies some mental functions by changing the physics and chemistry of his brain.

(vii) *Dualism is at best barren, at worst obstructive*. Since dualism has a ready explanation for every mental event, and, moreover, one that is immune to neurophysiological argument, it does not encourage psychological research. In particular, dualism discourages a close connection between psychology and neurophysiology, psychiatry and neurology, and human and animal psychology; and it disowns whole fields of research, such as physiological psychology, psychopharmacology and evolutionary psychology. It can tolerate only pure psychology of the traditional mentalistic kind—or at most behaviorism, which keeps silent about the mind and so does not really bother the dualist. (On the contrary, behaviorism, by denying the mental, facilitates the task of dualism.) On the other hand, dualism encourages beliefs in the arcane, such as psychokinesis, telepathy, and precognition. (For a good selection, see Ludwig, 1978.)

(viii) *Dualism refuses to answer the six W's of the science of mind*. Every science attempts to answer, in an intelligible and testable manner, questions of at least six kinds, namely those beginning with *what* (or *how*), *where, when, whence, whither,* and *why*: I call these *the six W's of science*. For example, chemistry is supposed to find out, among other things, *what* combines with what, and *where* and *when* (under which conditions) the combination occurs. By so doing it also explains the origin of compounds (*whence*), their dissociation (*whither*), and the combination mechanism (*why*). Likewise, psychology is supposed to find out, among other things, *what* feels (or perceives, thinks, wills, behaves, etc.), *where*, and *when* (under what circumstances) the feeling (or perceiving, thinking, willing, behaving, etc.) occurs. It should also account for the origin (ontogeny and phylogeny) and the loss of this faculty, i.e. its *whence* and *whither*, as well as its neural mechanisms (i.e. its *why*). The answer that there is no such thing as feeling (thinking, willing, etc.) is to renege most if not all of psychology. To answer that there is, only we should not care *what* does the feeling (or perceiving, behaving, etc.), hence *why* it occurs, is to curtail science and forgo all hope of understanding ourselves. And to answer that what does the feeling (perceiving, thinking, willing, etc.) is the mind, is no answer at all. (It is in fact to indulge in circularity if the mind is defined as that which feels, thinks, etc.) Therefore dualism, by refusing to face the six W's of science, is nonscientific.

(ix) *Dualism is not a scientific theory but an ideological tenet.* In fact neither parallelistic nor interactionistic dualism is a hypothetical-deductive system with its own technical vocabulary and its own technical, testable, and systematized assumptions. Both versions of dualism are vulgar opinions that can be stated in a few imprecise and ordinary words. Neither contains any law statements. In particular neither tells us what the lawful relations between bodily and mental events are. *A fortiori*, neither discloses the mechanism whereby the mental is either synchronous with the physical or interacts with it. Hence dualism is not a scientific theory: it is just part of an archaic, nay prehistoric, ideological package.

(x) *Dualism is inconsistent with the ontology of science.* In all the sciences, from physics through biology to sociology, properties are possessed by concrete entities (in particular systems), and events are changes in certain properties. (We are writing of course of substantial properties and changes thereof, not of properties of abstract objects.) Not so in the dualistic philosophy of mind, which remains detached from biology and neuroscience, and demands that an exception be made for mental properties and events. Whereas every scientific theory needs a single state space to represent the states of its referent(s), the dualist would need two disjoint state spaces if he were to attempt to formulate his fuzzy ideas in mathematical terms. Indeed, he would need one state space to locate brain states and another for locating mental states—and perhaps even a third space for the states of the elusive "liaison brain", which Descartes thought was the pineal gland, and Eccles (1977) has been looking for in vain. Psychoneural monism, on the other hand, fits in with the state space approach adopted in science, for it denies that there are mental properties that fail to be brain properties, and it denies that there are brain properties that are totally independent of all others. That is, it asserts that a single state space, namely that of the brain, is needed to account for both mental and purely bodily properties, states, and events (Bunge, 1977b). Psychoneural dualism is incompatible with such an approach and, in general, with the ontology of modern science.

In short, we have scored another 10 points against psychoneural dualism. So, the final score is 20 to nil.

We have examined ten of the reasons adduced in favor of psychophysical dualism and another ten against it. We found that every one of the former turned against it, and every one of the latter has been sustained. (For further objections, see Feigl, 1958; Doty, 1965; Quinton, 1965; Armstrong, 1968; Wade Savage, 1976; and Zangwill, 1976.) The overall conclusion is that psychophysical dualism is not a viable scientific option—not a doctrine that can be embraced by science or by a science-oriented philosophy. We must therefore give psychoneural monism a chance, the more so since dualism has had the best press for about two millennia.

5. Emergentist psychoneural monism

Emergentist psychoneural monism, or $\mathscr{M}$ in Table 1.1, boils down to the following theses (Bunge, 1977b; Bunge and Llinás, 1978):

  (i) all mental states, events, and processes are states of, or events and processes in, brains of higher vertebrates;
 (ii) these states, events, and processes are emergent relative to those of the cellular components of the brain;
(iii) the so-called psychophysical (or psychosomatic) relations are interactions between different subsystems of the brain, or between some of them and other components of the organism.

The first clause is the thesis of psychoneural monism of the materialist kind. The second clause is the emergence thesis: it states that mental facts are both organismic or biological, and molar, i.e. involve entire assemblies of interconnected cells. The third clause is a monistic version of the dualist myth of the interactionist variety.

If one accepts the above theses then one can talk about *mental phenomena* without leaving the biological ground: the mentalist vocabulary originally coined by religion and dualistic philosophy begins to make, or is hoped to make, neurophysiological sense. (Equivalently: psychology becomes a neuroscience.) In particular it now becomes possible to speak of *parallel sequences of events*—e.g. of processes in the visual system and in the motor system, or in the speech system and in the cardiovascular system. It also makes good scientific sense to speak of *psychosomatic interactions*, because these are now construed as reciprocal actions between different subsystems of one and the same organism, such as the cerebral cortex and the autonomic nervous system. For example, rather than say that love can color our reasonings, we may say that the right brain hemisphere can affect the left one, and that sex hormones can act upon the neural systems that do the thinking. In short, ironic though it may sound, the dualistic modes of speech, which encapsulate our undigested introspective experience and which are but metaphorical and vague in the context of psychoneural dualism, become literal, precise, and testable in the context of emergentist materialism. The latter salvages whatever can be salvaged from the shipwreck of dualism.

Emergentist materialism has many attractive features, the most important of which are that (a) it squares with the natural sciences by postulating that mental facts, far from being affections of an immaterial substance, are states of, or events and processes in, concrete organisms, whence (b) mental facts can be investigated through the normal procedures of science—a feature which turns psychology into a natural science instead of a supernatural one.

Emergentist materialism holds, then, splendid promise and, moreover, has already rendered distinguished service by being the driving philosophical force behind physiological psychology, psychopharmacology, and neurology. However, it has one important shortcoming, namely that it is still immature. In fact emergentist materialism is not a *theory* proper, i.e. a hypothetical-deductive system containing precisely formulated and detailed hypotheses accounting for a wide range of psychoneural facts. It is instead a *programmatic hypothesis*—one both scientific and philosophical—in search of scientific theories embodying it. So much so that emergentist materialism can be summed up in a single sentence, to wit: *mental states form a subset* (albeit a very distinguished one) *of brain states* (which in turn are a subset of the state space of the whole animal).

What is needed for implementing the program of emergentist materialism, i.e. for developing it into a mature scientific enterprise? Obviously not more undigested data, whether purely neurophysiological or purely behavioral—nor more disquisitions of an ideological nature. What we do need are two different though complementary batches of theories:

(i) *extremely general theories* (not just stray hypotheses or programs) of the mental conceived of as a collection of functions of the brain;
(ii) *specific theories* accounting for the functioning of the various subsystems of the brain.

The general theories of psychoneural activity would belong to the intersection of ontology and psychology, while the specific theories of the psychoneural would be the exclusive property of physiological psychology. And all of them should be stated in precise terms, i.e. should be mathematical in form.

It may be argued that the preceding plea for intensifying theoretical work in the fields of psychophilosophy and psychophysiology is impertinent because there is no dearth of theories in both fields. Let us see about that.

Certainly much has been written about the so-called *identity theory*. But none of the "theories" of the psychoneural that agree with the materialist hypothesis are theories proper, i.e. hypothetical-deductive systems, let alone mathematical ones. They are instead single and stray *hypotheses*. And they are verbal and often verbose. (This may be one of the reasons that most mathematical psychologists have not been attracted to materialism. Another is that it is easier to tackle behavior than to account for the entire process, of which behavior is only the tail end.) In other words we still do not have a general materialist *theory* of the mind. (See, however, the following chapters.) All we have is a hypothesis that functions in a programmatic or heuristic capacity rather than by systematizing a vast array of data and issuing specific predictions that can be checked in the laboratory or in the clinic.

As for specific theories in physiological psychology, the situation is different. Many have been proposed, particularly over the past quarter of a century. (See Hebb, 1949; Milner, 1970; Thompson, 1975; and Bindra, 1976.) However, (a) there are not enough of them, (b) those which are closely linked with experiment are for the most part verbal, and (c) those which are mathematical are often far removed from experiment. (Moreover, most theories in mathematical psychology are either (a) neobehavioristic learning theories that disregard the brain or (b) information-theoretic theories regarding the brain as a computer rather than a biosystem. Both skip the chemical and biological levels.)

So much for the shortcomings of emergentist materialism in its infancy. However many and great these may be, the emergentist materialist philosophy of mind seems to be the best we have, and this for the following reasons.

    (i) Because it eschews the mysterious mental substance (or independent mind), without thereby denying mental facts, emergentist materialism is far more *compatible with the scientific approach* than either dualism or eliminative and reductive materialism.

   (ii) Emergentist materialism is *free from the fuzziness* that characterizes dualism with its talk of mental entities and processes that cannot be pinned down, and of mysterious correlations or interactions between brains and minds.

  (iii) Unlike dualism, emergentist materialism is *consistent with the general concepts of state and event* that can be gleaned from all the sciences. (On the other hand, according to dualism mental states would be the *only* states that fail to be states *of* some thing, and mental events would be the *only* events that fail to be changes of state *of* some thing—this being why dualism agrees more closely with theology than with science.)

  (iv) Unlike dualism, emergentist materialism *fosters interaction between psychology and the other sciences*, in particular neuroscience and this precisely because it regards mental events as special biological events.

   (v) Unlike dualism, which postulates an unchanging mind, emergentist materialism *accords with developmental psychology and neurophysiology*, which exhibit the gradual maturation of the brain and behavior.

  (vi) Unlike dualism, which digs an unbridgeable chasm between man and beast, emergentist materialism *jibes with evolutionary biology*, which—by exhibiting the gradual development of behavior and mental abilities along certain lineages—refutes the superstition that only Man has been endowed with mind.

(vii) Unlike reductive materialism, which ignores the emergent properties and laws of the nervous system and its functions, and hopes quixotically that one day physics will explain them, emergentist materialism *acknowledges the emergent quality of the mental* and suggests that it should be approached with the help of all the sciences because the brain is a multilevel system.

None of the rivals of emergentist materialism can boast of so many important supports, direct and indirect, scientific and philosophical. And none of them promises to yield so many experimental and theoretical fruits. (In particular dualism is totally barren.) Therefore it is worth while to try to implement the program of emergentist materialism, i.e. to attempt to build theories of various degrees of generality, mathematical in form and agreeing with the known facts, that construe the mind as a distinguished subset of the set of brain processes. We shall propose one general theory of the kind in the succeeding chapters, but before doing so it may be appropriate to take a glimpse at the long history of the mind–body problem.

6. Brief history

No other conceptual problem has as many roots as the mind–body problem, and none has made so much trouble for philosophers, scientists, and laymen alike. For these reasons, to better appreciate the magnitude and ramifications of the problem it is necessary to take at least a hurried look at its history.

It all began at least twenty thousand years ago. True, nothing is known with certainty about the philosophy of mind of primitive man. However, we do know something about the beliefs of contemporary primitives, such as the Australian aborigines, the Amazonian indians, and the Eskimos: they believe in spirits of humans and animals, inhabiting them while they are alive, and wandering about disembodied after death. And there is also some evidence, mainly from funerary sites, that the idea of a disembodied soul was held by primitive man long before the Neolithic revolution. This belief was well entrenched in the religions prevailing at the dawn of civilization, about 5000 years ago. Indeed, religion and belief in an immaterial (possibly eternal) soul go hand in hand. In sum, psychophysical dualism seems to be the oldest philosophy of mind on record.

Psychophysical monism came much later, together with the first scientific attempts. It was conceived by the Ionian philosopher–scientists, particularly Epicurus, and the father of medicine, Hippocrates. These thinkers rejected supernaturalism and adopted a strictly materialistic world view which had no use for disembodied spirits. However, while the Hippocratic school took firm roots among physicians for a while, materialism came quickly under the fire of Plato and his successors and, except for Lucretius, it won no outspoken followers among the learned. True, the Hippocratic tradition was cultivated by Galen and his disciples, but stripped of its philosophical underpinnings. And Epicureanism grew to be a strong school during the days of the Roman Empire, but it did not attract any notable thinkers. Materialism, so obviously at variance with religion and idealistic philosophy, declined no sooner than it was born.

The most brilliant, vigorous, and influential opponent of psycho-physical monism and, in general, of the ancient materialistic and atomistic world view, was Plato. His was the first coherent philosophical system that enshrined psychophysical dualism. In the dialogues *Cratylus* (399–400) and *Phaedo* (64–68) Plato makes his teacher Socrates expound and refine the obscure Orphic doctrine that (a) man is a compound of body and soul, (b) the soul is immaterial and eternal, (c) the soul animates the body, (d) the soul is superior to the body, (e) the soul is imprisoned in the body and delivered from it at death, and (f) the soul can know absolute truth and enjoy absolute beauty only after such deliverance. This doctrine was adopted and considerably obscured by the Neoplatonists, and made official by the Christians a good while after Paul. Save for the occasional heresy it has dominated Christianity for fifteen centuries.

Plato's disciple Aristotle was one of the heretics, though not a clearly outspoken one. He taught that man is an animal and the soul the "form" of the organism. Hence the question whether body and soul are one "is as meaningless as to ask whether the wax and the shape given to it by the stamp are one" (*De anima*, Bk. II, Ch. 1, 412b). This shy version of psychophysical monism was adopted by Averroes and the Latin Averroists but never became popular wherever the arms of Rome or of Islam reached. (On the other hand Thomas Aquinas, in Christianizing Aristotle, taught the divine origin, immateriality and immortality of the individual human soul.)

Another challenge came from Descartes at the beginning of the modern era. In his *Passions of the Soul* (1649) he expounded an original version of interactionist dualism. While he upheld the mind–body duality, he denied that the rational soul animates the body and asserted instead that the body is a machine. Even feeling and perception he thought were mechanical—not so thought and consciousness. This doctrine had a liberating effect on biology and animal psychology, for it allowed scientists to investigate animals, even humans, as if they were watches—except of course in so far as their rational souls were concerned. It taught thus, contrary to Christian dogma, that the human body was not sacred, and so could be dissected and studied the way any other physical system could. On the other hand, Descartes accepted the official view that the rational soul was immaterial, autonomous, and immortal, hence accessible to philosophy and theology but not to science. (Yet in his *Traité du monde* and *Traité de l'homme*, published posthumously in 1662 and which exerted a strong influence on the French materialist philosophers, Descartes came often close to materialism. Because of this he has been called "the masked philosopher".) Because it effects a compromise between science and faith, and appeals to common sense, Cartesian interactionism became popular among scientists and philosophers, and is still the majority view in the West. For example, one version of it is expounded by the agnostic philosopher Sir Karl Popper and the Catholic neurophysiologist Sir John Eccles in their joint book *The Self and Its Brain* (1977).

Although Cartesian interactionism was adopted by all the *bien-pensant* thinkers, it has met many more eminent challengers than the popular histories of philosophy would have us believe. To begin with there is Hobbes (1651), who regarded thought as a motion of the particles of the brain. Then there is Spinoza (1677), who criticized dualism and identified the extended substance and the thinking one and noted that, since they are one and the same, they could not possibly interact. And Locke, though not a materialist, stated that "God can, if he pleases, superadd to matter a faculty of thinking" (1690, Bk. IV, Ch. 3, Sec. 6). Also Hume (1739), though equally far from materialism, rejected Cartesian dualism and poked fun at the notion of an insubstantial and eternal soul.

But of course the strongest challenge came from outspoken materialists such as the philosopher Thomas Hobbes (1665) and the chemist–theologian Joseph Priestley (1777). Even more militant and far more influential were the French materialists, who found inspiration in the posthumous works of Descartes, chiefly the *Traité de l'homme*. Those widely read philosophers, usually overlooked by Anglo-Saxon philosophers, were La Mettrie—famous for *L'homme machine* (1745)—Helvetius (1759), Diderot (1769), d'Holbach (1770), and Cabanis (1802).

From then on materialism became popular, not so much among the cautious academic philosophers as among scientists and the cultivated public (cf. Gregory, 1977). The philosopher of religion Feuerbach (1841), the biologists Karl Vogt (1857), Jacob Moleschott (1852), and Ludwig Büchner (1855), and the social scientists and political activists Karl Marx (1859) and Friedrich Engels (1877–8) were all influential materialists. So was Charles Darwin in the privacy of his *M* and *N Notebooks* (*apud* Gruber and Barrett, 1974). There he stated several times his conviction that "the mind is [a] function of [the] body"—and gave good arguments for it. Moreover, Darwin founded comparative and evolutionary psychology with his books *The Descent of Man* (1871), and *The Expression of the Emotions in Animals and Men* (1872).

However, most of the early evolutionists did not adopt Darwin's biological approach to the problem of mental evolution. In particular, George Romanes, who wrote extensively on mental development and evolution, held on to the Christian doctrine of the soul. Even now most psychologists pay only lip service to evolutionary biology. The studies on mental evolution are so few that there is no *Journal of Evolutionary Psychology*. Certainly there have been important recent advances in the study of the evolution of the anatomy of the nervous system, but they have only exceptionally been linked to the evolution of behavior and mentation. Psychology and even neuroscience are yet to experience the Darwinian revolution. Here again the grip of prehistoric myth is in evidence. *Le mort saisit le vif.*

By and large materialism remained, until recently, an extramural philosophy. For the most part neurophysiologists, psychologists, and philosophers have been either indifferent (or perhaps just cautious), or dualists—like Sherrington, Freud, and Popper. Some recognized the problem but thought it insoluble. Others failed to see it because they had no use for the nervous system: this was the case with behaviorists and psychoanalysts. (Extremes meet!) And some philosophers—e.g. Putnam (1960)—declared that the mind–body problem was really a pseudoproblem. To some it all boiled down to a choice of words—mentalistic or neurophysiological or perhaps even computeristic. These attitudes prevailed until about 1960.

In 1956 the psychologist Ullian T. Place rescued psychoneural monism from academic oblivion with a very influential article on consciousness as a brain state. He immediately commanded the enthusiastic assent of a vigorous phalanx of philosophers, particularly Herbert Feigl (1958), Jack Smart (1959), and David Armstrong (1968), each of which defended some version of the so-called 'identity theory'—which at that time was no more than a programmatic hypothesis. From then on psychophysical monism has been a respectable and much-debated doctrine. (Until then it had been held only by a few scientists and by the dialectical materialists.)

However, there was considerable diversity of opinion among the identity theorists. Thus while Smart, Armstrong, and their numerous followers are robust materialists and, moreover, physicalists (reductionists), Feigl seems to have been wavering between strict identity and neutral monism. (The latter had been advocated by his teacher Moritz Schlick, 1925, the founder of the Vienna Circle, under the name 'double designation'. However, it was never clear what the designatum was: Feigl, personal communication, 1977.) Feigl held that, no matter how much the concepts of psychology may differ from those of neurophysiology, they have the same referents. Moreover, he believed that a mere critical reflection upon the meanings of the terms 'physical' and 'mental' should eventually solve the mind–body problem (Feigl, 1960). However, it is not quite true that neurophysiology and psychology do refer to the same entities: the former deals with neural systems, the latter with entire animals (Hebb, 1959a). And big problems like the mind–body problem are not solved by semantic analysis but by building hypothetical-deductive systems (theories). There won't be an identity *theory* proper unless someone builds it, and this is a task for scientists, not philosophers—i.e. if we want the theory to be scientific.

At any rate, the so-called identity theory has been the object of vigorous philosophical discussion over the past two decades. This philosophical development was paralleled in science. First of all the same period saw a rapid decline of two powerful enemies of the neurophysiological approach to the mental, namely psychoanalysis—which finally began to be seen as a pseudoscience—and behaviorism, which an increasing number of people started to regard as narrow-minded, superficial, and even boring. The vacuum left by these mutually complementary doctrines was filled up by physiological psychology.

No sooner did psychologists change their ontological presuppositions concerning the mental, than they started to make a number of startling discoveries, such as the effect of sensory deprivation on ideation, the coupling of vision to the motor system, the existence of pleasure and pain centers, the effects of cortical ablation on speech and thought, and the mental effects of changes in the concentration of a large number of chemicals.

While psychologists bored the tunnel from one end, neuroscientists tried to reach the mind from the other. The effect of vision on the very organization of the visual cortex during development was shown; the columnar organization of the neurons in the sensory cortex was discovered; it was found that split-brain patients can be said to possess two minds; that behavior can be subjected to radio control and, of course, to surgical and chemical manipulation—and so on and so forth. During the same period behavior therapists started to cure phobias and other mental disorders, and psychopharmacologists and psychoendo-crinologists began to tackle psychoses and other neurological disorders. Last, but not least, an international offensive was launched by the Neurosciences Research Program and the International Brain Research Organization, that publishes *Neuroscience*. The mind–body problem has come scientifically of age, and psychophysical monism is acting as the philosophical driving force of its investigation.

To be sure psychophysical dualism, though now on the decline, is still the view that gets the most publicity. (Likewise parapsychologists, astrologers, flying-saucer mongers, and the like get a far greater press coverage than those who debunk them: see the complaints of *The Skeptical Inquirer*.) Dualism enjoys the support of eminent neuroscientists such as the late Wilder Penfield (1975), Sir John Eccles (1977), and (somewhat timidly) of Roger Sperry (1969), as well as that of leading philosophers such as Sir Karl Popper (1972, 1977), William Kneale (1962), and Stephen Toulmin (1971).

However, there are outstanding workers on the other side of the fence too, and, indeed, in greater and increasing numbers. For example, the neuroscientists Colin Blakemore (1977), Theodore H. Bullock (1958), Robert W. Doty (1965), Gerald M. Edelman (1978), C. Judson Herrick (1949), Vernon Mountcastle (1975), S. Ramón y Cajal (1923), T. Shallice (1972), and John Z. Young (1971, 1978); the psychologists Dalbir Bindra (1976), Kenneth Craik (1943), J. A. Gray (1972b), Donald Hebb (1949), Harry Jerison (1973), U. T. Place (1956), Jean Piaget (1968), N. S. Sutherland (1970), T. C. Schneirla (1949), W. R. Uttal (1978), and O. L. Zangwill (1976); and the philosophers David Armstrong (1968), W. V. Quine (1960), Richard Rorty (1965), and J. J. C. Smart (1963). For every authority in support of psychophysical dualism there is at least another one—usually younger—in support of psychobiology.

However, scientists and philosophers are not to be swayed by authority: they should examine the cogency of the views at stake and their empirical backing, as well as their compatibility with other scientific theories and even with the scientific world view. And they should also weigh the fruitfulness or barrenness of the various theories of mind, i.e. whether or not they suggest further experiments and theories, or merely provide comfort to entrenched superstition.

CHAPTER 2

The Organ

1. Basic framework

We shall deal throughout this book with systems of a special type, namely organisms endowed with subsystems of a remarkable kind, i.e. nervous systems. Therefore it will be convenient to start by characterizing the notion of a *concrete or material system*. We may define such an entity as a thing composed of parts or components that, far from being mutually independent, are coupled to one another. Every system σ has (i) a *composition* $\mathscr{C}(\sigma)$ (the set of its components), (ii) an *environment* $\mathscr{E}(\sigma)$ (the set of things other than the system components, and that act on or are acted upon by the latter), and (iii) a *structure* $\mathscr{S}(\sigma)$ (the set of relations, in particular links or couplings, among the components and among these and environmental items). Moreover, every system has *emergent properties*, i.e. properties not possessed by its components. In particular, biosystems have properties that their physical or chemical components do not possess. (For a discussion of systems in general, and biosystems in particular, see Bunge, 1979a.)

Animals possessing a central nervous system, or CNS for short, come in various degrees of complexity, from primitive worms with half a dozen neurons to flies with about 100,000 to humans with nearly a hundred billion (10^{11}). The corresponding behavior levels range from automatic to highly creative. And the varieties of inner life (or subjective experience) vary from nil to extremely rich. Since the lower forms of nervous system functioning and animal behavior are usually recognized to be explainable along strictly biological lines, we shall concentrate on the higher functions—i.e. on those which, according to popular belief, require the presence of a soul, spirit, or mind inaccessible to science.

Our main assumption is that behavior is an external manifestation of neural processes, and that the latter include some which are not ostensive, such as feeling, imagining, dreaming, willing, and reasoning. In either case neither psychic function nor behavior exists by itself. It is the organism as a whole, or some subsystem of it, that does the behaving. And it is the CNS, or some subsystem of it, that controls behavior, feels, imagines, wills, reasons, plans, etc. In other words there is no mind separate from the body, or even parallel to it or interacting with it. Mind is just a collection of functions (activities, events) of an extremely complex CNS. We shall formulate these ideas in terms of the state space framework, which is that of all science.

As we have seen, dualism cannot be formulated within that framework because it describes the mental in ordinary language terms. However, if it *were* possible to mathematize these terms, dualism would need *two* separate state spaces: one for brain states, the other for mind states (Fig. 2.1). And this would go against the grain of contemporary science.

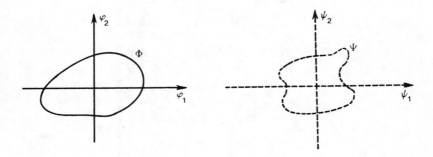

FIG. 2.1. Dualism needs two separate state spaces: Φ (physical) and Ψ (mental). The mental state space Ψ is mathematically ill-defined—hence the dotted lines.

On the other hand, monism requires a single state space for each animal species. But, whereas neutral monists and spiritualists would not know what (state) variables might describe the state of the neural or the mental substance, materialists should know, at least in principle, how to proceed (Fig. 2.2).

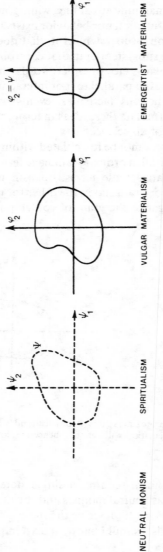

FIG. 2.2. Varieties of monism. Neutral monism: there is a single substance known only through its dual manifestations. Hence no state space for it. Spiritualism: all is mind. Vulgar materialism (eliminative and reductionist): all is matter. Emergentist materialism: some brain properties are mental. (That is either some of the axes of the state brain space, or some functions of theirs, represent mental properties.).

Note the difference between postulating two different state spaces (one of them hazy) and hypothesizing a single state space spanned by state variables some of which are mental even though all of them represent brain properties. In the latter case each mental state is a brain state but not conversely—i.e. *mental states form a subset of the collection of all brain states*, which in turn are included in the set of possible states of the whole organism. And each mental process is a brain process, and so representable by an arc of curve in the brain state space.

2. Neural units

During the heyday of behaviorism the nervous system was regarded as an uninteresting black box mediating in a mysterious way between stimuli and responses. Nowadays neurophysiology and physiological psychology view the CNS as an extremely complex biosystem that, besides "processing" inputs and controlling outputs, is in constant autonomous (and sometimes creative) activity. As a matter of fact these sciences are interested in systems at six different levels:

Subcellular: neuron membranes, synaptic boutons, dendrites.
Cellular: neurons and glial cells.
Neural microsystems: multineuronal systems (fixed or itinerant assemblies of hundreds, thousands, or even millions of neurons).
Neural macrosystems: systems of hundreds, thousands, or millions of neural microsystems. In primates, the following sublevels: somesthetic system, visual and hearing systems, temperature-regulating system, uncommited cortex, etc.; cerebral hemispheres; brain; central nervous system (CNS) or brain *cum* spinal cord; nervous system (NS), or CNS *cum* peripheral nerves; neuroendocrine system (NES), or CNS *cum* endocrine glands (e.g. pituitary and adrenals.)
Organism (animal).
Small group (system of animals interacting directly, e.g. family, horde, or work gang).

Every mental process presumably engages millions of neurons (out of a total of nearly one trillion in *Homo sapiens*). And it occurs not only at the neural (micro or macro) system level but also at the cellular and subcellular level. Indeed, contrary to what had been thought a few decades ago, what goes on at the synaptic cleft determines largely the overall behavior of the neuron. For example, a dopamine excess produces schizophrenia, while too little of it is manifested as Parkinsonianism—in either case a serious malfunction of the entire CNS. Therefore the old hypothesis that the neuron is just an all-or-none device acted on by an incoming current, and mimicked by an electric switch, has become obsolete (Bishop, 1956; Pribram, 1971 a, b, Kandel, 1976). In any case, the psychobiologist is interested in medium and large size neural systems possessing properties that are emergent relative to their components. We "must undertake the description of neural masses in terms peculiar to their own properties, arising out of but distinct from the properties of single neurons" (Freeman, 1975). As an eminent neuroscientist put it two decades ago: "One way of expressing our faith—and it is just that—is to say that there remain to be discovered new and emergent levels of physiological relations between neurons in masses, which will explain the gaps in our understanding of the phenomena of behavior, and that mind is simply a name for some of these relations or their consequences" (Bullock, 1958, p. 166).

The identification of neural systems, subsystems, and supersystems can be anatomical (topographical), physiological (functional), or anatomo-physiological, and is often done with the help of behavioral clues. Psychologists are interested in the functional characterization of neural systems, i.e. in finding out what they can do. Now, some such systems have permanent components while others don't. The best-known example of a neural system of the former kind (constant composition) is the visual system, composed of anatomically identifiable subsystems: the eyes, the optic nerves, the optic tracts, the lateral geniculate nuclei, and the visual cortex. On a much smaller scale we find the vertical columns of neurons across the layers of the visual cortex (Mountcastle, 1957; Powell and Mountcastle, 1959; Hubel and Wiesel, 1963). Whether neural circuits proper are real or fictitious, nobody seems to know (Bullock, personal communication).

The neurosurgeon may not be able to carve out some other neural systems because they do not have a constant composition: far from having a constant location, they may be itinerant neuron assemblies formed just for the occasion (Craik, 1966; Bindra, 1976). There are probably thousands of neural systems with more or less clear boundaries. And it is anyone's guess how many billion itinerant psychons (or *pexgos*, as Bindra calls them) may be formed during the lifetime of a primate (Fig. 2.3). Besides, psychons may be composed of neurons that, though coupled plastically to one another, are distributed among several anatomically distinct regions (Bechtereva, 1978).

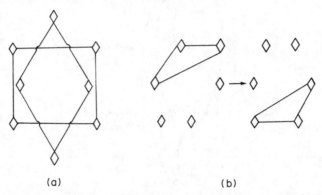

(a)   (b)

FIG. 2.3. (a) Two neural systems occupying roughly the same spatial region yet functionally detached: they "subserve" different functions. (b) Psychons can be itinerant even if their components stay in place, because their connections change in time.

Not only the subsystems of the CNS but also its supersystems command the interest of the neuropsychologist, and first of all the neuroendocrine system (NES). The coupling between the CNS and the endocrine glands, such as the pituitary (intracranial) and the adrenals (extracranial) is so intimate that, although the two can be distinguished anatomically, they cannot be separated physiologically. Neural systems activate endocrine organs via blood-borne hormones. In turn, hormonal signals activate neural systems in two ways: by changing behavior or by reacting on the same or other endocrine organs (Fig. 2.4). The CNS and the endocrine systems are so closely coupled that some neurons produce chemical messengers; this suggests the speculative hypothesis that the primitive neuron was both neural and a microgland that eventually became specialized. (Cf. Scharrer and Scharrer, 1963.)

EXTEROCEPTIVE AND
INTEROCEPTIVE STIMULI

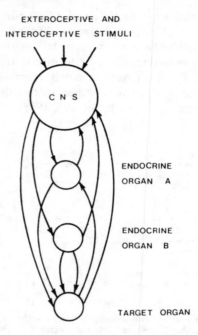

FIG. 2.4. Interactions among the CNS and endocrine glands.

What then is the justification for postulating that mentation is a neural function rather than a neuroendocrine one? Why not assume that mind is a collection of functions of the neuroendocrine system rather than of the CNS? For this reason: that hormones *influence* brain states but do not *do* the perceiving, feeling, willing, thinking, etc. For example, a change in noradrenalin (norepinephrine) concentration causes a change in mood or affection, and so facilitates certain brain functions while inhibiting others. But other systems, such as the cardiovascular and the digestive ones, are also intimately coupled with the CNS and yet we do not attribute to them any psychic functions. *A fortiori*, even though certain behavioral acts, such as locomotion, are done by the entire animal, we do not spread the mind all over the body. (These are just instances of the ever-present problem of tracing the boundaries of a system. Two things may be so tightly coupled that they form a system, yet each of them may in turn be a subsystem, as is the case with the atoms in a molecule and the persons in a society.)

We are on safe ground when stating that mental states and processes are states or processes of some brain. Uncertainty sets in when we try to localize the various mental facts, i.e. to pinpoint the subsystem "subserving" or "mediating" or "responsible for" a given mental fact. This is the problem of identifying the basic functional unit capable of being in a mental state. Barring the fruitless dualistic dismissal of the question, there are three stands on this issue: neuronism, holism, and systemism. Let us review them quickly.

3. Neuronism, holism, systemism

Neuronism (or *atomism*) attributes certain mental abilities to single neurons. For example, some neurophysiologists speak of *command neurons* capable of making decisions (cf. Kupfermann and Weiss, 1978). This hypothesis is suspect for a number of reasons. Firstly, because it eliminates the problem instead of solving it: indeed, if a single neuron is capable of discharging complex mental functions, then there is no need to study complex neural systems. Secondly, because there is not a shred of evidence for the hypothesis that a single neuron can execute complex operations such as that of issuing an instruction, couched in a symbolic language, to behave in a certain way—and, moreover, one that could be disobeyed only at a risk. The ability to make decisions and issue commands, and even the ability to obey the latter, seems to be the privilege of multineuronal systems (Llinás and Bunge, 1978). Thirdly, because histological examinations of neurons of mental patients of certain kinds have failed to exhibit any abnormalities at the cellular level: most neurological (or psychiatric) disorders are malfunctions of complex neural systems not of individual neurons. In short, neurons are not smart—they are not even dumb. Hence 'control neuron' may be a more suitable name than 'command neuron'.

In conclusion, neuronism seems to be false. Moreover, far from being illuminating, neuronism has often elicited an obscurantist backlash. In fact many an eminent neurophysiologist, having spent a lifetime pushing microelectrodes into individual neurons, reports having failed to find any mind in them, and jumps to the conclusion that mind must be immaterial. But of course all he has shown is that single neurons are incapable of mentation. He ought to have concluded instead that it takes complex neuronal systems (probably multimillionaires) to do that, just as it takes myriads of molecules to form systems possessing emergent properties such as solidity and opacity. In short, neuronism won't do. (See, however, Konorski, 1967.)

The polar opposite of neuronism, namely *holism*, attributes mental abilities either to the brain as a whole or to the immaterial soul or mind. Thus holists will favor a holographic theory of memory and other mental traits. And they will cite Lashley's "laws" of mass action and equipotentiality of the cortex. But, regardless of how they fare with rats, these "laws" do not hold even approximately for human beings. For example, if the Broca area is destroyed, no speech at all can be articulated; and if the Wernicke area goes, no speech can be understood. True, functional recovery does occur sometimes within limits because the right hemisphere takes over some left hemisphere functions. And it is also true that the various subsystems of the brain interact, so that the impairment of one of them is likely to result in the impairment of others. However, none of this proves that the brain is an amorphous body. Mental functions are not just a matter of amount of nervous tissue but of its organization. This is confirmed by comparative psychobiology: after all, porpoises have an even larger cortex than men, and yet they have not even tried to concoct myths about mind.

The alternative to both neuronism and holism is *systemism*, or the hypothesis that the brain, far from being either a heap of self-sufficient units or a homogeneous body, is a *system of specialized subsystems or organs*. There is multiple empirical evidence for the hypothesis that there are numerous brain "centers", "areas", or "organs" in charge of functions of definite types. For example, the brain stem regulates the activity of the cortex and can be manipulated in such a way as to induce sleep or wakefulness (Magoun, 1958). The limbic system may be said to be the organ of emotion, and the frontal lobe the organ of foresight. And the recovery patterns of bilingual aphasics suggests that each language engages a distinct neural system. The suggestion is particularly strong in the cases of total loss of one of the languages, and of antagonistic restitution, where the two languages are recovered successively but, as the second improves, the first regresses—as if the reactivation of one of the systems were inhibiting the other (Michel Paradis, personal communication).

There is also compelling evidence for the hypothesis that the various brain subsystems form a supersystem: (a) every sensory stimulus acts on all of the major "structures" (subsystems) of the brain, and (b) every response seems to be "mediated" (generated) by a number of distinct subsystems (cf. John, 1972). But from the fact that "all systems go" when performing particularly difficult tasks it does not follow that there are no specialized systems.

The systemist framework overcomes the difficulties of neuronism and of holism: it is intermediate between the thesis that a single ("pontifical") neuron can be "responsible for" every possible thought concerning grandmother, and the thesis that every single mental event engages the entire brain. According to the systemist viewpoint every mental function is a function of a neural system, whether permanent or itinerant. This hypothesis suggests looking for the smallest neural system capable of effectively discharging the function(s) concerned, and so encourages neural modeling as well as the design of experimental techniques, such as the measure of blood flow into the various subsystems as an indicator of their activity (Fig. 2.5).

Instead of asserting dogmatically that a given mental ability must be the function of either an individual neuron or the whole brain, systemism invites, then, looking for medium-size neural systems— presumably composed of at least 100 neurons—capable of possessing the emergent properties in question. The systemic framework is thus heuristically fruitful even if it supplies no precise answers to the specific questions it elicits. Whether the system suspected of performing the function(s) of interest contains a few neurons (as with insects) or billions of them; whether it involves always the same neurons (fixed neuron assembly) or keeps changing its composition (itinerant neuron assembly), is a question best left to detailed empirical investigation. In either case the programmatic hypothesis is that each mental function is performed by some neural system that is neither so small as to make emergence impossible, nor so big as to render analysis pointless.

(There is a superficial similarity between systemism and phren-

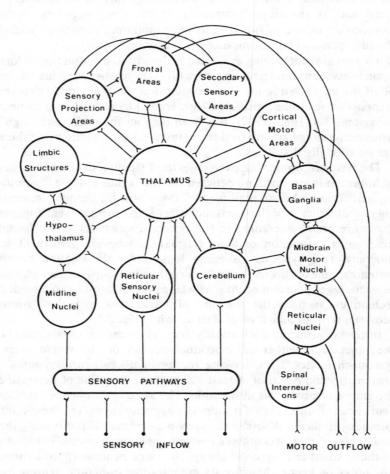

FIG. 2.5. A schematic drawing of the interactional model of brain function, as it appears to be emerging. Adaptive behavior is the outcome of simultaneously ongoing activity in several interacting neural systems. The presumed pathways of fairly direct interaction are shown here; not all the pathways shown have been anatomically verified. (From Bindra, 1976, p. 26.)

ology—a doctrine whose merits, incidentally, are only now being recognized: see Bynum, 1976. But whereas phrenologists did not acknowledge itinerant neural circuits, we do. And whereas phrenologists were wildly speculative and dogmatic, we can exhibit some empirical support for the existence of tightly knit neuron assemblies with a specific function, and make no bones about the programmatic nature of our framework.)

Each of the above three frameworks—neuronism, holism, and systemism—suggests its own brain research strategy. The neuronistic or atomistic strategy is to focus attention on the individual neuron, hoping that a more detailed knowledge of it will somehow eventually lead to a better understanding of the properties and activities of neural systems. The holistic strategy tackles the brain as a whole and looks at its "mass action", in particular the overall electrical potential (EEG pattern) and whole animal behavior. Finally, the systemist strategy consists in investigating the brain as a whole *as well as* every one of its subsystems and their relations with non-neural systems, in particular the endocrine one.

The atomistic strategy yields indispensable knowledge about the neural atom (or neuron) but must fail to discover anything about the cooperative or collective events and patterns that are so characteristic of every complex system—whether physical, chemical, biological, or social. Since the mental is not found in the individual neuron, the atomist may be tempted to supplement his knowledge of neurophysiological detail with a supernaturalistic doctrine of mind—as exemplified by Eccles. And the holistic strategy will yield valuable information about whole brain processes but it will be incapable of explaining their underlying mechanisms. (Analogy: try to explain the working of a TV set without inspecting its innards and making conjectures about its components and the interactions among them.)

Only the systemist strategy promises to describe, explain, and eventually predict the functioning of each neural system. It is the one Sherrington (1906) recommended under the name *integrative*, and is also the one fostered by Hebb (1949) and his school, as well as by the neurophysiologists who look for neuron assemblies (such as cortical columns) and the modelers who conjecture their activities. This strategy is no different from the one used successfully in other fields of science and technology. We shall adopt it for this reason. (More about the atomism–holism–systemism trilemma in Bunge, 1977d.)

4. Development and evolution

Most dualists depict the mind as an invariable entity: as one that may have its ups and downs but does not change significantly either ontogenetically or phylogenetically. They therefore hold that each person keeps his or her "personal identity" throughout his or her life: Jane Smith is identical to herself from infancy to old age and, according to psychoanalysts, even her dreams are predetermined by her infantile experiences (see, for example, Jones, 1961, p. 232). Long before developmental psychology attained maturity with Piaget, Hume (1739) found that model of mind grossly off the mark and emphasized the dynamic nature of mind. Even the mind of a healthy adult with regular habits, such as Immanuel Kant, changes from hour to hour: now alert and creative, in a while incapable of concentrating and solving the simplest of problems—e.g. because drowsy. Moreover, if Kant had disobeyed his king's orders to stop that irreligious nonsense, he might have been thrown into prison or even solitary confinement—in which case his brain would have deteriorated to the point of being unable to produce any more philosophy.

The variability of the mind—or rather the minding brain—is even more marked in the case of a developing animal, be it a puppy or a human baby, and it is immense and rapid in senility. Here certain dramatic changes are only too obvious, both anatomically and behaviorally. In particular, certain abilities or faculties emerge or disappear nearly overnight, as entire neural systems are set up or break down. Thus the baby who could say only a few stray words suddenly utters her first full sentence; and the senile scientist suddenly experiences a conversion to some Oriental cult. (In the first case there is evidence of dendritic growth, myelinization, and other anatomical changes. In the second there is marked shrinking of the brain.) In sum, if we consider periods of rapid development, or of quick degeneration, the illusion of invariability of the mind, or personal identity throughout life—in the sense of invariability of the mind—vanishes. Certainly there is continuity of the person, but this is not identity.

The ability of the CNS to change either its composition or its organization (structure), and consequently some of its functions (activities), even in the presence of a (roughly) constant environment, is called *plasticity* (cf. Paillard, 1976). Plasticity seems to be characteristic of the associative cerebral cortex from birth to senility, to the point that this system has been characterized as "the organ capable of forming new functional organs" (Leont'ev, 1961, *apud* Luria, 1966). In psychological terms, plasticity is the ability to learn and unlearn. From a monistic perspective learning is activating neural systems not previously engaged in the task in question, presumably by establishing or reinforcing certain synaptic connections. (According to Hebb, 1949, the neurons that fire together tend to stick together forming neuron assemblies or systems.)

The development of an animal is controlled (but not uniquely determined) by its genome. Ultimately this control is biochemical as it consists in the manufacture of enzymes and other proteins. And the genetic control is variable, for not all the genes "express" themselves (i.e. control the synthesis of proteins) all the time. Moreover, genetic control is not one-sided but is itself modified by environmental circumstances and by behavior, not in the sense that the latter can change the genic composition but that it can stimulate or inhibit gene "expression". To be sure it is now fashionable to assert that genes determine everything, in particular behavior. However, there is no empirical evidence for this hypothesis of genetic predetermination: it is a dogma. (For a criticism of this dogma, see Piaget, 1976.) The evidence points clearly to the joint control by genome and environment.

In particular neurophysiological changes—hence behavioral and mental changes—can be accelerated or slowed down by environmental stimuli, whether natural or artificial, as well as by the cessation of such stimuli. *Example 1*: Administration of thyroxine to the newborn rat advances by a couple of days its acquisition of swimming skills, whereas administration of cortisol delays by about the same time the maturation of the CNS of the animal (Schapiro *et al.*, 1970). *Example 2*: A protein deficiency during infancy will impair permanently (irreversibly) some brain functions, even the most basic sensorimotor ones (Cravioto *et al.*, 1966). *Example 3*: Animals reared in environmentally impoverished conditions may exhibit (a) a thinner cerebral cortex, (b) a higher concentration of free amino acids (which are not used to build proteins) and a corresponding lower rate of protein synthesis in the visual cortex and other areas, and (c) a diminution in the number of dendrites and synapses. Not surprisingly, the corresponding behavioral manifestations are quite noticeable. *Example 4*: Stimulation (in particular fondling) during infancy leads to brain asymmetries (lateralization) in rats (Denenberg *et al.*, 1978). *Example 5*: Smile patterns are the outcome of inborn muscle configuration and culture: the genome determines the former but not the way to use it. So much for the nature–nurture (or genome–environment–experience) interplay that pilots development.

The dependence of behavioral patterns and mental abilities on both anatomical and ecological characteristics becomes even more obvious when contemplated from a historical perspective, i.e. when behavioral and mental evolution are considered. All organisms are capable of regulating their own biofunctions and of coping with some environmental changes. A few plants—notably *Mimosa pudica* and the Venus flytrap—react and adapt effectively to rapid environmental changes: they possess a chemical (hormonal) information system outwardly (behaviorally) resembling the nervous system. However, these are exceptions and, anyway, the hormonal information system is too clumsy (slow and undifferentiated) to cope with multiple and quick environmental changes. The ability to react to them by adapting to them, as well as the capacity to explore and modify the surroundings in an active rather than a passive way, are typical of animals. And it is characteristic of the higher vertebrates to be able to form maps of the environment and to plan courses of action. Only a highly evolved nervous system can tackle such tasks.

Not surprisingly, many behavioral and mental abilities come in degrees, and these degrees correspond to the level of complexity of the nervous system when present. The following levels of organization or complexity of the nervous system have been distinguished:

(1) *Nerve net* or diffuse nervous system, as in *Hydra* and jellyfish: no neuronal specialization or specificity.

(2) *Ganglionic* nervous system, as in insects, molluscs, and crustaceans. The system is composed of relatively autonomous subsystems or ganglia (closely packed neurons), each of which specializes in a given function. (If in doubt about the relative

autonomy of such subsystems, watch the rhythmic contractions of a spider leg severed from the body.)

(3) *Central* nervous system composed of brain and spinal cord, as in vertebrates. The brain is a superganglion composed of several closely interconnected subsystems, each of which is composed of numerous neurons of different kinds or connected in different ways.

The above are not just levels of complexity of neural organization: they are also rungs in an evolutionary process that has presumably taken nearly one billion years. And, since complexity in neural organization must go hand in hand with behavioral and mental complexity, those are also stages in the evolution of behavior and mentation. To be sure evolutionary psychology is a young and neglected field of research (Bunge, 1979b). However, certain general trends of behavioral and mental evolution are well established (cf. Masterton *et al.*, 1976a, b). Among these are the overall increase in the value of the brain: body ratio along evolution, particularly among vertebrates: see Fig. 2.6. (The trend line is $E = kP^{2/3}$.)

In conclusion, the brain and its functions, far from being invariable, develop during the lifetime of the animal (ontogenesis) as well as in the course of the history of animal populations (phylogenesis). Therefore, to speak of the human mind as an immutable entity, and, moreover, one quite independent of the CNS, is preposterous: the mental abilities we are so proud of have very humble origins both phylogenetically and ontogenetically. Paradoxically, only this modest stance allows one to hope for vast improvements of such abilities, both in the individual and during the future evolution of our species. The believer in the invariability of the mind can hold no such hopes. On the other hand, he lives in blissful ignorance of the deterioration of the brain, hence of mental abilities, during senility.

Figure 2.7 gives a rough idea of the evolution of behavior and mentation.

5. Initial definitions

The time has come to define some of the key notions that have

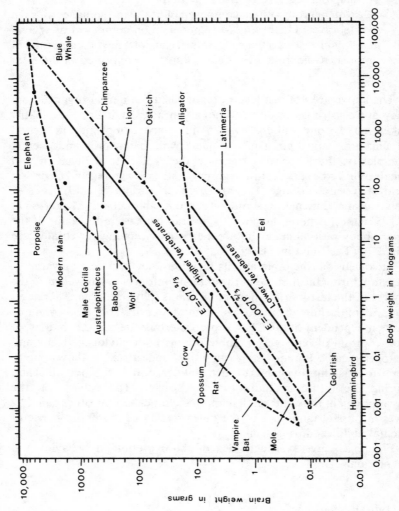

FIG. 2.6. Brain: body ratios in familiar vertebrate species. Both coordinates logarithmic. (From Jerison, 1973, p. 44.).

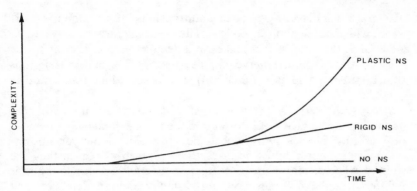

FIG. 2.7. Evolution of the degree of complexity of behavior and mentation. Only successful species are taken into account. Examples of orders with (nearly) rigid NSs: invertebrates, fish, reptiles; with plastic NSs: birds and mammals.

occurred thus far in this book and recurring in the remainder of it. To begin with we shall characterize a nervous system (or subsystem) as an *information system* in an animal. Certainly one must be wary of the much-abused concept of information. Thus the information language that pervades molecular biology as well as biology proper is metaphorical. At one time it was heuristically powerful but is now obstructive because it gives the false impression that everything is understood when it is stated, for example, that each RNA molecule "codes for" one or more proteins, or that development consists merely in the "expression of genetic instructions". Things are different when we come to organisms endowed with endocrine or, *a fortiori*, neuroendocrine systems. Here the environmental and internal inputs are not just nonspecific transfers: sometimes they generate specific signals conveying definite information about such events.

There is a definite "code"—a naturally evolved one of course—whereby stimuli of a certain kind (e.g. thermal) are "translated" (transduced or coded) as neural pulses in the organism; and these signals in turn activate other components, such as muscles or glands. These are signals proper, not just neutral energy fluxes: they carry information and they trigger the release of much greater quantities of energy than they transport. The nervous system, then, is a genuine information network, for it detects, generates, and transmits information in accordance with definite natural "codes". Thus when a sensor is activated by a stimulus, the latter is transduced in a definite manner specific to the sensor. And when the nerve impulse reaches a synaptic cleft it is transduced into a different (chemical) process according to still another "code".

Because the nervous system is an information system, it is legitimate to employ the language of information theory in *formulating* a number of neurophysiological and psychological problems. However, information theory won't suffice to *solve* these problems because they are specific, whereas that theory is extremely general, so much so that it is indifferent to the mechanism of information generation, detection, and transmission. Indeed, as far as the theory is concerned, the information could be mechanical, electrical, chemical, or what you will. For this reason the numerous attempts to understand the mental—and even to underpin psychoneural dualism (as in MacKay, 1978)—in terms of information system engineering are doomed to failure just as the turn of the century attempt to reduce everything to energy exchanges. In general, black-box theories provide only schemata useful in the preliminary stages of research.

Unlike general information theory, psychobiology happens to deal with living systems, in particular with information *bio*systems. Our definition is this:

DEFINITION 2.1. *A system is a* nervous system *if and only if it is an information biosystem(i.e. a living signal detecting and processing system) such that*

   (*i*) *it is composed of (living) cells;*
   (*ii*) *it is or has been a proper part of a multicellular animal;*
   (*iii*) *its structure includes (a) the regulation or control of some of the biofunctions of the animal, and (b) the detection of internal and environmental events, as well as the transmission of signals triggered by some such events.*

This definition is assumed to cover all nervous systems, from simple neural nets to human CNSs. The vertebrate nervous system has a third structural property: it interacts directly with every other system of the animal. And the CNSs of the higher vertebrates (mammals and birds) are more than information processors: they are also information generators. More on this in Ch. 7.

DEFINITION 2.2. *A biosystem is a* neural (*or* neuronal) system *iff it is a subsystem of a nervous system.*

For example, the auditory and speech systems are neural systems. On the other hand, a single neuron is not.

DEFINITION 2.3. *A biosystem is a* neuron (*or* nerve cell) *iff it is a cellular component of a neural system.*

Neural circuits and ganglions, cell assemblies (Hebb, 1949) and neuron populations (Freeman, 1973), working constellations (Luria, 1966), and *pexgos* or itinerant neural systems (Bindra, 1976) are neural systems. So are the functional neuronal columns identified throughout the primate cortex (see Szentágothai and Arbib, 1974; Goldman and Nauta, 1977; Mountcastle, 1978). Of particular interest are the smallest such units, or *minicolumns*, formed by about 110 neurons (except in the visual cortex, where they are constituted by about 260 neurons). The next unit is the *hypercolumn*, which packages about 225 minicolumns. The human neocortex seems to contain about half a million such hypercolumns, and 140 million minicolumns. A single module of either kind may be in turn a member of several distributed systems (Mountcastle, 1978). According to Szentágothai (1978), "the cerebral cortex has to be envisaged as a mosaic of columnar units of remarkably similar internal structure and surprisingly little variation of diameter (200–300 μm). What is different in these columnar units is that each unit has a unique set of specific connections with a number of other columns of the cortex, both in the same and generally also in the opposite hemisphere and also with a unique group of subcortical sites".

Little is known about neural systems compared with what is known about individual neurons. However, great strides are being made, particularly in invertebrate neurophysiology (Kandel, 1976; Fentress, 1976). One of the simplest and best known of all neural systems is the lobster cardiac ganglion. It is composed of only 9 neurons and it produces periodic bursts of electric signals that contract the heart. Another well-investigated system is the lobster stomatogastric ganglion, with 30 neurons and also characterized by periodic bursts. (However, the mechanism of burst production has not yet been disclosed in either case.)

The neuron systems capable of perceiving (detecting and interpreting) signals, imagining, or willing, are probably composed of millions or billions of neurons. However, even a neuron system composed of a few neurons is bound to possess properties that its components lack, i.e. *emergent* properties. Therefore neuron systems are ontologically irreducible entities even if they are (up to a point) epistemically reducible, i.e. explainable in terms of cellular composition and structure. And they are fantastically rich systems: assuming 10^{11} neurons per human brain, 10^3 synapses per neuron, and only two states (*on* and *off*) per synapse, the total number of possible brain states turns out to be 2 raised to 10^{14}, which is greater than the number of atoms in the explored universe.

The preceding remarks counter the dualist argument that, because all cortical neurons look alike (at least to the untrained eye), they cannot be attributed the diversity of functions imputed to them by the monists (Puccetti and Dykes, 1978). Actually no two neurons are strictly identical. (Bullock, 1978, estimates that there are at least 10^8 different kinds of neurons in the human CNS.) But even if they were identical, we know that they form systems (in particular columns)—and, as any child experienced with Lego or Meccano knows, there is no end to the variety of systems that can be formed with a few elements. (After all, the enormous variety of the universe results from combinations of a handful of fields and less than a hundred atomic species.) Besides, the messages from the peripheral receptors are preprocessed before they reach the cortex; for example, there are a dozen relays between retina and visual cortex, and probably just as many between the ear drum and the auditory cortex. So, the cortical neural systems linked to the peripheral sensors receive very different messages even if all are (perhaps) couched in Corticalese.

We emphasize the importance, in vertebrates, of the neural systems or pools composed of thousands, millions, or billions of neurons. Exclusive attention to the individual neuron and its "all or none" firing pattern is misleading for it favors focusing on discontinuous processes and therefore invites the search for analogs in digital computers. Mental processes involve presumably millions of neurons and therefore continuous or quasi-continuous processes. (The spatial and temporal summation of millions of slightly outphased actions results in quasi-continuous processes.) This is important for neural modeling, as it allows one to employ differential equations (MacGregor and Lewis, 1977) as well as to approximate sums by integrals (Rashevsky, 1972). And it disposes of the so-called "grain objection" to the psychoneural identity hypothesis, namely that whereas brain events are spatially and temporally discrete, we can have experience of continuous expanses of red, or of the musical note D. (Recall point (vii) in Ch. 1, Sec. 3.)

In any animal possessing several neural systems, these differ both in internal organization and in their mode of connection. We shall distinguish the following basic types of connectivity or mode of connection (Fig. 2.8).

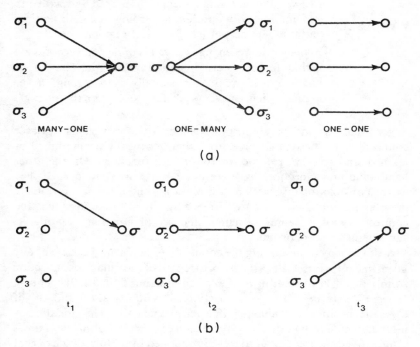

FIG. 2.8. Types of connection among neural systems: (a) constant, (b) variable in time.

Many–one: each afferent fiber synapses on to a single neuron of the receiving system. Unless all inputs are synchronized, the output of the receiving assembly is weak.

CONSTANT

One–many: each afferent fiber synapses on to every neuron of the receiving system. The latter can then act as a constant output transducer amplifying incoming signals.

One–one: each afferent fiber synapses on to one neuron of the receiving system and conversely. The output may be weak but is highly discriminatory.

VARIABLE

Regular: the receiving system is connected now with one system, now with another, according to a definite time pattern. The output is strong and regular.

Random: the receiving system is connected successively with different systems in a random fashion. The output is sometimes weak, occasionally very strong, never regular—hence never predictable except on the average.

We shall assume that constant connections, as well as variable connections of the regular type, are either genetically programmed or learned, and so serve routine (or routinized) functions. On the other hand, random connections have presumably creative functions, i.e. they are responsible for discovery and invention—and error. To formulate these assumptions we start by formalizing the intuitive idea that the connectivity of a neural system is the set of couplings among its subsystems or components.

A simple way of describing the connectivity of a neural system at any given instant is this. Call $C_t(m, n)$ the strength of the synaptic connection from neuron m to neuron n of a given system at time t. In general, $C_t(m, n) \neq C_t(n, m)$. The m–n connection is *excitatory* at t if and only if $C_t(m, n)$ is positive, and *inhibitory* iff $C_t(m, n)$ is negative. The excitation or inhibition caused by cell m in target cell n equals the output of m times $C_t(m, n)$. And the total input to cell n is obtained by adding all the partial inputs, i.e. by summing over m. The matrix $\| C_t(m, n) \|$ displays the total connectivity of the system at time t. The connectivity of a neural system with 1 million neurons is represented by a $1,000,000 \times 1,000,000$ matrix (lumping the hundreds of synapses of each cell into a single junction!).

Since we shall make frequent use of the concept of connectivity, which is usually handled in an intuitive way, we may as well define it explicitly with some care:

DEFINITION 2.4. *Let σ be a neural system and $\mathscr{C}_t(\sigma)$ the neuronal composition of σ at time t. Call*

$$C_t : \mathscr{C}_t(\sigma) \times \mathscr{C}_t(\sigma) \rightarrow [-1, 1]$$

the real valued function such that $C_t(m, n)$, for $m, n \in \mathscr{C}_t(\sigma)$, is the strength of the connection from neuron m to neuron n at time t. Then the connectivity of σ at t is represented by the matrix formed by all the connection values at t, i.e.

$$\mathbb{C}_t = \| C_t(m, n) \|.$$

(*The domain of the function C_t is the Cartesian product of $\mathscr{C}_t(\sigma)$ by itself, i.e. the set of all ordered pairs $\langle m, n \rangle$ of neurons in σ.*)

DEFINITION 2.5. *A* constant connectivity *is one that does not change once established (i.e. such that $\mathbb{C}_t$ is time-independent). A* variable connectivity *is one that is not constant.*

Finally, we can make

DEFINITION 2.6. *A neuron system is* committed (*or* wired-in, *or* prewired, *or* preprogrammed) *iff its connectivity is determined genetically and so is constant either from birth or from a certain stage in the development of the animal. Otherwise the neuron system is* uncommitted (*or* modifiable, *or* plastic, *or* self-organizable).

Note that we have defined neural, not behavioral, plasticity—i.e. we have characterized the changeability of neuronal connectivity, not the modification of behavior. The former entails the latter but not conversely. In fact even automata exhibit changed behavior when stimulated by new inputs (provided they are built to accept them). So, while we can safely assume that behavioral plasticity is universal in the animal kingdom (Davis, 1976), we shall reserve neuronal plasticity for some species only.

Finally, we propose

DEFINITION 2.7. *Every plastic neural system is called a* psychon.

So much for our first definitions. We are now ready for our first assumptions.

6. Basic assumptions on plasticity

Our first hypothesis is quite obvious:

POSTULATE 2.1. *All animals with a nervous system have neuron systems that are committed, and some animals have also neuron systems that are plastic (uncommitted, self-organizable).*

Apparently worms, insects, and other invertebrates have only totally (or nearly totally) wired-in neuron systems: they possess no psychons, hence no mental life. On the other hand, the uncommitted part of the CNS of man is the largest in any animal: it is a sort of vast reserve army ready to meet emergencies, most of which never happen in the course of the individual's life. In behavioral terms: whereas the behavioral repertoire of lowly animals is predetermined (programmed), that of man (and many other vertebrates) can evolve in the course of his life. But behavioral matters will have to wait till Ch. 5.

POSTULATE 2.2. *The neuron systems that regulate the internal milieu, as well as all the biofunctions of the newborn animal, are wired-in (committed).*

For example, the temperature and acidity of the intercellular fluid are regulated mainly by certain wired-in neuron systems, and so are the breathing and sucking movements of the newborn mammal. But those are not the only regulators: also the endocrine system plays an important role in internal control.

POSTULATE 2.3. *The plastic (uncommitted) neuron systems of an animal are coupled to each other forming another system. This super-system will be called the* plastic neural supersystem of the animal, *or P for short.*

POSTULATE 2.4. *Every animal endowed with plastic neural systems (psychons) is capable of acquiring new biofunctions in the course of its life.*

Finally, we adopt

DEFINITION 2.8. *Any neural function involving a plastic neural system (i.e. a psychon) that has acquired a regular connectivity (i.e. one that is constant or varies regularly) is said to be* learned.

In other words, learning is assumed to consist in the formation of new neural systems, i.e. in establishing permanent connections among neurons or facilitating ephemeral but repeatable neuron interconnections. Some such connections may be formed at random for the first time: if biovaluable they have a chance of becoming established (either gradually or at once) or of recurring. And they may involve a number of neural systems. Thus in man learning is sometimes assumed to engage the hypothalamus, reticular formation, extrapyramidal motor system, sensory cortex, and frontal cortex (cf. Pribram, 1971a, b).

In sum, what does the learning is the brain, and not even all of it. The relatively recent finding that it is possible to control (in particular to abate) one's heartbeats, intestinal contractions, and other functions regulated by the autonomic nervous system, does not invalidate our assumption. In fact such learning involves the will, hence it engages plastic cortical systems (psychons) presumably located in the forebrain. We submit that it is the latter, not the autonomic system itself, that learns to control the functions previously regarded as being totally insensitive to what goes on in the plastic neural systems.

The above ideas go back to Tanzi (1893), Ramón y Cajal (1895), and Sherrington (1897): all three conjectured that the existing pathways in the CNS are reinforced by use, that new pathways can be formed, and that some of them weaken by disuse. This is the so-called *use–disuse hypothesis*, refined and brought to the psychological fore by Hebb (1949). This hypothesis, which explains both learning and creativity, was not subjected to adequate tests for many years. For one thing only the spinal cord was investigated for modifiable synapses; for another only electrophysiological techniques were employed. Recent investigations on the synaptogenesis of neurons located higher in the nervous system, as well as finer methods (in particular electron microscopy and microchemistry), have reinforced confidence in the hypothesis (Giacobini, 1971; Moore, 1976; Rutledge, 1976; Greenough *et al.*, 1978;

Spinelli and Jensen, 1978; Cotman, 1978). These investigations have taught us that connectivity changes include changes in the size of the synapse, in the number and volume of the synaptic vesicles, and in the perforations in the synaptic plate. Besides, a few precise models of synaptogenesis are emerging (e.g. Malsburg, 1973; Cowan 1976).

Our definition of learning is neurophysiological rather than behavioral. Firstly, because we have not yet elucidated the notion of behavior. (First come the controllers, then the controlled system.) Secondly, because we need a definition of learning wide enough to include activities—such as evaluating and reasoning—that may have no overt manifestations. Thirdly and most important, because the appearance of a new pattern of behavior in response to stimuli of a new kind may or may not be a result of learning: it may be simply a result of the activation of previously unused nonplastic neural systems.

We close this subsection with a remark on the notion of an information biosystem, in preparation for our discussion of the brain–computer analogy. It has been tacitly assumed in the preceding that not all organisms are information systems, i.e. systems capable of receiving, processing, and transmitting signals of certain kinds. Unicellular organisms, most plants, and animals deprived of a nervous system proper, are not information systems. Hence they can be studied, nay ought to be studied, without the help of the concept of information. Having an endocrine or a neuroendocrine system changes it all, for such a system *is* an information biosystem.

Note that having sensors is not enough for constituting an information system, for any physical system may be said to detect or "sense" signals of some kind and react to them. The sensors of an information system are coupled to other subsystems, namely to transducers or encoders capable of processing and transmitting the input signals, so that these will reach other parts of the organism, which may in turn behave on the strength of that information. (Just think of the chain of processes constituting one of the simplest behavior types, namely the withdrawal reflex: Stimulus – Perception (recognition of obnoxious nature of input) – Muscle activation – Actual withdrawal.)

In sum, the CNS is a genuine information processor—but a living one, and so qualitatively different from an artificial information processor. Besides, as we shall emphasize in Ch. 7, Sec. 3, the CNS of the higher vertebrates is not just an information processor but also an information generator. For all these reasons, although neuroscience can derive some benefit from information theory, it cannot restrict itself to the latter. For, if it does, it won't be able to ask any specific (neurophysiological) questions. Moreover, wearing the information-theoretic straitjacket will suggest loaded questions. For example, if one asks "What is the storage capacity of the human brain?", one begs the question whether the brain stores information at all. However, the limitations of the brain–machine analogy deserve another section.

7. Is the CNS a machine?

The similarity between the functioning or behavior of the CNS and a complex machine, such as an automobile, is quite obvious—particularly in the case of malfunction or accident. Thus if the petrol filters get clogged, the engine stops; likewise if the blood supply to a brain stops, e.g. through heart failure, the brain ceases to perceive, imagine, and reason. If the steering system fails, the car will run aimlessly; likewise, if the frontal lobes of a man are destroyed, he loses foresight and remains at the mercy of circumstances. And if the panel instruments of an automobile are out of order, the latter ceases to monitor its own states; likewise, if the hypothalamus or the reticular formation of a human are destroyed or blocked, he ceases to be conscious. Only the dualist philosopher will fail to be impressed by this analogy—as long as he does not have to commit a mental patient to the repair shop.

The analogy between the brain and a complex information system, such as a digital computer, is even more impressive:

Brain	Computer
Neuron system	Subsystem
Nervous conduction	Information flow
Sensor	Terminal
Sensory input	Software input
Memory trace	Memory (storage)
Mental function	Information processing

The brain–computer analogy is so striking that it has inspired engineers to design and build "electronic brains" capable of mimicking certain brain functions. It has also misled some neuroscientists into believing that the way to understand the brain is to treat it as a machine and, in particular, a digital computer. This view is mistaken because (a) it ignores the specific biochemical and biological properties of neurons and neuron systems, (b) it ignores the spontaneous activity of neurons and psychons—so obvious in dreaming, hallucinating, and creating; (c) it ignores the plasticity of inter-neuron connections; (d) it conflates all the mental functions (feeling, imagining, thinking, willing, expecting, etc.) into a single function, namely computing (or information processing); (e) it ignores the creativity of the human brain, and (f) it ignores development and evolution.

The hypothesis that the brain is (or at least behaves like) a digital computer, was perhaps plausible in the 1950s (see, however, Bunge, 1956). But it has since been experimentally refuted with the discovery that neurons are not all-or-none elements. In fact neurons do much more than either remaining quiescent or firing; in particular, what goes on between synapse and cell body is at least as important as the electrochemical pulse that travels along the axon. The control functions of the brain and the mental functions consume together at least one-fifth of the total body oxygen intake and involve important energy transports and metabolic processes, such as turnover of proteins, nuclei acids, and phospholipids. (During excitation some such functions increase, whereas excessive stimulation can result in exhaustion, e.g. of neurotransmitters.)

For the above reasons the brain, though certainly an information biosystem, is not *just* an information processor. Even the more modest claim that, at least structurally, the brain works like a Turing machine, is false. Firstly, because the latter has a denumerable state space, whereas even atoms and molecules can be in any of a nondenumerable set of states. Secondly, whereas a Turing machine jumps from one state to another only upon receiving external inputs, the brain has a permanent autonomous activity. Thirdly, far from possessing a fixed state space, the primate brain keeps generating and annihiliating states. And, far from having a constant next state function, it has a variable one—as suggested by learning. Therefore when a given stimulus impinges on the animal, it may be matched to a new state or it may fail to be paired off to a state that used to be accessible. Hence a novel response, or else none at all, may ensue. For these reasons the approach to neural modeling via Turing machines or digital computers is extremely unrealistic and impoverishing, and therefore misleading.

A purely behavioral comparison between man and machine is not illuminating, for all it exhibits is certain superficial analogies and disanalogies. Moreover, Turing's famous criterion for deciding whether or not there is any difference between a robot and a human (Turing, 1950)—namely to concentrate on the net output or behavior of the systems being compared—is no criterion at all. Indeed, because it is confined to behavior it *ensures* that no difference be detectable. (Likewise Putnam, 1960, by *stipulating* that the CNS is a Turing machine, is able to conclude that there is no mind–body problem.) Of course there is no difference between man and robot if one stipulates that the only possible relevant difference could lie in behavior. But this stipulation is arbitrary and thus need not be adopted by the physiological psychologist or the neurophysiologist interested in finding out the neural controls of behavior. They may not be able to tell a robot from a human when looking at their behavior, but they will dispel any doubts if allowed to dissect them. Besides, even the most enthusiastic propounders of the thesis that man is a machine call a physician rather than a computer engineer (let alone an electrician or a plumber) when they feel unwell.

Worst of all, the machinist approach to the mind–body problem, being strictly structural and nonbiological, shifts attention from the unique biofunctions of the CNS and thus fosters psychophysical dualism, just as the view that the organism is a machine invites vitalism. In fact machinism has suggested at least three dualistic arguments:

(i) "Because the brain is a machine, and every machine may be said to be the *embodiment* of a design, the brain may be regarded as the embodiment of all possible ideas, i.e. of the human mind." (Even McCulloch, though intent on proving that the mental is a function of the brain, fell into that trap by treating the brain as a digital computer and writing of *Embodiments of Mind*, 1965.) But of course the very notion of embodiment is vague and makes hardly any sense except in the context of Platonic metaphysics, where ideas exist independently from ideation and can enter into things. (Yet Margolis, 1978, calls 'nonreductive materialism' his view on the embodiment of persons.)

(ii) "Because the brain is a machine, it has no consciousness. Hence consciousness must be a separate entity—the famous ghost in the machine ridiculed by Ryle (1949)." (Eccles, who calls the brain a 'neuronal machine' and regards the mind as immaterial, is a case in point.) Much the same holds for other mental states and events: not even the most enthusiastic workers in artificial intelligence (AI) believe any longer that they will ever build a machine capable of seeing red, or enjoying a scenic view, or feeling sorry for a fellow machine. Hence either they must claim that such facts do not really happen, or that they happen but fall outside the province of AI—or that they must be accounted for in nonscientific ways.

(iii) "Just as the computer hardware cannot work unless it is fed some software, so the brain must be given a mind to mentate. In other words, the mind is nothing but the software of the brain machinery—hence something separate from it." But of course this is mistaken: brains form their own functions by maturing and learning, and they are cleared of their minds only in deep sleep or in coma, or at death. Therefore in a living being "the software and hardware are not distinct as they are in a computer" (Young, 1971, p. 130).

However, something may still come out of the brain–computer analogy, not only for computer science but also for neuroscience. In particular, the machinist approach may yield a few organizational or structural principles. (However, so far very little has been learned after three decades of treating the brain as a gigantic information network. The exceptions seem to be two nonplastic subsystems of the human CNS, namely the cerebellum and the reticular formation.) Moreover, in principle it should be possible to synthesize miniature neurons and assemble them into mini-nervous systems. (The prefix 'mini' is suggested by this. Natural neurons perform a number of household functions that need not be discharged by synthetic neurons placed in a nutrient medium.) But such components would be biosystems, so it would not come as a surprise if they could function in a living brain as prostheses filling in for destroyed or removed neuron systems.

To conclude let us pack together some of our objections to the view that all animals, in particular men, are machines:

(i) no machine discharges biofunctions, even though some machines may be designed to imitate certain biofunctions;

(ii) whereas all neurons fire spontaneously, not only when they receive an afferent excitation, no component of a machine has a spontaneous activity—unless it goes out of order; in particular, whereas human memories are active (distorting), computer memories are passive (faithful);

(iii) machines are not subject to spontaneous mutation and natural selection: they do not evolve spontaneously but as a result of human (cultural) evolution;

(iv) while all machines have been designed by some men, no man has so far been designed by anyone, let alone by a machine;

(v) while some animal actions are purposeful and guided by foresight, the machines that act purposefully (i.e. that are goal-seeking) do so by proxy, i.e. on behalf of their designers or users;

(vi) since machines are not alive, they cannot possess any psychical properties: at most they can imitate the net result of some of them—much as cars imitate walking;

(vii) in the case of brains the hardware–software dichotomy makes no sense—or, if preferred, brains are largely self-programmed;

(viii) while computers are industrious and efficient, and can even be said to be smart, they can hardly be said to be imaginative, creative, or original: they can solve problems of certain kinds, apply some theories and value systems, but they do not invent or create them;

(ix) while computers and robots are the property of somebody (individual, corporation, or state), people are not—except of course under slavery; it is hard to imagine that anybody would wish to design and put together a robot yearning for freedom, feeling self-pity and moral indignation, etc.;

(x) the computer models of the brain are black box models that disregard the biological specificity of the brain components as well as their development and their evolutionary history: hence they do not tell us what makes them tick.

For these reasons, if we wish to understand mind we had better study animals rather than machines. (For further objections see Bunge, 1956; Clarke, 1967; Dreyfus, 1972; Watanabe, 1975; Weizenbaum, 1976.)

We close this chapter with a word on the old philosophical problem of other minds. How do we know that other people, unlike computers, are able to mentate? Just by analogy with our own subjective experience or overt behavior? These analogies doubtless suggest the hypothesis but do not establish it. What does justify us in attributing minds to other humans are the close similarities among all human brains as well as our knowing or conjecturing some lawful relations among mental processes and their behavioral manifestations. Such inference is similar to that involved in attributing hearts and lungs to the mammals and birds we see for the first time in the zoo (and abstain from dissecting). By the same token we would not be justified in attributing minds to computers for, since their components are radically different from living cells, their functions are bound to be dissimilar as well.

CHAPTER 3

The Functions

1. Brain functions

The *functions* of a biosystem, such as an organ, are the processes occurring in the system—i.e. what the system does. And the *specific functions* of the system are those the system but no thing of any other kind is capable of doing. (For a formalization of these notions, see Bunge, 1979a, Ch. 3.) Just as there is no system without functions (activities), so there is no function without some system that does the functioning. When a neuroscientist says that function X is "mediated" or "subserved" by "structure" (neuron system) Y, he means that Y *does* X and, more precisely, that X is among the specific or peculiar activities of Y. The structure–function (or system–process) separation is just as artificial as the separation of anatomy from physiology. Neither is understandable without the other.

Being a multibillion neuron system, the mammalian CNS engages in activities of a large variety, from synthesizing proteins to controlling the functions of other organs to performing higher functions such as forming a map of the surroundings. We shall not be concerned with the nonspecific or "household" CNS functions, such as protein synthesis, except to point out that, if anything, they are more intense in the brain than in other parts of the body, as judged from the rates of oxygen intake and protein turnover. We shall instead focus on the specific functions of the CNS, which may be grouped into two large classes: *control* and *cognition*. (Needless to say, distinction entails no detachment. For example, motor control is necessary for perception, hence for modeling the environment, which models are in turn necessary to behave successfully.) The schema in Table 3.1 may be of some help in this regard.

Table 3.1. *Classification of CNS functions*

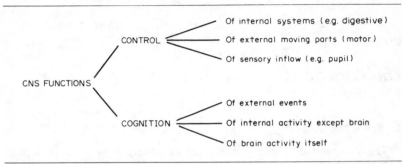

There are subcellular controls, such as enzymes, and cellular controls, e.g. that of neuron firing. Hence control is not peculiar to the CNS. What *is* peculiar to the control functions of the CNS is that they are ultimate and integrative: the CNS "says the last word" and it interrelates all control mechanisms and, through them, the entire body. In this manner it achieves, in the healthy organism, states close to synergy or harmonious functioning of the various subsystems.

The chain of events subject to biocontrol is (wrongly) said to be "hierarchical" because, far from being all on the same level, those events are grouped into different sets ordered by the relation of controlling. Indeed, a typical biocontrol chain of events looks like this:

(1) imbalance of some sort (e.g. water deficit);
(2) imbalance detection (e.g. by the hypothalamus);
(3) onset of regulatory mechanism (e.g. drinking behavior); failing this,
(4) residual imbalance detection;
(5) onset of higher level regulatory process (e.g. search for water), etc.

We shall say next to nothing about the control activities of the CNS, not because they are uninteresting but because they are of little philosophical import. Indeed, few dualists will deny them since Descartes dissipated the animal spirits and declared the body to be a machine. (Nevertheless, something will be said in Ch. 5, Sec. 1.) We shall focus instead on the cognitive activities of the CNS and shall group them as follows.

(1) *Knowledge of the external world*, i.e. of the immediate surroundings of the animal. This can be obtained in a direct manner, namely perceptually, or indirectly, namely intellectually. We shall deal with the former in Ch. 4 and with the latter in Ch. 7.

(2) *Self-knowledge*

   (2.1) *Feeling and emotion*, i.e. the information the brain receives from the rest of the body (and processes and integrates). Thus fear, an activity of the amygdala, may be regarded as the monitoring of accelerated pulse beating, sweating, diaphragm contraction, etc. Fear—like anger, hate, love, and well-being—is diffuse. Other modes of bodily self-cognition, in particular stabs of pain and pleasurable skin sensations, are localized. But whether diffuse or localized, feelings and emotions are brain functions. (No apologies to the radical rationalist for subsuming feeling and emotion under cognition. Feeling fear or desire, sadness or elation, are ways of knowing one's dispositions or reactions to certain events in the body or in the environment.)

   (2.2) *Self-consciousness*, i.e. the brain's cognition of its own states. It may be regarded as a function of certain "closed circuits" in the brain, i.e. processes without an immediate output. We shall deal with this function in Ch. 8.

We proceed now to explain a mode of representing CNS functions that tallies with the state space approach as well as with the definitions and principles laid down in Ch. 2.

2. Representation of CNS activity

Consider an arbitrary neuron system, be it a small neural column (fixed or itinerant), a sizable subsystem of the CNS (such as the hippocampus), or the entire brain. Like every other system, it can be represented by a state function $\mathbb{F} = \langle F_1, F_2, \ldots, F_n \rangle$ which, for the sake of simplicity, may be taken to have a finite number n of components. (See e.g. Bunge 1977a or 1977b.) If we are not interested in the precise localization of the system and its components but only in its overall spatial properties, we can assume that $\mathbb{F}$ is only a time-dependent function whose values are *n*-tuples of real numbers. That is, we can set $F: T \to \mathbb{R}^n$, with T included in the set $\mathbb{R}$ of real numbers. (We take the host of the neuron system, e.g. its skull, as its reference frame.)

Each component F_i of the state function can be decomposed into a constant part F_i^c and a variable part F_i^v (Fig. 3.1). Obviously, either can be zero during the period of interest. But the point is that, while the rate of change of F_i^c vanishes at all times (i.e. $\dot{F}_i^c = 0$), that of F_i^v does not. The latter may therefore be taken to represent the activity of the neuron system in the *i*th respect. For this reason we make

DEFINITION 3.1. *Let* $\mathbb{F}: T \to \mathbb{R}^n$ *be a state function representing a neural system v, and let* $\mathbb{F} = \mathbb{F}^c + \mathbb{F}^v$, *with* $\dot{\mathbb{F}}^c = 0$ *(nil rate of change) for all* $t \in T$. *Then*

  (i) *v is* active *at time t iff* $\mathbb{F}^v(t) \neq 0$;
  (ii) *the* activity *of v over the time lapse* $\tau \subset T$ *equals the fraction of components of v active during* τ.

In neuroscience it is common to measure the activity of individual neurons by either their action potential or their firing frequency. But these are not the only possible activity measures and they are not suitable for neuronal assemblies. A good measure of the activity of such multineuronal systems is the extra blood inflow, which can be monitored with the help of radioisotopes. Let these remarks suffice concerning the problem of measurability of neuron system activity.

Every state of activity of a neural system is then a value of the variable part of the state function of the system; hence every process occurring in the system is a list of successive states of activity of the system as a whole. In other words, we adopt

DEFINITION 3.2. *Let* $\mathbb{F}^v: T \to \mathbb{R}^n$ *be the variable part of the state function of a neural system v. Then*

  (i) *the state of activity of v at time* $t \in T$ *is* $s = \mathbb{F}^v(t)$:
  (ii) *the (total)* process *(or* function) *v is engaged in over the time interval* $\tau \subset T$ *is the list (ordered set) of states of activity of v:*
$$\pi(v, \tau) = \langle \, \mathbb{F}^v(t) \,|\, t \in \tau \, \rangle.$$

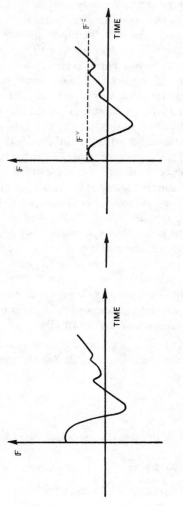

Fɪɢ. 3.1. Decomposition of a state function $\mathbb{F}$ into a constant part $\mathbb{F}^c$ and a variable part $\mathbb{F}^v$. The latter represents the functions (i.e. the activity) of the system. (The decomposition is a particular case of a linear coordinate transformation.)

Whereas single neurons may pass twice through roughly the same state of activity, it is most unlikely that a neural system composed of a million neurons will do the same. We may assume that there are no two identical states of activity of a medium-size neural system and, *a fortiori*, of a gross neural system such as, say, the hippocampus or the olfactory area. Since mental states will be identified with some such states of activity, it follows that no mental event ever recurs in exactly the same form. (To be sure one can neglect such variations to a first approximation. Thus Stevens' power law $\psi = k\phi^n$, relating the intensity ψ of the subjective experience of a sensory stimulus ϕ, makes no provision for the state of the animal at the time of stimulation, let alone for its experience and expectation. Yet since these additional factors do play a role, they will have to be incorporated into a more sophisticated law statement. By the way, it may be conjectured that the intensity ψ of the subjective experience equals the firing frequency of the neuronal system processing the corresponding sensory stimulus (see Thompson, 1975). This is of course in tune with the psychoneural identity hypothesis.)

We now introduce the concept of specific activity of a neural system. The processes characterizing a neural system are those it alone, of all the subsystems of a given animal, can engage in. In order to formalize this concept we introduce the notion of a scrambled process or, rather, scrambled representation of a process. This representation exhibits the successive states that make up a process without their order: it is a plain set rather than an ordered set or list. Formally:

DEFINITION 3.3. *Let $\pi(v,\tau) = \langle \mathbb{F}^v(t)|t \in \tau \rangle$ be the (total) process that a neural system v in an animal b engages in during the time interval $\tau \subset T$. Then the corresponding*

(*i*) scrambled process *is*
$$\bar{\pi}(v,\tau) = \{\mathbb{F}^v(t)|t \in \tau\};$$
(*ii*) specific scrambled process (*or* specific function) v *engages in during τ is*
$$\bar{\pi}_s(v,\tau) = \bar{\pi}(v,\tau) - \underset{\mu < b}{\cup}\bar{\pi}(\mu,\tau), \textit{ with } \mu \neq v,$$
where $A - B = A \cap \bar{B}$, and '$\mu < b$' stands for "μ is a subsystem of b".

(*Caution*. The holist will probably object that the organism breathes, digests, feels, etc., with its whole body, in the sense that no individual subsystem of the latter can function properly in isolation from the rest. Granted. However, it is only a certain subsystem that is "in charge" of a specific function, all others being in this respect supporting subsystems. In particular, we think with the brain not with the pituitary, the thyroid, and the adrenal glands, even though the former would not function normally without the latter. The coupling among the various components of a system should not lead to denying that they are different entities, and that some of them have different functions.)

There are two main views concerning CNS activity: we shall call them the *causal* and the *autogenic* views. According to the former, the CNS is normally quiescent, being activated only by stimulation coming either from other subsystems of the body or from the environment. This is the view of Sherrington, Pavlov, S–R psychology, and the computer models of the CNS as an information processor or as a deterministic automaton. The causal view enjoys no experimental support whatever and is just an example of the Peripatetic maxim *Omne quod movetur ab alio movetur* ("Whatever moves is moved by another"). Indeed, neither physics nor chemistry nor, *a fortiori*, biology know of any systems that change only when acted on by outside inputs (cf. Bunge, 1959, 1977a, 1979a). For this reason we may postulate that every thing changes spontaneously in some respects, inductively in others.

Research on single neurons, such as the motoneurons of invertebrates, has provided strong confirmation of this hypothesis. (Moreover, the intrinsic fluctuations of the membrane electric potential are quite patent and measurable.) At the other end of the scale, the experiments on sensory deprivation have shown that the CNS is active even when the sensory inflow stops. (But they have also shown how important sensory stimulation is for the *normal* functioning of the CNS: the subject cut off from the external world does not even have a correct image of himself.) We shall therefore adopt the hypothesis that the CNS, and every neural subsystem of it, is constantly active even in the absence of external stimuli; and that the latter modify or modulate the ongoing activity of the system rather than being its only source of change.

To obtain a general principle of spontaneous central activity consider m neurons synapting on to a given neuron i. The rate of change of the latter's state of activity can be assumed to consist of an autonomous (spontaneous) part and another proportional to the signals of the afferent fibers:

$$\dot{F}_i^v(t) = A_i(t) + \sum_{j=1}^{m} C_t(j, i) F_j^v(t),$$

where $C_t(i, j)$ is the strength of the i–j connection. This system of equations is undetermined (incomplete). It has to be supplemented with a system of equations for the rates of change of the connectivities. A popular hypothesis is

$$C_t(i, j) = c_{ij} \exp(-|x_{ij}|/b),$$

where the c_{ij} and b are real numbers, and $|x_{ij}|$ the distance between the units i and j. Another interesting candidate would seem to be

$$\dot{C}_t(i, j) = c_{ij} F_i^v.$$

(For some mathematical models of the dynamics of cortical systems, see Marr, 1970; Wilson and Cowan, 1973; and Nass and Cooper, 1975.)

However, here we are interested only in the general principle, which can be stated thus:

POSTULATE 3.1. *For any neural system v of an animal, the instantaneous state of activity of v is decomposed additively into two functions:* $F^v = A + E$, *where* A *does not vanish for all* $t \in T$, *and* E *depends upon the stimuli impinging on v from other subsystems of the animal.*

DEFINITION 3.4. *Let* $F^v = A + E$ *be the active part of the state function of a neural system v. Then* $A(t)$ *is called the* state of spontaneous activity *of v at time t, and* $E(t)$ *the* state of induced (*or* stimulated) *activity of v at t.*

(Contrast Postulate 3.1 with the McCulloch and Pitts, 1943, model, where $A = 0$.)

Once we know, or pretend to know, how a neural system works, we may attempt to find out how two or more neural systems combine to form a supersystem. Suppose v_1 and v_2 are two neural systems of a given animal with the same number m of neurons each (e.g. two cortical columns), with active state functions F_1^v and F_2^v respectively. And suppose further that the neurons in v_1 synapse on to those in v_2 so that v_2 has a stimulated or induced activity in addition to its spontaneous activity. The simplest assumption is of course that the induced activity E_2

of v_2 depends linearly upon $\mathbb{F}_1^v$, i.e. $\mathbb{E}_2 = C\mathbb{F}_1^v$, where C is an $m \times m$ matrix representing the inter-system connectivity. This connectivity changes in time: we assume that it strengthens with use and weakens with disuse. If v_1 fails to activate v_2, the value of C will have decreased, after one time interval, to $C(t+1) = aC(t)$, with $0 < a < 1$. After k time intervals, $C(t+k) = a^k C(t)$, which approaches zero as time goes by. If, on the other hand, v_2 is activated by v_1, the connectivity will be strengthened in proportion to the simultaneous activity of the two neural systems (Hebb's hypothesis). That is, the increment in connectivity will be $\delta C(t) = b\,\mathbb{F}_1^v\,\mathbb{F}_2^v$, where b is an $m \times m$ matrix of real numbers, some positive, others negative. Hence in general the connectivity value at time t will be

$$C(t) = aC(t-1) + b\,\mathbb{F}_1^v\,\mathbb{F}_2^v,$$

so that the state of activity of v_2 at t will be represented by

$$\mathbb{F}_2^v(t) = \mathbb{A}_2(t) + aC(t-1)\,\mathbb{F}_1^v(t) + b\left[\,\mathbb{F}_1^v(t)\,\mathbb{F}_2^v(t)\,\right]\,\mathbb{F}_1^v(t).$$

This is just a speculative proposal for the building of a whole class of neural models. (For a similar model, see Cooper, 1973; for a simpler one, Amari, 1977.) However, models of this sort are experimentally testable and, moreover, they suggest their own tests. Thus by controlling the stimulated part of $\mathbb{F}_1^v$ and measuring the spontaneous activities of v_1 and v_2—i.e. $\mathbb{A}_1$ and $\mathbb{A}_2$—as well as the total output $\mathbb{F}_2$, one may check the above model. The philosophical interest of this model lies in showing that it *is* possible to construe mental states and events as states and events of neural systems provided one makes use of the appropriate mathematical tools. On the other hand, the ordinary language version of the psychoneural identity hypothesis sounds just as paradoxical as the ordinary language version of the hypothesis that light is (identical with) a propagating electromagnetic field, or that hereditary traits are encoded in DNA molecules.

3. Mental states and processes

Every fact experienced introspectively as mental is identical with some brain activity: this, in a nutshell, is the so-called *psychoneural identity theory*, or *psychobiological hypothesis of the mental. Example 1:* Vision (normal or hallucinatory) consists in the activity of neural systems in the visual system (including the visual association cortex in higher vertebrates). *Example 2*: Learning is the formation of new neural systems (or connections). *Example 3*: Recall is the reactivation of neural connections.

Not all brain activity is mental, and not all neural systems are capable of carrying out mental functions (activities, processes). For example, only some of the activities of the cortical component of the visual system are mental: those of the committed or wired-in components (e.g. the retina and the optic nerve) are not mental. (Recall Postulate 2.2.) Only the uncommitted neural systems are capable of learning; i.e. learning is an activity of the associative cortex, or the portion of the cortex that is neither sensory nor motor. Moreover, we shall hypothesize that the uncommitted (or plastic) neural systems are the "seats" or "neural correlates" of the mental. More precisely, we shall assume that every mental state or process is a state of activity or process of some uncommitted (plastic) neural system modulo its household functions: i.e. the mental is the *specific* function of some such system. Our assumption takes the form of

DEFINITION 3.5. *Let b be an animal endowed with a plastic neural system P. Then*

(i) *b undergoes a* mental process (*or* performs a mental function) *during the time interval τ if and only if P has a subsystem v such that v is engaged in a specific process during τ (i.e. $\overline{\pi}_s(v, \tau) \neq \phi$);*
(ii) *every state (or stage) in a mental process of b is a mental state of b.*

Example 1: Acts of will are presumably specific activities of neuronal modules in the forebrain. *Example 2*: Reading is an activity of the visual system together with Broca's speech area and the supplementary motor area. *Nonexample*: Hunger, thirst, fear, rage, and sexual urge are processes in subcortical systems (mainly hypothalamic and limbic), hence they are *nonmental* according to our definition. What *is* mental is the consciousness of any such states—which consciousness is a process in some subsystems of *P*.

Some immediate consequences of our definition follow.

COROLLARY 3.1. *All and only the animals endowed with plastic (uncom-*

mitted or not-wired-in) neural systems are capable of being in mental states (or undergoing mental processes).

Since most species lack plastic neural systems, most organisms have no mental life. In particular, plants and insects have none. (Hence, stop talking to your ferns and ants.)

COROLLARY 3.2. *All mental disorders are neural disorders.*

That is, not only the "organic" but also the "functional" disturbances are nervous tissue disorders—not necessarily cellular though. Therefore the current separation between neurology, psychiatry, and clinical psychology is unnatural.

COROLLARY 3.3. *Mental functions (processes) cease with the death of the corresponding neural systems.*

COROLLARY 3.4. *Mental functions (processes) cannot be transferred directly (without any physical transmission lines) from one brain to another.*

That is, extrasensory perception is out of the question if one admits that the mental is a brain function. On the other hand, only technical difficulties are currently in the way of inter-brain communication with physical means other than optical, acoustical, tactual, and other conventional signals. However, telepathy via electromagnetic waves emitted, received and decoded by brains is impossible if only because the radiation emitted by the brain is far too weak for that purpose (Taylor and Balanovski, 1979).

Using Definition 3.3(ii) of specific activity we make

DEFINITION 3.6. *Let P be a plastic (uncommitted) supersystem of an animal b of species K. Then*

(i) *the mind of b during the period τ is the union of all the mental processes that components of P engage in during τ:*

$$m(b, \tau) = \bigcup_{v < P} \overline{\pi}_s(v, \tau);$$

(ii) *the K-mind (or mind of species K) during period τ is*

$$M(K, \tau) = \bigcup_{k \in K} m(k, \tau).$$

Since the members of the set called 'mind' are brain functions (processes), it makes no sense to say that the brain is the "physical basis" of the mind. (Besides, that expression is dualistic: it suggests that, whereas the brain is material, the mind is immaterial.) And since the human mind is nothing but the union of all the individual human minds (clause (ii) of the above definition), it makes no sense to talk about the *collective mind* of mankind as if it were an entity or even a functional system.

On the other hand, the mind of an individual animal does have a functional unity. In fact recall that the components of the plastic or uncommitted plastic neural supersystem, far from being uncoupled, form a system (Postulate 2.3). This is the "neural basis"—pardon me—of the unity of the individual mind, on which many philosophers have insisted. In our framework this unity is expressed by

COROLLARY 3.5. *The mental functions of (processes in) the plastic neural supersystem of an animal are coupled to one another, i.e. they form a functional system. (That is, for every animal b and every period τ of its existence, $m(b, \tau)$, if nonvoid, is a functional system.)*

Consequently, when the neurosurgeon cuts a living primate brain into two, he splits the plastic system into two, and thus also the corresponding mind of the animal. More on this in Sec. 4.

Our last convention is

DEFINITION 3.7. *Let x be an object and b an animal endowed with a plastic neural system. Then*

(i) *x is in the mind of b iff x is a mental state or a mental process of b (i.e. if b has a plastic neural system engaged in a specific process containing x as a member or as a subset);*

(ii) *x is in the mind (or is mental) iff there is at least one animal y such that x is in the mind of y.*

Remark 1. Our concept of the mental hinges on our previous definition of the concept of a specific process in some plastic (nonpre-wired) neural system. Actually there is no such thing as a specific process but only a specific *feature* of a process. Indeed, in Definition 3.2 a real process in v during τ is denoted by $\pi(v, \tau)$: it is only by abstracting from whatever is common to other processes in the same animal that we manufacture the notion of a specific process $\overline{\pi}_s(v, \tau)$—or rather the specific features of a process (Definition 3.3). Thus each mental process will be accompanied by a host of other processes in the same neural system, such as protein turnover and blood flow. Consequently, although we can represent a neural process in a neural system by an arc of a curve in the state space of a brain, we cannot represent in a similar way the corresponding "pure" mental process. (Unless of course we shrink the state space, disregarding all the axes representing "household" functions.) Which is just as well because there are no purely mental processes. (Cf. Ch. 7, Sec. 1.) Therefore when reading a state space diagram such as Fig. 3.2 we must remember that the arc of a curve in it represents the entire process, of which the corresponding mental process is just one feature or aspect.

Remark 2. A mental state, or state of mind, may be roughly constant—e.g. one of perceiving a stationary thing for a while. However, any such state is a state of *activity* of some neural system: no such activity, no mentation. In other words, mental states are more like states of motion than like static states such as the state of a gas in a rigid enclosure placed in a constant environment.

Remark 3. We have stated that mental states are neural states (or features of such), not that every neural state has a mental "correlate". Although different mental states are different neural states, the converse is not true: one and the same mental event could now be a process in one itinerant neural system, now in another. To be sure there will be some differences: even when doing routine sums for all we know we may engage a different itinerant neural system each time—but we won't notice the difference introspectively (Bindra, 1976). (Calling N the set of neural states that happen to be mental, and M the set of mental states distinguishable introspectively, we shall find that M is the quotient of N by the relation of introspective equivalence, i.e. $M = N/\sim$.) Introspection is as coarse a means of looking inwardly (into our brain) as vision is one of looking outwardly. Just as we do not see much of the external world without the help of microscopes, telescopes, and scientific theories, so we do not succeed in "seeing" much of what goes on within our skulls without the help of all the instrumental and theoretical paraphernalia of neuroscience.

Remark 4. In our framework a *change of mind* is a neural event, i.e. a

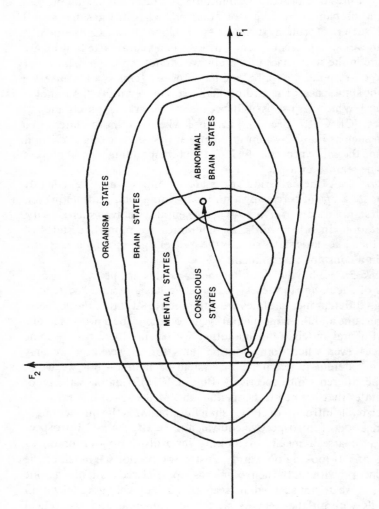

FIG. 3.2.   Projection of state space of human being. Both axes represent neurophysiological properties, but one of them or some function of both is identical with a psychological property. Arc of curve represents mental process, which is only partly conscious and may even have an abnormal segment.

change in the state of some neural system or other. For example an animal faced with n different alternatives may prefer now one, now another, perhaps with different propensities (probabilities) in each case. His mental states and changes of state with regard to such options may be represented by the $n \times n$ matrix $\|P_{ij}\|$ of the transition probabilities, where P_{ij}, for $i \neq j$, is the probability of the change of mind from state i to state j, whereas P_{ii} is the probability that the animal sticks to the ith alternative.

Remark 5. Our Corollary 3.2, that all mental disorders are neural disorders, contradicts the standard dichotomy between organic and functional (or behavioral) disorders. This dichotomy, and the accompanying division of labor (into neurology and psychiatry), is inspired by psychoneural dualism. According to psychophysical monism all mental states, whether normal or abnormal, are organic: they are all states of the CNS. The difference is not one between organic and psychological disorders but one between sickness originating at the *cell* level (e.g. dopamine deficiency or thyroid deficiency) and sickness at the *system* (or subsystem) level—i.e. wrong connections. Because of the plasticity of a large part of the human cortex, systemic or behavioral disorders can often be cured by relearning (e.g. behavior therapy, or mere change of environment), at least as long as the corresponding neural connections are not too rigid. On the other hand, sick neurons call for a biochemical (or psychopharmacological) approach instead of logo-therapy: cells do not listen. In short, we propose replacing the organic/behavioral dichotomy of mental illness by the following classing:

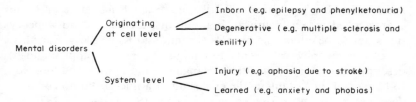

Remark 6. So far we have asserted only that an animal has a mind just in case it has got a plastic neural system, i.e. if and only if its nervous system can do something that is not genetically predetermined in all

detail. But we have not mentioned any species complying with this condition—nor shall we do so here. Neuroscience does not know yet for certain which animal species, other than primates, do have a mind, i.e. possess plastic neural systems. To be sure everyone has his own ideas in this respect, but the problem has not been investigated scientifically except with a few standard laboratory animals. Even in these cases there is uncertainty due to the dual habits of denying the mental and of characterizing it in mentalistic terms. Our previous assumptions and definitions allow for a neurophysiological investigation of the problem—one which, incidentally, belongs to comparative and evolutionary psychology.

Remark 7. The human child is not so much plastic as remarkably immature at birth as compared with other animals. The growth and maturation of the child's brain—in particular its neocortex and corpus callosum—consists in progressive dendritic ramifications and in myelinization. Because of the immaturity of its CNS, the newborn child cannot be attributed a mind—but of course it does have the capacity of forming one, and quickly. Yet psychoanalysts still speak of intrauterine mental life—not to speak of the alleged "sexual experiences" of the infant, which would be the origin of the adult's neuroses. (See, Jones 1961, p. 232.)

Remark 8. We have not characterized mental states and events independently of brain states and events, as is usually done. We have not proceeded this way for a number of reasons. Firstly, because mentalistic predicates, such as "sees red" and "thinks hard" are, though indispensable, coarse and vulgar rather than exact and scientific. Secondly, because the whole point of the neurophysiological approach to mind should be to get away from the ordinary knowledge approach and render mind accessible to science. Thirdly, because, if mental events are characterized independently of brain events, then the identity theory turns out to be either idle or false (Brandt and Kim, 1967). Fourthly, because some physical events too might be given (simple-minded) descriptions in everyday mentalistic language, and so would be "proved" to be mental. For example, the explosion of a nuclear bomb could be described as the most frightening experience. (See Davidson, 1970, for the strange claim that *all* physical events might be described in mentalistic terms and so might seem to *be* mental events. In the same paper mental events are declared to be lawless—unlike physical events.

These strange results come from (a) failing to define the concept of an event, (b) confusing events with their descriptions, and (c) believing that ordinary language descriptions are relevant to the problem.)

Remark 9. The dualist's claim that the mental must be nonphysical because it cannot be described in physical terms, such as 'pressure' and 'conductivity', misses the point. Firstly, although such events as nightmares and feeling a sour taste are not describable in strictly physical terms, they are—at least in principle—describable in neurophysiological terms. Secondly, in ordinary life we may never care to describe mental states or events in neural terms, just as we do not care to describe such ordinary physical events as a car crash and the burning of a light bulb with the paraphernalia of physical theory. It would not be worth our while to do so; we are satisfied knowing that, if need be, such events (or some of their features) could be accounted for in scientific terms.

Remark 10. Mind and brain are not identical: there is no more brain–mind identity than there is lung–respiration identity. In our version of the identity "theory", the set of mental events is a subset of the events in the plastic neural systems of the animal.

Remark 11. We shall continue to put double quotes around the term 'theory' as long as the neural systems (e.g. neuron columns, circuits, itinerant cell assemblies) engaged in mentating are not identified the way neural systems (and sometimes even individual neurons) "responsible" for motor functions are being identified by invertebrate neuroscientists. We have just produced a *framework* for a theory proper—or rather a matrix for a whole class of specific theories of the mental. Only the latter are empirically testable and in particular refutable: extremely general theories are at best only confirmable (Bunge, 1973a).

Remark 12. We may now speak of *the mental* and even of *the mind* without cautionary quotation marks. On the other hand, we should be wary of the words 'soul' and 'spirit', and even more so of the expressions 'objective spirit (or mind)' and 'absolute spirit', supposed to denote a supraindividual mind existing by itself. The idea of an unembodied soul, spirit, or mind, is just an *asylum ignorantiae*. Presumably it was unavoidable ten thousand years ago, when there was no science to explain the world, but there is no justification for using it in what passes for the Age of Science.

Remark 13. Philosophers have debated for centuries the question whether the mind is passive (empiricism) or active (idealism), i.e. whether it is totally dependent upon environmental stimulation or totally self-reliant. As soon as the focus is shifted from the mind to the brain and its activities, the entire issue evaporates. Like every other biosystem, the brain is *both* autonomous (self-starting) in some respects and dependent upon the environment.

Remark 14. Definition 3.7 of "being in the mind" suggests the following philosophy of mathematics. Mathematical objects, such as classes and functions, are objects that *can be only in some mind*. That is, mathematical objects are patterns of possible brain processes: they do not exist elsewhere nor by themselves, apart from thinking brains. Likewise mythical objects, such as Zeus and Mickey Mouse, are no more than that—and also no less for, after all, brain processes are real or can be actualized. The mind is finite: we can think only finitely many mathematical objects. But we make up for this finiteness by *pretending* that all those possibilities that are not actualized exist (formally). Thus although we shall never be able to derive all the infinitely many theorems of a theory, we feign that they exist: this alone authorizes us to speak of *the theory*. This, in a nutshell, is our fictionist and materialist philosophy of mathematics.

Remark 15. Pegasus and Maxwell's equations are in the mind (of somebody at some time). Both exist then as brain processes (and only as such); in this they are alike. But they are unlike in that, whereas Pegasus is a concept and an image with an empty extension (i.e. no counterpart in the external world), the Maxwell equations represent fairly well (truthfully) all possible real electromagnetic fields. This, then, is a difference between myths and scientific constructs: although both exist only in some minds, the former do not represent while the latter do represent real things.

Remark 16. The difference between the internal and the external worlds is not absolute but relative to the brain: what is internal to mine is external to yours and conversely.

Remark 17. Some physicists claim that quantum mechanics concerns only objects subject to observation or measurement; and, since these operations can only be carried out by conscious beings, quantum mechanics would necessarily include reference to conscious processes, and thus be supraphysical. Even the most cursory examination of quantum mechanics shows that it is not concerned with mental processes: none of its variables refers to any mental trait, and none of the problems that the theory solves successfully is a psychological problem (Bunge, 1973b). But even if quantum mechanics, or some other theory, did refer in part to mind, it would not therefore be nonphysical, for mental processes are physical processes in the large (etymological) sense of 'physical'.

Remark 18. Because the human brain is composed of a number of subsystems that can function in parallel (though with some mutual interference), it can perform several mental tasks at the same time—such as seeing, hearing, and having flashbacks while thinking.

Remark 19. The lack of confidence of philosophers in the ability of matter to think may be due to their regarding the stone, rather than the gyroscope or some other self-controlled system, as the paradigm of matter: indeed anyone who has held a spinning top in his hands cannot help being impressed by its activity and persistence.

4. Mind–matter interaction

The interactionist variety of dualism, from Descartes (1649) to Popper and Eccles (1977), holds that matter and mind, though separate and heterogeneous, act upon one another. We have seen in Ch. 1, Secs. 2 and 4, that this doctrine can hardly be stated because interactions are well defined only for concrete things. Thus to speak of mind–body interaction is just as mistaken as speaking of shape–body, or motion–body, or composition–system, or behavior–animal, or property–thing interactions.

However, it does make sense to speak of mental–bodily interactions provided this expression is taken to abbreviate "interactions among plastic (uncommitted) neural systems, on the one hand, and either committed neural systems or bodily systems that are not part of the CNS". *Example 1*: The interactions between cortical and subcortical regions of the CNS, between sensory and motor areas, between ideational neural systems and external receptors, between the visual cortex and the pituitary, etc. *Example 2*: Yogis learn to regulate their heartbeats, intestinal contractions, and even rate of oxygen intake (cf.

Miller, 1969). *Example 3*: A person's train of thought can be interrupted by the hearing of a scream, the onset of pain, or the intake of a drug.

Paradoxically enough, while the dualist has no right to claim that mental events influence nonmental bodily events (because he has no clear notion of such influence), the monist is entitled to this opinion: he makes sense when speaking of psychosomatic effects. Indeed, since mental events are for him neural events of a kind, they can influence and even cause other events in any subsystem of the same body because of the integrative action of the CNS. In short, because mental events are neural events, and the causal relation is defined for pairs of events in concrete things (Bunge, 1977a, Ch. 6, Def. 6.23), we have

COROLLARY 3.6. *Mental events can cause nonmental events in the same body and conversely.*

Consequently disturbances of nonmental (e.g. metabolical) bio-functions may influence mental states and, conversely, mental events, such as acts of will, may influence nonmental bodily states. This is what neurology, neurochemistry, psychiatry, education, and propaganda are all about.

Example 1: A blow on the head can "knock out the mind" of the patient, erasing all memory of events immediately preceding the accident. An equally familiar example is the stroke, or cessation of motor and mental activities as a result of the flooding of a brain hemisphere. (The dual event is artery clogging, e.g. by bacteria or parasites, which has similar effects.) *Example 2*: By implanting electrodes in selected sites of the brain, and sending electric currents through them, the neurophysiologist can control some mental states and, through them, elicit or block behavior such as rage (cf. Delgado, 1969). *Example 3*: By cutting certain nerve fibers, or removing entire CNS areas, the neurosurgeon can eliminate malfunctioning neural systems that prevent the normal functioning of the rest of the body—e.g. causing epileptic seizures.

Example 4: Suggestion, with or without hypnosis, seems to consist in inducing a brain process of a certain kind (a belief) that in turn elicits a somatic change such as a movement or a skin reaction (Barber, 1978).

The most dramatic and revealing of all surgical interventions is of course commisurotomy, or the sectioning of the bridge between the two cerebral hemispheres, or corpus callosum (Sperry, 1964, 1966,

1977a, b; Gazzaniga 1967; Bogen 1969; Gazzaniga and LeDoux 1978). The study of split-brain patients has shown that "the mechanisms of human consciousness *can* be split and doubled by split-brain surgery" (Gazzaniga and LeDoux, 1978, p. 145). For example, while the patient's left hemisphere may wish to read, his right hemispher may wish to go for a walk, and so a conflict arises within one and the same skull. This is not surprising in our framework: indeed, according to Corollary 3.5 there is a single mind as long as there is a single plastic system. But if the latter is cut into two then two plastic systems emerge, each with its own mind or system of mental functions:

COROLLARY 3.7. *Let b be an animal whose plastic nervous system is split into two detached parts, L and R. Then the mind of b during any time interval τ posterior to the splitting is split into two disjoint functional systems:*

$$m(b, \tau) = m_L(b, \tau) \cup m_R(b, \tau), \text{ with } m_L(b, \tau) \cap m_R(b, \tau) = \phi.$$

Hence the results of commisurotomy do not support dualism (*pace* Puccetti, 1977). On the contrary, they show conclusively that there is no immaterial mind that holds the hemispheres together. Dualism could be saved only by invoking divine intervention at the time of splitting the corpus callosum. God would have to replace the original single soul by two new independent souls—each of which would have to remember something of the past history of the original soul. This looks like an easy solution but it is not, for it poses the grave theological problems of which if any of the three souls deserves being saved, and what to do on Resurrection Day with three souls and one body. Even assuming that this theological difficulty could be resolved, the dualist is in an awkward position. If he denies that the split–brain patient has two minds—as Eccles (1965) has done—he defies experience. And if he acknowledges that a physical entity such as a surgeon's scalpel can slice a mind into two, he contradicts himself (Bunge and Llinás, 1978). But enough of hair splitting about brain splitting.

As for chemicals with mental effects, they may be classed into those synthesized by the body, and drugs. Among the former we find brain cathecholamines (dopamine, epinephrine, and norepinephrine) and endorphins. Excessive levels of the former seem to cause schizophrenia (cf. Kety and Matthysse, 1975). And endorphins, being opiate-like peptides, seem to relieve pain. As for drugs, they range from mild stimulants such as tea through spirits, sleeping pills, and hallucinogens (such as marijuana, opium, and LSD) to drugs producing psychoses (like cocaine)—or abating them (like haloperidol). All such chemicals affect mental functions by modifying the CNS metabolism in various ways, from changing properties of the neuron membrane to taking part in biochemical reactions. Thus by modifying membrane conduction this drug produces amnesia and another one facilitates recall; and by blocking the synthesis of certain neurotransmitters this drug produces schizophrenia while that one cures it. (See Groves and Rebec, 1976; and Siegel and West, 1976.)

Finally, the purely behavioral or psychological manipulation of mental activities is no less physical, because the sensory inflow and the behavioral output controlled by the teacher (or preacher or propagandist or psychiatrist) modulates the neural connectivity, reinforcing certain connections and weakening others. In sum, the mental can be controlled, nay *is* being controlled, in various ways precisely because it is not immaterial: if it were it should be immune to all attempts at manipulating it. (For a list of kinds of deliberate modifications of brain activity and behavior, see Omenn and Motulsky, 1972. For behavior modification through education, see Skinner, 1953; Bandura 1969.) (Fig. 3.3.)

But if the physical control of the mental can sound amazing, the mental control of the body—as in the cases of some religions and political martyrs—is wonderful and has often been cited as proof of the superiority of Spirit over Matter. Yet this kind of action remains mysterious unless one adopts a neurophysiological view of mind. Consider just three well-known phenomena: hunger, anger, and yoga. The process in which the hunger feeling occurs is normally this: sensors in the digestive tract send signals to the hypothalamus, which in turn alerts the cortex. The motor cortex (and the cerebellum) control the muscles intervening in searching and reaching for food, and in eating. (This is the usual process in the healthy animal. A lesion or merely an electrical stimulation of the hypothalamus may produce hunger. And in man and some other animals the mere sight of appetizing food may produce hunger even if the animal is sated.) The dualist thinks he can afford to skip all these links: he discards the process ensuing in the

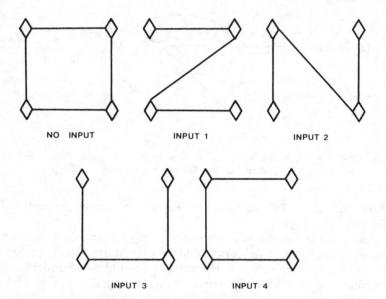

FIG. 3.3. Changing people's minds and behavior. Different stimuli may alter the connectivity of one and the same set of neurons. Outcome: different ideas, attitudes, behavior, etc.

cortext urging the body to eat, and speaks of the direct action of the mind on the muscles. His account is far simpler—and unscientific.

Consider anger next. The dualist is satisfied with "explanations" like this one: "She kicked him because she was angered by his words." The physiological psychologist analyzes this ordinary knowledge account in the way schematized in Fig. 3.4, showing a causal chain of bodily events.

Finally, consider the yoga techniques for controlling heartbeats, oxygen intake, body temperature, and even pain threshold—or else the biofeedback techniques for moving external things without the intervention of any muscles (but by using exclusively the electic brain waves). None of this is evidence for the power of Mind over Matter: to rate as such, a definite mechanism of the alleged action of an immaterial object upon the physical ought to be advanced. What such phenomena do show is that the autonomic system is not as fully autonomous as we used to

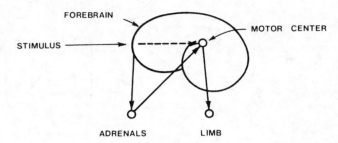

FIG. 3.4. From mind to action—or from forebrain to limbs. Forebrain
→ adrenal glands → motor center → limb.

think: they show that there is a two-way traffic between the cortex and the subcortical systems.

Likewise the "meditation" practiced by the yogis and their disciples is not evidence for the superiority of Mind over Matter, let alone for the thesis that "consciousness is the basis of the universe". Indeed, such "meditation" consists in suppressing thought altogether—i.e. in inhibiting the activity of what is probably the most recently evolved subsystem of the brain. By the same token such a state of blank mind and abnormal metabolic rate cannot be characterized as "expansion of consciousness" or "experiencing pure consciousness", for it is nothing but the lowest, and thoroughly *nonmental*, state of the brain. (Incidentally, the dictionary tells us that 'to meditate' is identical with 'to think deeply and continuously'. Hence 'meditation' is a misnomer for what is a nonmental activity of the brain. 'Relaxing' is a more adequate term.)

In sum, we *can* talk of mind–body (or psychosomatic) interactions provided we only intend to abbreviate the longer expression 'interactions between brain events of the mental kind and other events in the body'. But literal talk of mind–body interaction is (a) fuzzy, because interactions are well-defined only for material entities, and (b) a remnant of prehistoric animism (that has been traced back to the Neanderthal man of 50,000 years ago).

5. Where is the mind?

It is a dualistic tenet that, whereas the physical is extended, the mental is not: hence the Cartesian synonymy of 'body' and *res extensa* (extended thing), on the one hand, and of 'mind' and *res cogitans* (thinking thing), on the other. The *prima facie* evidence for the nonspatiality of the mental is of this kind: when a person thinks of a problem he does not feel his thoughts to be located anywhere. However, as long as we remain on the ordinary knowledge level we may also cite evidence for the thesis that the mind is coextensive with the body—e.g. when your foot hurts you feel pain there, not in your brain. So, ordinary experience is ambiguous: it supports now the thesis of the nonspatiality of the mental, now the thesis that the mind can wander throughout the body. This suggests that the nonspatiality thesis is confused, and that introspective evidence is insufficient. We must examine both.

The thesis of the nonspatiality of the mental contains two different hypotheses. One is that *mental events are unextended*, the other that *they occur nowhere*—except of course "in the mind", which is immaterial and therefore unextended. While the latter hypothesis obviously implies the former, the converse is not true. Indeed, mental events might be unextended yet occur somewhere—say in the brain. Likewise, a physical event that takes no time occurs at some time or other (relative to some reference frame). In the ontology of science there are no events in themselves but only events in some concrete thing or other (cf. Bunge, 1977a). Hence the question of the space "occupied" by an event is the question of the extension of the changing thing; thus not the *firing* of a neuron but the *firing neuron* is spatially extended.

Events occur wherever the "eventing" things may be. In particular, mental events occur in some plastic neural system or other. So, in principle, and often also in practice, the neurophysiologist *can* determine the location of a thought process, e.g. by eliciting it with electrical stimulation at precise sites in the cortex (Penfield, 1958). Hence the philosopher's claim that "it makes no sense at all" to talk about mental states and events as being located somewhere in the body, has been experimentally refuted. Mental events are just as localized as the corresponding plastic neural systems. If the latter have a fixed location, so have the mental events they engage in. And if the neural system in question happens to be itinerant, the mental event itself will be itinerant. In short, mental events occur in the brain. But this does not entail that the mind, as the set of all mental events, is in the head: being a set, it is nowhere. (Sets are not in space unless they happen to be sets of spatial points.)

What about the pain in the limb, particularly in the limb that has been amputated (phantom limb)? The short answer is that, just as we see the stars in the sky, not in our brain, so we locate pains in several parts of the body, and sometimes either localization is mistaken. A long answer is that the cortex of the adult human has a map of the entire body (the *somatotopic* representation). It is here that the signals coming from various parts of the body are decoded and located. If they come from the stump of an amputated limb, the patient can feel them as originating in the missing part because he has formed since childhood a comparatively unalterable map. (For alternative neurophysiological explanations of phantom limb experiences, see Ch. 4, Sec. 6.)

In sum, mental processes are located wherever the corresponding psychons (mentating neural systems) are located; likewise, they occur in time and they take some time to happen. This generalization from contemporary neuropsychology comes as no surprise to the psychophysical monist, for whom the *res cogitans* is *res extensa*, namely the brain. That Wittgenstein (1967, p. 105e) should have regarded that thesis as "one of the most dangerous of ideas for a philosopher" only goes to show the abyss between his philosophy and science.

What about ideas: are they too in space-time? The answer to this ambiguous question depends on the construal of 'idea'. If taken as ideation processes, ideas *are* in the brains that happen to think them up—but only there and only at the time they are being thought. On the other hand, the so-called *product* of any such process, i.e. the "idea in itself", is nowhere in space-time because it does not exist by itself; we only feign it does. For example, although thinking of the number 3 is a brain process, hence one located in space-time, the number 3 is nowhere because it is a fiction existing by convention or fiat, and this pretence does not include the property of spatiotemporality. What holds for the number 3 holds for every other idea—concept, proposition, or theory. In every case we abstract from the neuropsychological properties of the concrete ideation processes and come up with a construct that, by convention, has only conceptual or ideal properties.

In summary: the mental is in some head or other; but ideas in themselves, having no being of their own, are nowhere. (More in Ch. 7, Sec. 4.)

6. Mentalist predicates

Apparently the most formidable objection against psychophysical monism is this: "The materialist claims that all mental events are brain events, but he cannot offer a clear description, let alone definition, of a mental event without the help of mentalist concepts such as those of self, privacy, and immediate accessibility. Consequently he cannot even state his identity thesis. In other words, the materialist cannot consistently state the identity of phenomenal and physical predicates because he refuses to buy the former at their face value."

Actually the above is not an objection specifically addressed to the psychoneural identity thesis but one that can be raised against all science conceived of as a cognitive enterprise reaching beyond the ordinary language description of appearances. Our rejoinder is this:

(i) Science attempts to account for reality behind appearance—or for appearance as a smallish part of reality—so it either does not employ phenomenal predicates or, if it does, regards them as derived, not as basic. To be sure phenomena, in particular mental phenomena, are experientially immediate, but they are neither ontologically nor scientifically primary: they are something to be explained.

(ii) Appearances (phenomena) can be explained by psychology, at least in principle, in strictly nonphenomenal terms. For example, the various visual illusions can be explained either as results of incomplete or inadequate information, or as results of the fatigue or the inhibition of certain neurons, or the faulty connection of others. (Cf. Ch. 4, Sec. 6.)

(iii) A rigorous formulation of the monistic thesis must not employ ordinary phenomenal or mentalist predicates—nor fuzzy expressions such as 'mental–neural correlation'. (At any rate ours does not.) The monistic thesis is that every mental process is a brain process, not that every mentalist sentence is identical with some neurophysiological sentence: the identity is ontological, not linguistic. (This important point has been obscured by the nonmaterialist version of the "identity theory" defended by

Schlick, 1925, and Feigl, 1958, namely the "double designation" view—a version of neutral monism.)

In other words, we must not demand that science descend to the level of common sense but, instead, must strive to raise the latter to the level of the former. After all, this is what we do when shopping for breakfast cereal and, instead of allowing ourselves to be goaded by the advertisement that "X peps you up", look at the protein, vitamin, and calorie content of X—or when shopping for a car and, instead of remaining satisfied with the assurance that "X is spirited", inquire into the acceleration of X. We should behave similarly with regard to mentalist predicates. More precisely, we should adopt

RULE 3.1. *Whenever possible dispense with mentalist predicates: either replace them by, or define or deduce them with the help of, neurophysiological predicates.*

Example of elimination: "The idea of an immaterial mind controlling the body is vitalism, no more, no less; it has no place in science" (Hebb, 1974). *Example of reduction*: The degree of introversion of a person equals the activity of his or her frontal cortex–medial–septal area–hippocampal system (Gray, 1972a).

Rule 3.1 invites either of the following strategies with regard to mentalist predicates: elimination, definition, or deduction with the help of neurophysiological concepts. Of these the second, i.e. definition (identification), has been commended by the so-called identity theorists (e.g. Smart, 1959). That is, they have proposed that, for any mentalist predicate M, there is a neurophysiological predicate N such that $M = N$, where $=$ is the relation of ordinary (or strict or necessary) identity. Ordinary language philosophers have claimed that this cannot be, for "it makes no sense" (Malcolm, 1964). An obvious rejoinder is that no scientific hypothesis at all makes sense to them, for they insist on restricting themselves to ordinary language.

A related objection to the identity thesis is as follows (Kripke, 1971). If the identity is to be taken just as seriously as "Heat is the motion of molecules", then it must be a necessary identity, in the sense that it must hold in all possible worlds—whatever these may be. However, this cannot be, for "it seems clearly possible" (to Kripke) that M (e.g. pain) could exist without the corresponding brain state N, or that N could exist without being felt as pain—whence the identity is contingent and therefore flimsy. Rejoinder: (a) scientists and science-oriented philosophers do not waste their time speculating about (logically) possible worlds: they want to explore the real world (Bunge, 1977a); (b) the distinction between necessary (strict) identity and contingent identity is unclear and does not occur in logic or in science. In sum, the sophistic objection to materialism holds no water. (For additional shots, see Valdés, 1979.)

To be sure, our Rule 3.1 is not a summary of the current state of the art but rather a programmatic injunction, i.e. one that can guide scientific research. As such it can be confirmed but not refuted. And it should be discarded (or simply forgotten) if found barren. But, far from being so, it is behind many a success in contemporary physiological psychology and neuroscience.

Note that Rule 3.1 is the *weak*, not the strong, reductionistic thesis: we favor the *partial* reduction (definition or deduction) of the mental to the neurophysiological, not the elimination of its emergent properties (cf. Bunge, 1977b, c). Thus we do not state that a frog enjoys listening to a Beethoven quartet, or that what a human feels when listening to it is no different from a frog's feeling on hearing a mating call. We only say that enjoying Beethoven is a process in a human auditory system educated to face such experience.

The partial reducibility (definability or deducibility) of mentalist predicates does not entail that *every* ordinary language sentence concerning mental events is translatable without further ado into a (possibly very complex) scientific formula. Nor, *a fortiori*, does it entail that every mentalist sentence is identical with some neurophysiological sentence. If this were so then there would be only a difference in degree between the scientific and the mythical accounts of the mental. In short, genuine psychoneural monism (unlike the linguistic "identity theory") does *not* assert that, given any mentalist sentence m, there is one neurophysiological sentence n such that $m = n$.

The best one can do about mentalist sentences is either to eliminate them altogether or to try to cleanse, deepen, and refine them. For example, the phrase 'The soul survives', which makes sense in some theologies, makes none in our framework, where *soul* does not occur at all while *mind* is defined as a set of neural processes. (Sets are neither alive nor dead.) And those ordinary language mentalist sentences that *are* translatable into Neurophysiologese—e.g. 'Her mind is at work', or 'I am having a yellow afterimage'—may be so only roughly. As for the converse translation, of neurophysiological and psychophysiological sentences into ordinary language (mentalist) sentences, it is more often than not impossible, as should be obvious from looking at any of the mathematical models of mental processes published over the past few years.

In short, the various languages employed to describe mental events—in particular Mentalese, Behaviorese, and Neurophysiologese—are not mutually translatable on the whole. This is because, save exceptions, their sentences do not express the same propositions. For example, 'She is happy', 'She is grinning', and 'Her pleasure center is active' are, though related, quite different. In fact, although they have the same referent (She), and each describes one aspect of one and the same process, they have different senses and therefore they are inequivalent.

The inequivalence of most mentalist and neurobiological propositions is no obstacle to the building of bridges between them. The entire science of psychophysics is an attempt to disclose some such bridges, e.g. the relation between sound intensity and felt loudness. Psychophysical laws are of the form: "For all x, if x is an animal of species K, then: if physical stimulus p impinges on x, then x feels mental phenomenon m." Such generalizations may eventually be deepened by expressing m in neurophysiological terms, such as nerve firing frequency.

Neurology, too, looks for bridges between the mental (and also behavioral) states reported by neurological patients in phenomenal language (e.g. 'I suffer from migraine'), on the one hand, and sentences describing the corresponding malfunction of the CNS, on the other. Some neurological laws are of the form: "For all x, if x is human, then: If x is in neurological condition n, then x feels mental phenomenon m." Here again, m lumps a number of properties of some neural system(s) that may or may not coincide with the one possessing property n.

Finally, note that we have not mentioned any so-called "criteria of the mental", such as "Something is a mental event if and only if it can be described only in mentalist terms—e.g. 'I felt ashamed when she looked reproachfully at me'" (cf. Davidson, 1970). We do not need such ordinary language criteria—nay we do not want them, because by their very wording they presuppose the myth of the autonomy of the mind and thus block the search for the neural "basis" or "correlate" of the mental.

On the other hand, we do have some use for behavioral and physiological *indicators* or *tests* for finding out what is going on in a subject and whether she is actually having the mental experiences that she claims. Exams, interviews, lie detectors, and electroencephalographs are among the means devised so far for "reading the mind", i.e. inferring (with uncertainty) mental states from behavioral or physiological events. These tests, far from enshrining psychophysical dualism, bridge the gap between the physical and the mental erected by millennia of common sense and ideology.

So much for the general and basic concepts and assumptions of our version of the psychobiological theory, or rather framework for theories, of the mental. We proceed now to examining a few particular and rather typical kinds of mental process.

CHAPTER 4

Sensation and Perception

1. Sensors and sensing

Perception is a favorite subject of philosophical speculation, and such speculation has exerted an influence, for better or worse, on psychological theorizing. In particular, two traditional philosophical views are still alive in psychology. One is *innatism*, or the doctrine that sensory inputs can only evoke preexisting mental schemata or images; the other is *empiricism*, or the doctrine that the mind is initially a clean slate (*tabula rasa*) on which external inputs are inscribed. There are, to be sure, even more outlandish views on perception, e.g. the claim that linguistic analysis shows perceiving not to be a state or process at all (Ryle, 1954). We shall ignore these other views and shall come up with a sort of synthesis of innatism and empiricism.

The very first point to realize is that perception is not just sensation or detection. You feel cold, or hungry, or in pain, but you do not perceive coldness or hunger or pain. Feeling or sensing is detecting in an immediate way: it is what sensors or feelers do. Perceiving, on the other hand, is deciphering or recognizing a sensory message: it is seeing a round brown patch *as* a ball, hearing the ululation of a siren *as* an alarm signal, feeling the edge of a razor *as* a cutting tool. Sensing takes only detectors or sensors; perceiving takes, in addition, organs capable of interpreting what is felt or sensed. Let us then begin with sensors and their specific function—sensing.

All things react to external stimuli, but some react more selectively than others. The things that react to but few stimuli are said to detect them. Detection consists sometimes in filtering out all inputs but a few, and at other times in combining with entities of just a few kinds. The general concept of specific reaction, or detection, is elucidated by

DEFINITION 4.1. *A system detects things or events of a certain kind (or is a detector for them) if and only if it reacts to them only.*

Multicellular organisms have a variety of detectors grouped into systems called *selective systems* (or also, mistakenly, *recognition systems*). For example, the immune system can detect a large variety of molecules because it is composed of detectors (antibodies) of many kinds. And the CNS can detect a huge variety of internal and external events. Such detection is often a chemical process triggered by a stimulus (e.g. a molecule or a photon) in a chemoreceptor attached to some sensory system, such as the visual or the taste and smell system. Such chemoreceptors, or components of them, admit stimuli of certain kinds and ignore all others: they are selective. In particular, chemical detection is of the lock-and-key kind, i.e. only those molecules are detected by a receptor component, that match with them (Fig. 4.1).

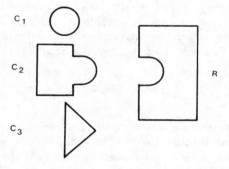

FIG. 4.1. Chemoreceptor in an organism. R detects (binds with) signals C_1 and C_2 but does not react with (detect) C_3. Hence C_3 is not detected. The detection process consists in the formation of a receptor–chemoeffector complex capable of having some effect on other parts of the organism through the intermediary of hormonal or nervous signals.

For an animal it is not enough to possess detectors: it must be able to do something about the events it detects—e.g. escape from them or neutralize them or, on the contrary, look for more of the same. This necessitates amplification and transmission of signals in a uniform fashion, so that each signal can be "read" unambiguously by the CNS. This is what neurosensors or neuroreceptors do. A mammal has myriads of neurosensors: sensors for motion, pressure, heat, rate of secretion, acidity changes, muscle contraction, novelty, etc. The general concept is this:

DEFINITION 4.2.   *A detector is a* neurosensor (*or* neuroreceptor) *iff it is a neural system or is directly coupled to a neural system.*

(The second term of the disjunction makes allowance for artificial sensors that could make up for the loss or damage of natural neurosensors.)

Example 1: The frog's eye has detectors that respond exclusively to moving insects (Lettvin *et al.*, 1959). *Example 2*: The visual cortices of cat and monkey (and probably also of man) contain neurons that specialize in detecting vertical lines and others in horizontal lines (Hubel and Wiesel, 1959, 1962). These are called *feature detectors.*

In higher animals neurosensors come in systems, and the specific function or activity of such systems is to perceive. For example, the olfactory system of a higher vertebrate contains more than odor detectors: it processes the signals emanating from them and turns them into percepts (Fig. 4.2). This suggests the need for

DEFINITION 4.3.   *A sensory system of an animal is a subsystem of the nervous system of it, composed of neurosensors and of neural systems coupled to them.*

The higher vertebrate sensory systems are rather complex. For one thing they do not function properly in isolation from other subsystems of the CNS, such as the motor system. For example, the immobile eye is blind: vision involves active exploratory movements of the eyeball. For another, the neurosensors are not just detectors of environmental inputs, like the thermocouple and the photoelectric cell. They are under the constant action of the CNS by way of the gamma efferent fibers (Fig. 4.2), so that their state depends not only upon external stimulation but also on the state (and history) of the CNS. This explains why we do not perceive the same stimulus twice in exactly the same manner. And it shows that any model of perception contrived in imitation of purely physical or chemical detectors, such as photographic cameras, is bound to fail.

We are now ready for

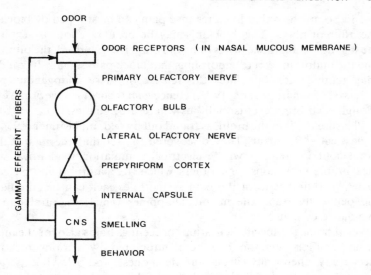

FIG. 4.2. The large-scale organization of the olfactory system in mammals. The odor receptors in the cat involve about 100 million neurons. Note the distance between odor reception and smelling (odor perception). Note also the action of the CNS on the receptors.

DEFINITION 4.4. *A* sensation (*or* sensory process *or* feeling) *is a specific activity(process) of a sensory system.*

Feeling cold or hot, hungry or sated, tired or vigorous, is having sensations without perceptions. Likewise feeling pain. Painful stimuli act on special receptors of three kinds: mechanoreceptors, heat receptors, and others that detect stimuli of both kinds. The information they gather concerning stimuli acting upon them is carried by C fibers in the case of slow and poorly localized pain, and by $A\delta$ fibers in the case of sharp and well-localized pain. (These are the fibers specialized in conducting painful impulses. But pain can also result from the excitation of nerve fibers of other kinds.) Some of these fibers enter the nucleus gigantocellularis (in the bulbar reticular formation) and others reach the spinal cord dorsal horn (see, for example, Liebeskind and Paul, 1977). So pain is (identical with) the activation of certain neural systems in either the nucleus gigantocellularis or the spinal cord dorsal horn. (So much so that in either case pain can be stopped by blocking the afferent fibers. This blocking may be brought about by external means such as analgesic drugs or by the brain itself. Indeed, the pituitary and the midbrain secrete endorphins that block pain signals. It could be that acupuncture stimulates the release of these endogenous pain killers: see Pomeranz et al., 1977.) Hence pain is always in the brain, even though such brain events "tell" us where it originates.

Pleasure too is in the brain, as found out by Olds and Milner (1954) in a classical experiment. They discovered in fact that the mammalian brain contains regions whose electrical stimulation is identical with pleasurable sensations, and others which are painful. (The pleasure system is different from the pain system, i.e. each can be stimulated independently. Hence the pursuit of happiness is no less natural than the avoidance of pain.)

What holds for specific sensations or feelings holds also for the mood of an animal: this too can be manipulated by various means— electrically, chemically (drugs and hormones), and behaviorally (gestures, etc.). Thus electrical stimulation of the septal region of the brain can change depression into exhilaration, and alcohol can bring joy or sadness according to the dose and the initial state of the brain. Hence to claim that joy and sadness, love and hatred, exhilaration and depression, are not scientifically analyzable and need not be understood, for everyone can feel them (Sacks, 1976), is sheer obscurantism.

In sum, from the monistic perspective a sensation or feeling of some kind is the specific activity of a certain sensory system (i.e. a subset of the event space of the latter).

2. Perception

Perception is not just detection or specific reaction to internal or external stimuli (i.e. detection). Remember that the frog's eye has "bug detectors" that respond exclusively to moving insects. So, in the case of the frog, "the eye speaks to the brain in a language already highly organized and interpreted, instead of transmitting some more or less accurate copy of the distribution of light on the receptors" (Lettvin et al., 1959). The signals emitted by the sensors are then "preprocessed" in them and become further processed in the brain. Such processing may be defective temporarily or permanently—as in dyslexia, where the patient sees 'and' but reads 'dan' or 'nad'.

The degree of sensory processing or "interpretation" depends not only on the complexity of the sensory message but also upon the structure of the brain—not just the inborn one but the organization acquired during the development of the animal in its environment. The primate brain has extensive sensory cortical "areas" which can be subdivided into three parts: the primary, secondary, and tertiary "areas". Only the primary sensory cortical area should be regarded as a component of the corresponding sensory system, for its specific function (activity, process) is sensing. Presumably, this area is plastic only during the early stages of development. In the cat it seems to have lost its plasticity by the time the animal is three months old (Hubel and Wiesel, 1962). On the other hand, the secondary and tertiary cortical sensory areas seem to be more or less plastic throughout the animals's life. We shall call them the *plastic neural systems directly attached to the sensory system.*

The difference between the primary and the plastic sensory cortical areas is a clue to the difference between sensation and perception in the higher vertebrates. Indeed, we shall assume with Hebb (1968) that, whereas sensation is the specific activity of a sensory system including the primary sensory cortical area, perception is this activity together with the activity elicited by the former in the plastic neural systems directly attached to it (Fig. 4.3).

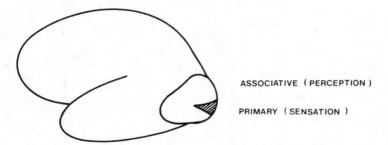

ASSOCIATIVE (PERCEPTION)

PRIMARY (SENSATION)

FIG. 4.3. Schematic diagram of visual primary and associative systems in man: the former senses (detects), the latter perceives (interprets) visual stimuli. Both are in the occipital lobe.

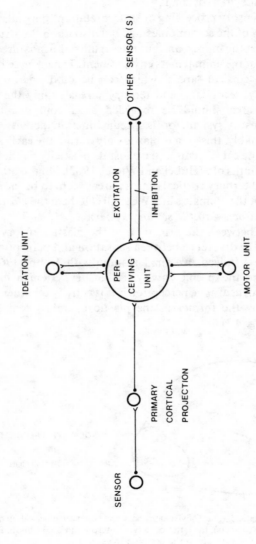

FIG. 4.4. Schema of a perceptual system: a modification of Bindra's (1976), in turn a modification of Hebb's (1949).

Figure 4.4 summarizes the following features of human perception: (a) the perceiving is done by a neural system located in a secondary sensory projection of the brain cortex; (b) the functioning of the central perceiving unit is strongly influenced by some motor unit or other—as shown by the experiment of Held and Hein (1963)—as well as by ideational units and by sensory inflows of various modalities; (c) the central perceiving unit can be activated by any other units coupled to it (e.g. dreams, hallucinations, phantom limb experience, eidetic images); (d) perception can guide motion as well as ideation. Caution: the central perceiving unit need not be a permanent (anatomically detachable) system but can be an itinerant one, i.e. it can be freshly generated at each perceptual act, as conjectured by Bindra (1976).

We feel then justified in making

DEFINITION 4.5.

(i) *A* percept (*or* perceptual process) *is a specific activity* (*process*) *of a sensory system and of the plastic neural system(s) directly coupled to it*;

(ii) *a* perceptual system *is a neural system that can undergo perceptual processes*.

An anesthetized animal senses but does not perceive: the sensory signals do not reach the secondary and tertiary sensory areas because the brain stem arousal system has been inactivated.

We assume—in line with Bindra (1976)—that, whereas a sensory system has a roughly constant neuronal composition, the corresponding perceptual system has a variable part. This explains why the same stimulus can activate different perceptions (as in the cases of the duck–rabbit and the Necker cube figures) and why different stimuli can give rise to the same perception (as in the case of size constancy) (Fig. 4.5). To put it in other words: two percepts in an animal are *equivalent* if and only if they are elicited by (roughly) the same sensation and involve (roughly) the same plastic neural system. (This problem is treated in the psychological literature under the heading *stimulus equivalence*.)

Now, unlike feeling, which is sensing bodily events, perceiving is detecting and interpreting signals that normally originate in events

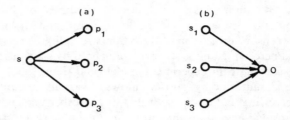

FIG. 4.5. Sensation and perception. (a) Same sensation elicits different perceptions according to the plastic neural assembly that is being activated. (b) Different sensations give rise to same perception by activating the same plastic neural system.

external to the CNS. Thus seeing a thing *as* a bird and hearing the noise it makes *as* its song are modes of perceiving the thing—which may or may not be a bird. Perceiving is always perceiving some thing (or rather events occurring in a thing) in a given way. The schema is always: *animal x in state y perceives object z as w.* Thus the princess, when drunk, perceives the frog as a prince (or conversely). In short, to perceive is to construct, not just to copy (Neisser, 1967). The bricks of such perceptual contructions are sensations, memories, and expectations. The external stimuli are the referents and triggers of perceptions rather than their causes.

The causal theory of perception, according to which perceptions are fully determined (caused) by the perceived objects, ignores not only the fact that we (mercifully) fail to perceive most of the things that surround us: but it also ignores the essential contribution of the plastic component of the perceptual systems. However, that theory (or rather view) does have an important grain of truth, namely the hypothesis that the perception of an external object is the distortion it causes in the ongoing activity of a perceptual system. The apparatus introduced in Ch. 3 allows us to express this idea in a somewhat more precise way, namely as

POSTULATE 4.1. *Let v be a perceptual system of an animal b and call* $\bar{\pi}_s(v, \tau) = \{ \mathbb{F}^v(t) \,|\, t \in \tau \}$ *the specific process (or function) that v engages in during the time period τ when in the presence of a thing x external to v, and call* $\pi_s^0(v, \tau)$ *the specific process going on in v during the same length of time when x does not act on v. Then b perceives x as the symmetric difference between the two processes. That is, the perception of x by b during τ is the process*

$$p(x, \tau) = \bar{\pi}_s(v, \tau) \Delta \pi_s^0(v, \tau).$$

(The symmetric difference between sets A and B is $A \Delta B = A - B \cup B - A$.)

According to Definition 4.5 perception does not require the presence of an external thing perceived: hence it covers both normal perception and hallucination. On the other hand, the previous axiom is limited to situations in which there are things external to the perceptual system concerned (not necessarily external to the whole animal). Our postulate accounts for the active or creative nature of perception, and thus for the fact that one and the same perceptual system in different states will perceive differently one and the same object. (In particular, one and the same person will perceive the environment differently in different stages of his or her development. Remember how big things appeared in childhood.) Clearly, our postulate disagrees with the direct apprehension doctrine of empiricists and intuitionists (in particular Gestalt theorists). But it is consonant with the current neurophysiology of perception. External and internal stimuli do not set the CNS in motion but modulate or control its incessant activity. That is, the environment enhances or dampens, and in general controls the activity of the CNS rather than causing it.

3. Interlude: *Ding an sich* versus *Ding für uns*

Postulate 4.1 highlights the difference between the *thing in itself* and the *thing for us*, i.e. between the autonomous object and our perception (or conception) of it. Take the philosopher's favorite, yet usually misunderstood, case of the planet Venus and our sightings of it at dawn (Morning Star or MS) and at dusk (Evening Star or ES). Some philosophers have argued that, since there is a single thing to be seen, namely Venus, MS = ES. This move eliminates subjective experience and, in particular, phenomena, so it looks very scientific. But science is only partial if it cannot accommodate subjectivity, i.e. us.

MS is Venus *as seen* in the morning, when the world looks young. And ES is Venus *as seen* at sundown, when the world looks old. One and the same *Ding an sich*, i.e. Venus, is perceived differently, so there are two distinct phenomenal objects (Fig. 4.6).

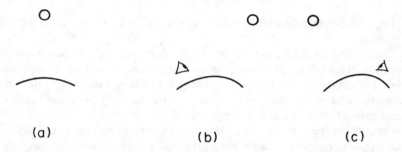

(a)   (b)   (c)

FIG. 4.6. The physical object (a) and two phenomenal apprehensions of it: (b) and (c).

Your seeing the planet at dawn, through a clear atmosphere and with fresh eyes, is not the same as your seeing it at the end of the day, through a dirty atmosphere and with tired eyes—and neither is identical with Venus, which has changed but little between the two sightings. Your seeing Venus is identical with the simultaneous firing of certain neurons in the visual area of your cortex as a consequence of the arrival of inputs transmitted by the optical nerve and originating in the retina (Milner, 1974). Since the inputs differ in the two cases, and the perceptual system is not in the same state, it is no wonder that MS ≠ ES. And since seeing is a neural process rather than a purely physical one, neither MS nor ES is the same as Venus.

The moral of the above story for epistemology should be clear: although perception gives some information about reality, it shows us only the skin of it, i.e. appearance—or reality-as-perceived. Disentangling the object (thing in itself) from the subject (percipient subject) calls for a different kind of brain process, namely hypothesizing and theorizing about things in themselves. And the moral of this moral for psychology is equally obvious: Although perceiving does involve constructing (rather than passive recording), it is not the same as conjecturing. Hence the view that perceiving is tacit hypothesizing or inferring (Gregory, 1970), though attractive, must be false. What *is* probably true is that perceiving is creative and influenced by hypothesizing and conversely—as must be expected from the systemic nature of the brain.

The realist (nonphenomenalist) thesis, that appearance is only a part of reality, can be summarized in

POSTULATE 4.2. *Let Φ be the totality of possible facts occurring in an animal b and its environment during the lifetime of b, and Ψ the totality of possible percepts of b (or the phenomenal world of b) during the same period. Then Ψ is properly included in Φ.*

This assumption suggests two rules:

RULE 4.1. *All sciences should investigate possible real facts and should explain phenomena (appearances) in terms of them rather than the other way around.*

RULE 4.2. *A science-oriented ontology and epistemology should focus on reality, not appearance.*

The phenomenalist philosophies of Richard Avenarius (1888–90), Ernst Mach (1886), Bertrand Russell (1914), Alfred North Whitehead (1919), Rudolf Carnap (1927), and Nelson Goodman (1951) violate both rules and are therefore at variance with the scientific approach. And the philosophers who, like Thomas Nagel (1974) and most British Philosophical psychologists, deny the very possibility of giving a neurophysiological account of the phenomenological features of human experience, do nothing to help the attempts of physiological psychologists to do just that—namely to explain what appears to a subject in terms of both the state of his CNS and events in his immediate surroundings.

4. Perceptual maps

What do we perceive and how? The naive realist answer is: We perceive things as they are. Yet consider Parmenides' homogeneous and eventless universe. An observer would be unable to perceive anything in it, because there would be nothing to discriminate from anything else, and because nothing would be stirring. He would be unable to see, because only things that bounce photons back can be seen; he would hear nothing because only moving things can generate sound waves; and he would have no tactile sensations because touching is disturbing—and being disturbed. The observer himself must be changeable, because perception is a process in an animal equipped with perceptual systems.

So, we do not perceive things but events, and not all events but only some of those that affect us: the light bouncing off this page and hitting our retina, the honk of the automobile, generating sound waves hitting our ear-drum, the dog's licking our hand, and so on. Whatever we perceive is an event or a sequence of events, and not just any event but an event originating in a neurosensor or acting on the latter and, in any case, belonging to our own event space (or set of events occurring in us). And our perceptions are in turn events in the plastic part of our own sensory cortex.

In other words, our answer to the question "*What* does animal b perceive?" is "Animal b perceives *events* in the event space $E(b)$". $E(b)$ is included in $S(b) \times S(b)$, i.e. the set of ordered pairs of possible states of b. (See Bunge, 1977a or b.) And our short answer to the companion question "*How* does animal b perceive events in $E(b)$?" is this: "Animal b *maps* events in $E(b)$ onto events in some subsystem of its own perceptual system (e.g. sensory cortex) c, i.e. in $E(c)$." Admittedly this map is not the simple projection imagined by Kepler and Descartes: it is partial, distorted, and changing. Still, it *is* a map, i.e. a representation of certain sets (of events) on to another set (of events).

Actually in mammals there are two sets of perceptual maps: the somatosensory and motor maps (or body schemata), on the one hand, and the external world maps, on the other. The former represent in the cortex events happening in the limbs, on the skin, and in other parts of the body: they are the famous sensory and motor *homunculi* (little men) depicted as sprawling on the sensory–motor cortex (cf. Penfield and Rasmussen, 1950). To be sure these maps are not simple: points that are close in the body may have distant cortical images and conversely; and while some large body areas are poorly represented in the cortex, certain small body areas (e.g. the thumbs) project on to large cortical areas. However, the point is that every set of points (not every point) in the body does have a single image in the sensory–motor cortex. Likewise external events that happen to activate neurosensors are mapped on to the sensory cortex, or perhaps somewhere else in the brain. (See O'Keefe and Nadel, 1978, for the conjecture that the locus of spatial maps is the hippocampus.)

The assumption concerning the representation or projection of bodily events in the cortex can be elucidated with the help of the general mathematical concept of a function, which is far more general than the concept of a proximity-preserving function or map used in geography. In fact it can be clarified by

POSTULATE 4.3. *Let b be an animal equipped with a perceptual system c and call S(b) the state space of b and S(c) that of c. Moreover, let E(b) ⊂ S(b) × S(b) be the animal's event space, and E(c) ⊂ S(c) × S(c) its perceptual event space. Then there is a set of injections (one to one and into functions) from the set of bodily events to the set of perceptual events. Each such map, called a* body schema, *depends on the kind of bodily events as well as on the state the animal is in. That is, the general form of each body map is*

$$m \colon S(b) \times 2^{E(b)} \to 2^{E(c)},$$

where 2^S is the power set, or family of all subsets, of S.

This assumption does not specify the body schemata; it does not even say how many they are. We leave these tasks to psychobiology. We only emphasize that the body maps are not proximity preserving, let alone distance preserving. (Werner, 1970, assumes, on the other hand, that the somatosensory map is a continuous topological transformation.)

It would seem at first glance that phantom limb experiences refute the postulate. They do not, because the body schemata are learned. If, before the amputation, events occurring in the limb were projected on to certain cortex events, then after the operation events in the stump are represented by the same cortex events: the body image is remarkably constant once learned. More in Sec. 4.

DEFINITION 4.6. *Let b be an animal with state space S(b), bodily event space E(b), and perceptual event space E(c). Then b, when in state s ∈ S(b), feels the events in the collection $x \in 2^{E(b)}$ if and only if b has a body schema m such that $m(s, x) \in 2^{E(c)}$ (i.e. if those events project on to the cortex c of b). Otherwise b is* insensitive *to x.*

Note that an animal may lack the proper sensors or may have them but not properly connected to the sensory cortex. For example, humans cannot detect magnetic fields or the plane of polarization of plane-polarized light. And humans with lesions in the visual cortical area are unable to see certain things in their visual areas or may even be totally blind.

The external world maps are similar to the body schemata. Only in this case the bodily events are caused by external events, and the maps are far more numerous than the body schemata. For example, it seems that there is a dozen or so visual maps, each representing one feature—shape, color, motion, etc. Our assumption is

POSTULATE 4.4. *Let E(e) be a set of events in the environment e of animal b equipped with a perceptual system c. Moreover let E(b) ⊂ S(b) × S(b) be the animal event space, and E(c) ⊂ S(c) × S(c) its perceptual event space. Then there is a set of partial maps k from sets of external events in E(e) to ordered pairs ⟨ state of b, set of bodily events in b ⟩, and another set of partial maps p, from the latter set to sets of perceptual events. Furthermore, the two sets of maps are equally numerous, and each map k composes with one map p to form an* external world map *of b in e, or ε. That is,*

$$\varepsilon : 2^{E(e)} \overset{k}{\to} S(a) \times 2^{E(b)} \overset{p}{\to} 2^{E(c)}.$$

Look at the commutative diagram:

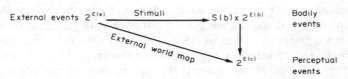

It is likely that external world maps are largely if not wholly learned. And it is sure that, once learned, and barring brain damage, they help guide behavior, in particular locomotion.

DEFINITION 4.7. *Let b be an animal with perceptual system c in environment e. Moreover, call S(b) the state space of b and E(e) that of e. Then b, when in state s ∈ S(b), perceives* external events in *x ∈ 2^{E(e)} iff [these cause bodily events that are in turn projected on to the sensory cortex c, i.e. if] k(x) = ⟨s, y⟩, with y ∈ 2^{E(b)} and in turn p(s, y) ∈ 2^{E(c)}. Otherwise the events in x are* imperceptible *to b when in state s [i.e. imperceptible events either do not cause any bodily events or cause them but do not get projected on to the perceptual system].*

Note that, like the body schemata, the external world maps are not point-to-point correspondences but set-to-set ones. Moreover, we emphasize that there is a whole atlas of perceptual maps, one set for each modality. In other words, there is a number of perceptual spaces: visual, auditory, haptic, etc.—probably each with its own distinctive topology.

However, these various external world maps are interrelated. This integration of the various perceptual modalities is easily accounted for, at least in principle, within the psychobiological framework. Indeed, it may be assumed to consist in the simultaneous activation of two or more perceptual systems. This can be achieved by sensory inflow to receptors of two or more kinds, or by sensory inflow to a single receptor, and activation of other perceptual systems via associated neural systems. For example, a total or cross-model perception of a familiar hand may be had just by its haptic perception, because the tactual receptors activate others. Such integration, in which the angular gyrus participates centrally, is learned. (Recall the observations on the visual perception of persons who were born blind and acquired vision after having educated their haptic system.)

Not only does the organism learn to integrate the activities of its various perceptual systems—i.e. its perceptions in different modalities; it also learns to perceive in each modality. In particular the young vertebrate learns to touch, hear, smell, and see. Here again the psychobiological viewpoint can teach us something, while the dualistic one cannot. In fact, from a neurobiological point of view learning to perceive is a process of organization of the synaptic junctions in the sensory cortex. This developmental process, far from being determined genetically in all detail, is at the mercy of experience to such a point that an animal prevented from having sensory experiences of a certain kind during its early life will never be able to sense or perceive in the same modality. (For the pioneer experiments, see Hubel and Wiesel, 1962; Wiesel and Hubel, 1965. For mathematical models, see Wilson and Cowan, 1973; Malsburg, 1973; Pérez et al., 1975; Nass and Cooper, 1975; Metzler, 1977.)

5. Visual adaptation and pattern recognition

Postulate 4.4 does not define with precision the external world map of an animal and is thus of a programmatic nature. There are several ways to implement this program. One of them is to assume that the map is a conformal representation (Schwartz, 1977)—which presupposes that the visual area is a two-dimensional sheet. This proposal has two attractive features. One is that conformal representations are angle preserving, an invariance required by shape recognition. Another interesting feature of this hypothesis is that it accounts for the puzzling size constancy phenomenon, although this fact could also be accounted for by the action of the tactile system on the visual system.

A deeper, hence riskier, implementation of the program is the work of Cowan and Wilson (Cowan, 1976) on visual adaptation. Consider a subject looking at a figure and assume that both the cortical event space and the perceptual field event space (i.e. the collection of events that the subject can see) are mapped on metric spaces. In other words, assign each event (or set of events) a coordinate. Call X a point (or region) in the visual cortex of the subject, and X' a point in her visual field. Then the response of the cortex to an external light pattern will depend on the excitation and the inhibition as well as on the stimulus itself. Two relatively simple models suggest themselves. In the first, the response is proportional to the excess of the excitation over the inhibition; in the second, the inhibition is modified by the response itself. (That is, the first is a feedforward, the second a feedback model.) In the first case, the response $r(X)$ at point X to a light stimulus at point X' is

$$r(X) = k_e(X - X') - k_i(X - X'),$$

where k_e (excitation) and k_i (inhibition) are real valued functions, and $X - X'$ is the distance between the stimulus event and the response (perceiving) event. The response to an arbitrary light stimulus spread over the entire visual field of the subject, with intensity $s(X')$ at point X', is obtained by summating the weighted excitation and inhibition:

$$r(X) = \int dX' \, s(X') k_e(X - X') - \int dX' \, s(X') k_i(X - X') \qquad \text{Model 1}$$

The second model is obtained as a correction to the preceding one by noting that inhibition acts only around the points that get excited. (This is the hypothesis of lateral inhibition, which has been abundantly confirmed. Incidentally, lateral inhibition seems peculiar to nervous tissue.) Moreover, the contribution of the inhibition is the greater, the greater the response itself. Hence the second occurrence of the stimulus in the previous equation must be replaced by the response, so that we are left with the integral equation

$$r(X) = \int dX' s(X') k_e(X - X') - \int dX' r(X') k_i(X - X') \qquad \text{Model 2}$$

So much for the two hypotheses linking the physiological response to the stimulus, the excitation, and the inhibition. Both are couched in neurophysiological terms. On the other hand, the experimental results are couched in different terms—but these happen to be just the Fourier transforms of the former functions. Let us then obtain the Fourier transforms of the preceding equations with the help of the convolution theorem. The results, in obvious symbols, are

Model 1 $R(k) = [K_e(k) - K_i(k)]S(k)$
and $R(k) = K_e(k)S(k) - K_i(k)R(k)$,   whence

Model 2 $R(k) = \dfrac{K_e(k)S(k)}{1 + K_i(k)}.$

In these formulas k is the spatial frequency (in cycles per degree of visual angle), the stimulus $S(k)$ is at the discretion of the experimenter, and the response $R(k)$ (in spikes per second) is measurable with the help of microelectrodes. Apparently the experimental results favor Model 2.

Whether or not any of the above models is true, the important points are that there are such maps and that they can be investigated mathematically and experimentally. So, the sensory cortex *is* a sort of screen after all. Moreover, a brain map of a chunk of reality represents not only some of the events occurring in the surroundings but also their mutual relations, i.e. a part of the structure of reality.

In particular, perception tells us something about the spatiotemporal structure of appearance. But of course appearances are deceitful: perception may not even preserve the time order of events, as we know from cases like that of lightning and thunder. *A fortiori*, perceived time intervals will in general differ from physical time lapses: biological clocks are less reliable than physical clocks. The two can be compared as follows with the help of the duration function t_f introduced elsewhere (Bunge, 1977a, Definition 6.15). Let f be a clock and x a thing, possibly the same as f, with event space $E(x)$. Then the metric duration is a map t_f of events into real numbers satisfying certain conditions. When comparing physical time with psychological time we use two specializations of that function:

$$t_f : E(x) \times U_t \to \mathbb{R}, \quad \text{and} \quad t_a : E(a) \times U_t \to \mathbb{R},$$

where f denotes a physical clock and a an animal, and U_t is the set of time units. The set $E(x)$ of events is one of public events, some of which the animal can perceive; it includes the set $E(a)$ of private events occurring in the animal's brain. The relative discrepancy between physical and psychological time, for each event $x \in E(a)$ and a fixed time unit $u \in U_t$, is defined to be

$$\delta(t_f, t_a) = |t_f(x, u) - t_a(x, u)| / t_f(x, u).$$

In turn, this quantity should depend on certain neurophysiological variables. This removes all mystery from Bergson's suggestive but obscure distinction between physical and psychological time. It also sheds light on the experiments on time perception, in particular the findings that sensory deprivation, as well as certain drugs, increase the discrepancy between perceived duration and clock duration, and that perceived waiting time is proportional to the square of clock duration.

Another subject that becomes clearer from a monistic perspective is pattern recognition. The concept of pattern involved in the studies of pattern recognition, both in psychology and in artificial intelligence, is the rather special one of spatial pattern or regular arrangement of perceptible things or events in space, such as the ripples in a pond, the tiles in a floor, or the letters in a book. We can elucidate the concept of spatial pattern as follows. Let E be a nonvoid set of events and R a set of spatial relations defined on E. Then $\mathscr{E} = \langle E, R \rangle$ is a *spatial pattern*. And we shall say that an animal can *recognize* a spatial pattern provided it can perceive the events in it in their proper relations, i.e. if it is capable of mapping the pattern on to its own sensory cortex. More precisely, using the notions occurring in Postulate 4.4, we make

DEFINITION 4.8. *Let $\mathscr{E} = \langle 2^{E(e)}, R \rangle$ be a spatial pattern of events in the environment of an organism b and let $E(c)$ be the perceptual event space of b. Then b can recognize $\mathscr{E}$ iff, when in some state, b maps $\mathscr{E}$ homomorphically into a neural pattern $\mathscr{N} = \langle 2^{E(c)}, S \rangle$, where S is a collection of relations (not necessarily spatial) among cortical events in b.*

Thus if R_i is in R, then there is a relation S_i in S such that, for any sets x and y of external events,

$$h[R_i(x, y)] = S_i[h(x), h(y)],$$

where h is the homomorphism that represents external patterns as neural patterns.

6. Abnormal perception

Whereas to the nonscientific mind hallucinations are pranks of an autonomous mind, to the psychobiologist they are brain processes— rare perhaps but not lawless. Some of them can be induced artificially by neuroactive drugs such as LSD and alcohol—and they can be eliminated by further drugs such as thorazine. Furthermore, drug-induced halluci- nations are remarkably constant in content across individuals belonging to the same culture. For example, most of the shapes seen a couple of hours after the administration of the drug are lattice tunnels. And all of the Huichol Mexican Indians seem to perceive roughly the same geometric patterns when under the action of peyote—namely those found in their embroidery (Siegel and West, 1975). So, there is no doubt that there are psychotropic drugs which, upon changing the brain metabolism and the action of the neurotransmitters, distort in a lawful way the perception processes.

But of course hallucinations can occur without such metabolic alterations. The most common are the after-effects, such as the visual after-images and the weight illusions. Consider the classical experiment of J. J. Gibson (1933) sketched in Fig. 4.7. One explanation of this illusion attributes it to the habituation or fatigue of the neurosensors that detect tilted lines (Blakemore and Campbell, 1969). Call this a malfunction of the perceptual system if you will; still, it is a perfectly lawful process even though it results in an erroneous map of things.

The perception of ambiguous figures, such as Necker's cube, the vase–profile drawing, and Escher's bewildering etchings, might be explained in a similar way. The subject switches from one perception to the other as soon as the neurons engaged in one of them have become habituated (fatigued). This explanation seems more plausible than the

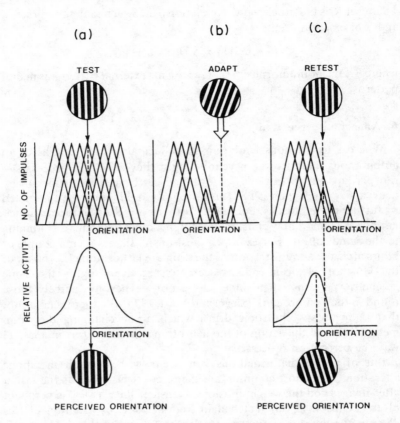

FIG. 4.7. The Gibson illusion. (a) Normal perception of vertical grating. (b) Habituation ("adaptation") to tilted grating. (c) Illusion: when sight shifts from (b) to (c), the vertical lines seem tilted in the opposite direction. Illusion presumably produced by fatigue of neurons exposed for about one minute to stimulus object (b). (From Blakemore, 1973.)

one according to which the phenomenon is rational, namely one of oscillating between two equally likely hypotheses (Gregory, 1973). However, in order to decide between the two we should be able to produce such Gestalt switches in subhuman primates and monitor the activity of their visual cortical neurons. But this seems currently technically unfeasible.

Other illusions, such as the size–weight one (where the bigger thing is perceived as the heavier although it is actually lighter) may call for different explanations. Some illusions probably involve ideational systems producing an expectation—based on experience—that distorts perception. These illusions are sometimes attributed to wrong strategy (or software) rather than to the activation of the wrong neural system (Gregory, 1973). However, even wrong expectations and mistaken inferences must ultimately be explained as neural processes, so that the malfunction–strategy distinction is not a dichotomy any more than the hardware–software one in the case of animals.

An illusion that has captivated philosophers of mind is the phantom limb experience. There are several possible neurophysiological explanations of this phenomenon, and some of them are mutually compatible. One is that, since the phantom experience is not found before age 4, it must be learned. And, if so, it may consist in the activation of the area of the cortical somatotopic map that used to record the signals coming from the limb before amputation. Another possible explanation is this: although after amputation there is no sensory input coming from the usual peripheral sites, the same excitation can arise higher in the pathway by spontaneous firing of neurons (Hebb, 1968). A third: the nerve endings on the stump, not being primary receptors but just transmitters, can transmit only messages of a certain kind—e.g. "Pain in large right toe"—no matter how stimulated. A fourth: the phenomenon is of the projective kind, as when we feel the events occurring on the tip of the pen as happening there and not on our fingertips (Pribram, 1971). Whichever explanation may turn out to be correct, it will tell us what happens in the CNS of the patient experiencing phantom limb, not what is "on his mind".

What about the out-of-the-body experiences reported by subjects who have taken LSD "trips" or who have been on the brink of death? Do they prove that the mind can get detached from the body and actually see the latter from the outside? Exosomatic experiences are real, but their animistic explanation is incorrect because there is no way of seeing without the visual system. If one could do without the latter then he should not value it so highly and, instead of wearing spectacles to correct some of its malfunctions, he should have his mind repaired. Exosomatic experience is not different from any other retrospection, in which we "see" (i.e. imagine) ourselves as others—e.g. walking on a beach. In both cases we supplement our actual perceptions, or our recollection of them, with inventions—particularly so in the age of mirrors, cinema, and television. After all, we supplement even our normal sensations all the time.

Finally, a word on after-images and dreams. A visual or auditory after-image, like any other after-effect, is a case of inertia and thus explainable in neurophysiological terms. The inertia consists in that an activity that had been elicited by a past event continues for a while after the extinction of its cause and is superposed to the new activity triggered by the new event. This phenomenon refutes the causal theory of perception but not the psychoneural identity hypothesis. In any case, after-images have declined in status as supporters of psychoneural dualism ever since it was discovered (Scott and Powell, 1963) that even monkeys can have them.

Likewise dreams do not support the prehistoric myth of the existence of nonembodied spirits entering our body during sleep, or the psychoanalytic myth of the Unconscious taking advantage of the censor's slumber. Dreams may well prove to be hallucinations on a par with those produced by sensory deprivation during wakeful life. In both cases the

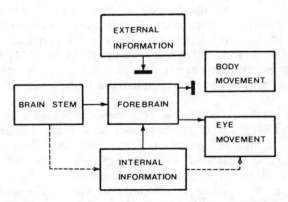

FIG. 4.8. The Hobson–McCarley theory of dream state generation. The brain stem stimulates the forebrain, which "makes the best of a bad job in producing even partially coherent dream imagery from the relatively noisy signals sent up to it from the brain stem" (Hobson–McCarley, 1977, p. 1347).

control of sensory inflow is lacking, and both illustrate the autonomous and relentless activity of the brain. (Computers, on the other hand, do not hallucinate or dream when switched off: they just "go dead".) A recent psychophysiological theory implicates the pontine brain stem and the forebrain in the generation of dream states, in accordance with the block diagram in Fig. 4.8 (Hobson and McCarley, 1977). Far from being immaterial entities, dreams are closed circuited brain activities; and far from having a purpose, they are aimless and usually sloppy activities.

In brief, abnormal perception and dreaming are lawful brain activities.

CHAPTER 5

Behavior and Motivation

1. Definitions and principles

Every animal, however simple, has a variety of outputs—movements, secretions, heat, long electromagnetic waves, etc. In its narrow construal, behavior equals the set of motor outputs of an animal, whether global as in locomotion or partial as in grasping or grinning, moving the eyeballs or excreting. Since this excludes interesting behavior such as secreting, the light output of a firefly and the electric discharge of an electric eel, we adopt the wider construal:

DEFINITION 5.1. *For any animal b,*

- (i) *the* behavioral state *of b at time t is the output of b at t;*
- (ii) *the* behavior *of b during the time interval τ is the set of all behavioral states of b throughout τ.*

Because behavior is output, the recording of behavior is a matter of physical or chemical recording, such as taking motion pictures, and the description of behavior one of kinematics. In and by itself pure behavior is of little interest to biology, psychology, or philosophy. These disciplines take (or ought to take) an interest in behavior only as a complex outcome and indicator of hidden bodily processes of various kinds—neural, endocrine, muscular, etc. The proper unit of study is therefore the entire cycle: stimulus on an animal in a given state – neural process – conduction of signal – response – outcome (i.e. effect of behavior) – feedback on neuroendocrine system. *Example*: Seeing a reference to an article, walking to the library to consult it, reading it, and making a note of some of its content—rather than just walking in response to an indifferent visual stimulus.

When inherited, or when learned and successful, behavior is stable or recurrent. In this case it is often called a 'behavior pattern':

DEFINITION 5.2. *A behavior pattern is a recurrent behavior.*

The "behavior plans" discussed by Miller *et al.* (1960) are actually behavior patterns. The term 'plan' is apposite only when there is deliberate choice. A behavior pattern is a result of laws (genetic, developmental, etc.) and circumstances. A genuine behavior *plan* requires some knowledge of such laws and circumstances—something only the higher primates seem capable of acquiring. But this is a topic for Ch. 8.

Animals belonging to different species can do different "things", such as swimming or flying, burrowing or building nests, preying or fleeing from predators, grooming or hoarding. And even when they do the same "thing" (i.e. go through the same motions) they may do it in different fashions or styles—some of them species-specific, others idiosyncratic. In short, there are different kinds of behavior and every animal species is characterized by some of them to the exclusion of others. All this is spelled out by

DEFINITION 5.3. *Let b be an animal of species K and let A be the union of all animal species. Then*

  (i) *the (possible) behavior of type i of animal b, or $B_i(b)$ for short, is the set of all (possible) behaviors of b associated with the ith biofunction (in particular neural biofunction) of b;*

  (ii) *the (possible) behavior of animal b is the union of (possible) behaviors of all types of b:*

$$B(b) = \bigcup_{i=1}^{n} B_i(b);$$

  (iii) *the (possible) behavior of type i of species K, or $B_i(K)$ for short, is the union of all the (possible) behaviors of the members of K, i.e.*

$$B_i(K) = \bigcup_{b \in K} B_i(b);$$

  (iv) *the behavioral repertoire of species K, or B(K), is the union of all (possible) behavior types of K:*

$$B(K) = \bigcup_{i=1}^{n} B_i(K);$$

(v) *the* specific behavioral repertoire of species *K is the behavioral repertoire exclusive to members of K*:

$$B_s(K) = B(K) - \underset{X \subset A}{\cup} B(X), \quad \text{with} \quad X \neq K;$$

(vi) animal behavior *is the union of the behavioral repertoires of all animal species, i.e.*

$$B = \underset{X \subset A}{\cup} B(X).$$

Caution. All of the above definitions are understood to hold at a given time in the development of the individual and the evolution of the species. As an animal develops, its behavioral repertoire changes, not just by adding new abilities but also by suppressing some behavior types or transforming them. (For example, in primates lip smacking develops from sucking.) The same holds, *mutatis mutandis*, for the evolution of behavior.

All animals behave in some way or other, but only those endowed with a CNS can coordinate their behavior and face new situations with some success. Thus while the jellyfish does not have a CNS and moves rather erratically, the starfish has one and exhibits coordinated behavior. All animals endowed with a CNS have muscles that, by contracting, move parts of the body—i.e. do the behavior. (Actually it is the NES, rather than the CNS, that controls motion, because hormones turn on or off many neuronal circuits, particularly motor ones, which they release from their normally inhibited state.) In turn, all muscles are activated by at least one excitatory axon. (Insect muscles are often innervated by just one or two neurons.) (Fig. 5.1.) (But the converse is generally false. Thus most of the neural systems of the human brain do not innervate muscles. Hence the study of human behavior can tell us but little about the human brain. See Welker, 1976.)

We compress the above into

POSTULATE 5.1. *The behavior of every animal endowed with a NS is controlled ("mediated", "subserved") by the latter. (That is, for every behavior type B_i of animals endowed with a NS, the latter contains a neural subsystem that controls the motions in B_i.)*

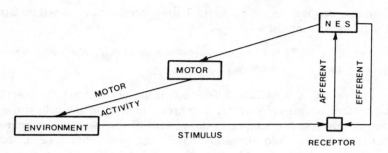

FIG. 5.1. The bare bones of a behavior cycle. The motor output depends not only upon the stimulus (if any) but also upon the state of the NES and the outcome of immediately preceding behavioral acts. For a feedback model, see Powers, 1973.

(An equivalent formulation is this: For every species K there is a family of functions $\phi_i\colon K \times S_i \times E \to M_i$, where S_i is the state space of the ith control neurosystem, E the set of external stimuli impinging on members of K, and M_i the set of type i behavioral outputs.)

An immediate consequence is

COROLLARY 5.1. *Any change in (nonredundant) neural systems is followed by some behavioral changes.*

Example: Rats whose cerebral ventricle is injected with THP become alcoholic (Myers *et al.*, 1977).

Behavior, then, is not primary but derivative—hence something to be explained rather than explanatory. But of course since behavior is (in principle) observable in an immediate fashion, it is the very first datum we can obtain about an animal's brain functions: it is a valuable indicator or the latter. (In other words behavior, though ontologically derivative, is epistemologically primary.) And data, far from explaining, are the very items to be explained.

Caution: Behavior is not usually a means to some end, for it is not often purposeful. In most cases the animal cannot help behaving the way it does: it is compelled by its genetic program, which in turn activates or defuses the neuroendocrine and sensory mechanisms that control behavior. This is the case with all inherited (or instinctive) behavior.

Now there are no two exactly identical NSs—not even two physical systems identical in all respects. This generalization, together with Postulate 5.1, entails.

THEOREM 5.1. *No two animals behave in exactly the same manner [even if they are conspecific]*.

The individual behavioral differences are usually of little interest to the laboratory scientist. However, they are of interest to the field-worker and of immense importance to the student of the evolution of animal behavior (cf. Roe and Simpson, 1958; Tinbergen, 1965). Indeed, such individual variability is no less than the raw material of natural selection.

We saw before (Postulate 2.1) that a nervous system may contain a plastic (uncommitted) subsystem, i.e. one capable of learning new patterns of behavior or mentation. This assumption, together with Postulate 5.1 and Definition 3.1, entails

THEOREM 5.2. *The behavioral repertoire of an animal endowed with plastic neural systems splits into two parts: the one controlled by the committed (or prewired) part of the NS of the animal, and its complement, i.e. the behaviors controlled by the plastic part of the NS.*

DEFINITION 5.4. *The part of the behavioral repertoire of an animal that is controlled by the committed part of its NS is called its* inherited *(or* instinctive *or* stereotyped *or* modal *or* rigid) *repertoire, and the one controlled by the plastic part of its NS its* learned *repertoire*.

Remark 1. Inherited must not be equated with *inborn*. The inborn behavioral repertoire of an animal is the part of its inherited behavioral repertoire that is available at birth, i.e. that does not wait for development to become operant. For example, while all mammals can suck from the start, some do not walk until they are a few months old: the motor system, largely programmed, is not mature at birth. Only the adult organism is in possession of its full inherited behavioral repertoire. In short, we have the inclusions: *Inborn* ⊂ *Inherited* ⊂ *Total*. (Chomsky, 1968, has not drawn a distinction between "innate" and "inborn" in claiming that the universal grammar is an "innate schematism": he seems to say that the *ability to learn* such a universal grammar is inborn, while the actual learning process occurs after the babbling stage is over. If so then he is far from being an innatist.)

Remark 2. There is nothing wrong with the concept of an instinct as long as it is not used to explain behavior (Hinde, 1974). Instinct (or inherited behavior) is something to be explained—in genetic and evolutionary terms.

Remark 3. Because natural selection eliminates most types of behavior resulting in backfiring (though not in misfiring), instinctive or programmed behavior looks marvelously suited to goals, i.e. purposeful. In particular the successive stages in the reproductive behavior cycle in birds and mammals look purposeful to the layman—and are often described in teleological terms by eminent ethologists (e.g. Tinbergen). However, biologists are quickly replacing teleology by causation and chance, e.g. by showing that birds build nests, mate, and brood, as a result of complex interactions between neuroendocrine, social, and environmental processes (cf. Erickson and Lehrman, 1964). They have also found that surgical and chemical intervention can destroy instinct. For instance, ablation of the olfactory bulb in the mouse eliminates the so-called maternal instinct (Gandelman *et al.*, 1971), whereas injection of testosterone into the medial preoptic area of a male rat evokes maternal behavior in it.

An immediate consequence of Theorem 5.2 and Definition 5.4 is

COROLLARY 5.2. *The behavioral repertoire of an animal deprived of plastic neural systems is totally stereotyped.*

Most inherited behavior has been selected because it is adapted to a certain environment, i.e. is biovaluable in the latter. (Not all: recall the moth's compulsion to circle about a flame.) But should the environment change drastically, some of the behavior types would be devalued. Joining both statements we have another axiom:

POSTULATE 5.2. *Provided the environment does not change radically during the lifetime of an animal, most of its inherited behavioral repertoire has a positive biovalue for it.*

The great biovalue of possessing a nervous system with plastic neural subsystems is, of course, its capacity to learn new behavior types and thus improve its chances of surviving environmental changes. So, we make

POSTULATE 5.3. *Some of the inherited capabilities of an animal endowed with plastic neural systems are modifiable by learning.*

Example: Birdsong improves with exposure to the song of conspecifics and even to the song of birds of different species (Marler and Tamura, 1964).

So much for our neuroethological concepts and principles. For an alternative but congenial set of notions and hypotheses, see Hoyle (1976).

Let us finally compare behavioral repertoires. There are at least four ways of doing so:

(i) If K and K' are species of the same genus, then it makes sense to say that the behavioral repertoire of K is *richer* than that of K' iff $B(K)$ includes $B(K')$. This won't do for species belonging to different orders. For example, although we cannot hear ultrasound like bats, and cannot fly like them, we have a far more varied (and powerful) behavioral repertoire than theirs. This concept is elucidated next.

(ii) A behavioral repertoire is the *more varied* the greater number of behavioral types it includes. A third possible comparison of behavioral repertoires is in respect of elasticity or capacity to innovate. The more gifted an animal, the less typical it will be— i.e. the more original or creative. The definition we want is this:

(iii) A behavioral repertoire is the *more elastic* the more behavior types it can incorporate or learn. Finally, we may assume that

(iv) A behavioral repertoire is *the more advanced* (in the evolutionary scale) the greater the number of learned (nonstereotyped) behavior types it contains. Thus although man, gorilla, and chimpanzee have comparable inherited behavioral repertoires, the human one is far more advanced than the others because man can learn many more behavior types than his cousins. Notice that advancement does not coincide with maximal adaptation: the saint and the genius, by behaving in extremely atypical ways, act often in a maladaptive fashion. Maladjustment is sometimes an asset rather than a liability. More on this in Ch. 9.

2. Drive, value, choice

What drives behavior? The traditional (teleological) answer, still heard much too often, is that goals do it, i.e. that all behavior is goal directed. This primatomorphic answer ignores the fact that only animals capable of forming a representation of their aims can possibly behave that way. (More on teleology in Ch. 6, Sec. 3.) The behaviorist answer, on the other hand, is that external stimulation drives behavior, i.e. that every action is stimulus bound. This answer ignores the fact that behavior is controlled by the NS, so much so that many behavioral acts—e.g. searching for food or mate—need have no external causes whatever. Whether or not an animal will engage in behavior of some type, in the presence of an external stimulus of some kind, depends on the state of its NES—which in turn depends on the outcome of its preceding behavior as well as on the state of the environment. Thus a food pellet will stir a hungry rat but perhaps not a sated one. Moreover, in certain states the animal will actively seek certain stimulations rather than waiting to react passively to what may happen. (Recall the so-called Zeroth Law of Rat Psychology: In any carefully controlled experimental situation, the repeated application of a given stimulus will elicit whatever response the subject damn well pleases.)

In any case animals must be motivated in order to initiate behavior, and often even to react to external stimuli: they must feel an *inner drive* to behave in a certain fashion rather than another. In short it is not that external stimuli *cause* behavior but that the state of the NES drives its owner to seek, avoid, or ignore external stimuli. Moreover there is little doubt that drives, as well as drive control mechanisms, are specific functions of fairly localized subsystems of the NES (Heath, 1977).

Hull (1943), who started the revolt against radical behaviorism, attempted to explain all behavior (in particular learning) in terms of drives—positive as in the case of the urge to sleep, negative as in the case of the urge to escape. He stated that animals move because they feel a drive to move, eat because they feel a drive to eat, and so on. Hull hypothesized that there is a single general drive. We now think of a multiplicity of drives not all of which are equally strong. (On the whole, defense overpowers hunger, which above a certain level dominates sexuality, and so on.)

Explanations of behavior in terms of drives are of course purely verbal, i.e. no explanations at all, as long as the drive concept remains an occult hypothetical construct. But this need not be so: drives may be identified with imbalances (deficits or superavits) of certain physiological variables such as sugar or noradrenaline levels in blood. In this case the hypothesis that behavior X is caused by drive Y can be put to the test, namely by manipulating the imbalance and watching behavior changes. The entire drive theory can be compressed into one definition and one assumption. First the convention:

DEFINITION 5.5. *A drive (or motivation) of kind X is an imbalance in the X component(s) of the state function of the animal. (More precisely: the intensity $D_X(b, t)$ of drive X in animal b at time t equals the absolute value of the difference between the actual and the normal values of X for b at t.)*

In the case of animals endowed with a CNS this definition should be changed into *"drives are detected imbalances"*, i.e. imbalances mapped into some CNS or other. (Exploratory behavior is no exception, for it may be regarded as resulting from a knowledge deficit, which is a kind of imbalance.) (Fig. 5.2.)

And now the hypothesis:

POSTULATE 5.4. *For every drive in an animal there is a type of behavior of the animal that reduces that drive (i.e. that decreases the imbalance in the corresponding property).*

We are not asserting the converse because there are behavior types which are not known to be regulatory or balance restoring. However, the inverse implication can be used as a drive indicator. That is, having assumed that *Drive* ⇒ *Behavior*, when watching behavior we may suspect (but not establish) that it has been motivated by the corresponding drive.

The adoption of the drive hypothesis (Postulate 5.4) allows one to explain many behavior patterns without resorting to teleology. Thus a bird engaged in nest building exhibits inner-driven behavior. It does not allow random sensory stimuli to divert it from its job: if it did, it would behave just as randomly as the stimulation it gets. The persistence of much of behavior can thus be explained in terms of programmed autonomous activity of the CNS without resorting to imaginary goals. (For further examples of the physiological approach to motivation, see Gross and Zeigler, Eds, 1969.)

The preceding should help dispose of the dogmatic objection to the biological approach to psychology, that motivation cannot possibly come under the sway of natural law—and so must be treated as an attribute of immaterial Mind or else denied altogether. A similar objection is to the scientific study of value. Biologists admit that certain

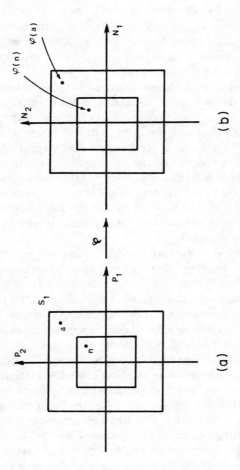

FIG. 5.2. Motivation in animals endowed with a CNS is neural mapping of a physiological imbalance. (a) Part of the state space of some extraneural subsystem of an organism: point *n* represents normal state and point *a* abnormal state. Points beyond the outer rectangle represent lethal states. (b) Mapping of normal and abnormal states into some subsystem of the CNS. The intensity of the drive is some function of the absolute value of the difference $\phi\,(a)-\phi(n)$.

states and events are valuable to the organism whereas others are not. We may take a further step and conjecture that all animals are equipped with receptors enabling them to evaluate some incoming stimuli as harmful, favorable, or indifferent. Even bacteria can swim towards nutrients and away from toxic substances. Presumably they do so because such stimuli activate certain sites in such a way that the foreign chemical binds more or less strongly with molecules in those sites if it is good for the organism, while it does not bind at all if it is noxious.

There is nothing nonscientific about attributing to all animals the ability to prefer some things over others and to avoid harmful stimuli. Those organisms that made the "mistake" of consorting with nocent chemicals or other harmful stimuli did not live to reproduce: they were weeded out. On the other hand, those animals that happened to be constituted in an adaptive manner did survive long enough to reproduce and pass such advantageous traits on to their progeny. In general, the preference of animal b for stimulus x over stimulus y can be explained by the greater adaptive value for b of x over y. In short, we can postulate that *all animals are capable of evaluating certain internal and environmental items* (things, states, events, etc.).

This does not entail that evaluations are always correct: in fact sometimes they are not. However, there is a strong selection pressure to perform the correct evaluations—e.g. to learn aversion to poisonous chemicals or to enemies. Nor does the above hypothesis entail that all animals can form value judgements. The latter are complex neural processes that only man and a few other higher mammals can engage in: all others evaluate without making value judgements.

The human brain is at the same time the organ of control, integration, perception, motivation, imagination, reasoning, and valuation. This gives it the chance to reason about values as well as evaluate reasons. Other animals do not have the proper CNS for performing such syntheses of reason and value: they flee, fight, or behave in a friendly manner without weighting behavior. Their value system has evolved by trial and error, i.e. the hard way—at tremendous cost. The human rating system is partly inherited and partly learned, and is in principle subject to control and revision. We value a number of things that our ancestors abhorred or just ignored and, conversely, abhor or ignore a number of others that our forebears delighted in doing. Not so other organisms:

their brains, if they have them at all, are not as plastic as ours, and their functioning is not as strongly influenced by society as ours.

Saying that an animal is capable of evaluating items of a certain kind amounts to saying that it has a *value system* built into it, whether from birth or from a certain time on. A characterization of this concept is

DEFINITION 5.6. *Let S be a set of items (things, states, or events) and b an animal. Further, let* $\gtrsim_b$ *be a partial order on S. Then the structure* $\mathscr{V}_b$ = $\langle S, \gtrsim_b \rangle$ *is a value system for b at a given time iff, at that time,*

(i) *b can detect any member of S and discriminate it from all other items in S;*

(ii) *for any two members x and y of S, b either prefers x to y* $(x \gtrsim_b y)$ *or conversely* $(y \gtrsim_b x)$ *or both* $(x \sim_b y)$.

This is a comparative concept of value and one involving the preference relation. A quantitative concept is that elucidated by utility theory and occurring in decision theory. (Utility may be construed as a function $U : A \times B \times T \to \mathbb{R}$ whose value $U(a, b, t) = u$ for an object $a \in A$ and an organism $b \in B$ at time $t \in T$ is the value b assigns to a at t. With the help of this function we can redefine the concept of a value system, namely thus: The *value system of the group of animals B* (species, population, community, or what not) is $V_B = \langle A, U \rangle$, where A is the set of objects (things, states, events) valued by the B's).

Note the difference between this concept of value and that of biovalue of a subsystem a of an organism b (Bunge, 1979a, Ch. 3). The *biovalue* of subsystem a for organism b at time t is the objective value that a *possesses* for b at t. On the other hand, the utility (or *psychovalue*) of item a for organism b at time t is the value b *assigns* to a at t. This assignment may be biologically mistaken even though it is a biological event; that is, an animal may attribute great value to biologically harmful items and little value to biologically valuable ones. In short, psychovalues may *conflict* with biovalues.

The psychophysical dualist would speak of a conflict between Mind and Matter—but he would then be forced to admit that sometimes the former is inferior to the latter. On the other hand, the psychophysical monist would regard that as a conflict between the brain (or part of it) and the rest of the body. In any case such a disparity between biovalue and psychovalue is presumably accentuated at the higher evolutionary stages, and it suggests that we should not attempt to reduce one kind of value to the other but keep them both on the same footing—the more so since psychovalue is a very special kind of biovalue. Moreover, we should add a third independent function, namely that of social value, or value to a community. But let us not wander from our subject.

Preferences are often automatic and constant, particularly in the case of primitive animals. Those capable of learning can learn to prefer and even change their preferences against their inherited value system. A rat learns by trial and error to prefer the most healthy foods and avoid the harmful ones in a single trial; and it can also learn to overcome the fear of electric shock if this is the price for good food. In sum, the more advanced an animal the more plastic its value system is bound to be. But, whether instinctive or learned, rigid or plastic, valuation is a function of the CNS in animals equipped with one. (Whether or not there is a special subsystem of the CNS in charge of valuation is still a matter of speculation. My hunch is that, the more complex the valuation act, the more subsystems of the CNS it is likely to engage.)

Our assumption can be formulated as follows:

POSTULATE 5.5. *All animals are equipped with a value system, and those capable of learning can modify their value system.*

Finally we introduce the notion of choice. An animal presented with a set of alternatives will probably abstain from choosing among them unless some exhibit an attractive feature, such as the appearance of edibility. If the animal tries out some of the options and finds out which lead to the most valuable outcomes, it may be said to have learned to choose. But in all cases there must be some freedom in order for there to be genuine choice. That is, the animal must be able to choose any of the alternatives open to it, and some choices must be (at least initially) mistaken for there to be choice learning. Hence we make

DEFINITION 5.7. *Let* $\mathscr{V}_b = \langle S, \gtrsim_b \rangle$ *be a value system for an animal b at a given time, and call $A \subseteq S$ a set of alternatives open to b, i.e. belonging to the behavioral repertoire of b. Then b chooses (or selects) option $x \in A$ iff*

   (i) *b prefers x to any other options in A;*

(*ii*) *it is possible for b to pick* (*i.e. do*) *any alternative in A* (*i.e. b must be free to choose*)*; and*

(*iii*) *b actually picks* (*i.e. does*) *x*.

Note the difference between preference and choice: the former underlies and motivates the latter. Choice is valuation in action, or overt valuation—hence an indicator of valuation, not a definition of the latter. (Most of the ethological literature on choice is marred by the conflation of choice and preference. This confusion is an unavoidable consequence of operationalism.) Note also that, since choice presupposes valuation, the expression 'random choice' is mistaken. Finally, note that not every choice implements a decision. Decisions are deliberate or reasoned (even if not always rational), and reasoning is the privilege of only a few animal species. Most choices, even in ordinary life, are not preceded by any decision-making process.

A possible application of the concept of choice or selection is to perceptive selection or attention, such as listening or looking in contrast to hearing or seeing. Consider a peripheral sensor sending messages to the corresponding neural systems in the secondary cortical sensory area. If all of these systems function at the same time, confusion is likely to result. Normally only some will be activated, all others being inhibited. It may be conjectured that this inhibition (or activation) is effected by a neural selector controlled by a neural motivating system. Thus if we want to listen to a particular conversation in the midst of a noisy party, we "tune in" the selector in such a way that it will drastically attenuate the recording of all the sounds but those we value most (Fig. 5.3).

Selective recall may be similar: the recall stimulus activates only the neural systems "tuned in" by a selector, controlled in turn by a motivating system. (For example, young bachelors have a selective recall capacity for the phone numbers of single girls.) In any case, paying attention to x is selecting or choosing x out of a number of possible items (stimuli, behavioral acts, memories, etc.). Hence attention is not a thing that selects stimuli but a state of activity of a neural system:

DEFINITION 5.8. *An animal b* attends to *item x iff the CNS of b is engaged in perceiving or doing x in preference to all other items accessible to b at the same time.*

There are degrees of attention, and they depend on the state of the

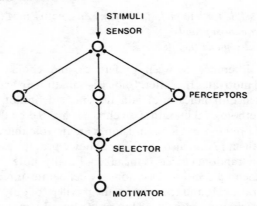

FIG. 5.3. Possible selector mechanism. Each of the three perceptors is tuned to one of three kinds of stimuli. The motivator inhibits the lateral perceptors, so the subject perceives only stimuli of one kind.

animal as well as the nature of the items that are being paid attention to. One way of defining the degree of attention paid by an animal to item x over a period T is the summation of the frequency of firing in the neural system engaged in processing (perceiving or doing) x during T (Fig. 5.4). However, we must attend to other matters.

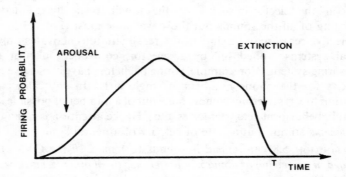

FIG. 5.4. Attention = the integral of the firing probability function.

CHAPTER 6

Memory and Learning

1. Memory

Memory is often defined in terms of learning, viz. as the retention of learning. If this were so then the study of memory should be just an aspect of that of learning—which it is not. Besides, only animals capable of learning—i.e. endowed with plastic neural systems—would be able to memorize incidents of their lives. But we know that many a complex physical system, such as a razor blade and a magnet, as well as many a chemical system, has "memory" of some of its past states. In such cases one says that the system undergoes a hereditary process of some kind. (Cf. Bunge, 1977a, Ch. 5, Def. 5.20.) For these reasons we must treat memory separately from, and even prior to, learning. A general definition is

DEFINITION 6.1. *A system σ at time t has* memory *of* (*or* memorizes) *some of its past states iff the state of σ at t is a function(al) of those past states.*

A system with memory can of course be called a memory system. The peculiar properties of a memory system are these: (a) it records ("commits to memory"), (b) it "stores", and (c) it recalls when suitably stimulated. Actually the second property may well be imaginary: instead of keeping a trace or engram of a state or event, the system may either (a) acquire the disposition or propensity of recalling the state(s) or event(s) concerned, or else (b) undergo a process without outlet. More on this in a while.

Since all organisms have genes, and the latter record part of the history of the species, all organisms can be said to have some memory of it, i.e. are hereditary systems. Besides, all organisms seem capable of at least short span memory. Bacterial chemotaxis is a case in point. This process

135

consists in the fact that bacteria can move up an attractant (e.g. nutrient) gradient, or down a repellent gradient. They seem to discover the right direction of motion as they move, namely by comparing concentrations of places separated by from 20 to 100 body lengths, so they must have a short span memory. Since bacteria are primitive unicellular organisms, their memory mechanism is most likely purely chemical and possibly this one (Koshland, 1977). The chemoreceptors, upon receiving a signal, synthesize a response regulator (which could be a molecule). The latter activates the response if the outcome is beneficial, and inhibits it otherwise; this response regulator breaks down as soon as the stimulus ceases. Whatever hypothesis may turn out to be true, it seems that bacteria do use memory to control their behavior.

What holds for the memory of bacteria must hold for all animals: otherwise they would be unable to survive long enough to reproduce. Memory, then, seems to be universal in the family of animals. But so is forgetting, or the erasing of memory "traces". So, we can lay down

POSTULATE 6.1. *All animals have memory of some of their past states, and none has memory of all of them.*

There is probably a large variety of memory systems or mechanisms. We are interested in two classes of them: fixed systems and itinerant ones. While invertebrates and lower vertebrates have probably only fixed memory systems, higher vertebrates have also itinerant memory systems, i.e. systems that are formed just for the occasion. Young's model of a fixed memory system is a good candidate for the first category (Young, 1965). According to this model the memory system is composed of a number of memory units or modules (mnemons). Each of these modules consists in turn of the following components: a classifying neuron that classes detected events (e.g. into good, bad, and indifferent), memory cells, and motor cells (controlling behavior). For example, in the octopus, whose main movements are attack and retreat, the mnemon could look like Fig. 6.1. Whether or not invertebrates, or even all animals (as Young believes) remember in this way, they do not "store" past events *in their memory*, let alone *in their minds*: if they store anything at all it is in their CNSs.

Let us now turn from invertebrates to vertebrates and, in particular,

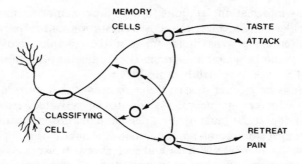

MEMORY
CELLS

TASTE
ATTACK

CLASSIFYING
CELL

RETREAT
PAIN

FIG. 6.1. The octopus mnemon: redrawn from Young (1965). If the incoming signal is "good", the classifying cell activates the attack control neuron. Following this action, signals indicating its outcome (positive or negative) arrive and either reinforce or inhibit that action, i.e. leaving the successful pathway open and closing the unsuccessful one.

humans. There are a number of models of memory in vertebrates. They all seem to fall into one of the following four categories:

(1) *Storage models*
   (1.1.) Localized engrams or traces.
   (1.2.) Global or holographic inscription.
(2) *Dynamical models*
   (2.1.) Strengthening or weakening of fixed connections.
   (2.2.) Strengthening or weakening of synaptic connectivities, i.e. dispositions to form similar connections.

The most popular memory model is of course (1.1) or the localized storage similar to the phonograph record, that can be replayed on demand. This is a favorite with the artificial intelligence crowd, because computers do have "memories" that store information that can be retrieved at will. But human memory is not like a computer's: far from faithfully reliving the past, recall introduces important changes in it, now unwittingly embellishing the story, now impoverishing it, almost always giving it a coherence and plausibility that was not there in the beginning (cf. Bartlett, 1932). In short, human recall involves reconstruction, creation, and destruction. On the other hand, a computer is not supposed to destroy information, let alone to have false memories. Therefore it seems unlikely that memorizing consists in storing, and correspondingly recall in retrieving. What holds for localized engrams holds also for global engrams or neural holograms. (For criticisms of the holographic model of memory, see Arbib *et al.*, 1976.)

If there is no storage of past states or events, then there must be a *propensity* for certain neural systems to be activated, either spontaneously or under stimulation by others. And this propensity may reside in the stronger connections among certain neurons than among others— a strength that increases with use and decreases with disuse, according to Hebb's hypothesis. For example, my uttering the word 'cloud' often makes me recall the word 'window' and conversely, probably because I have always had some difficulty in remembering these two household words in English and German. Probably, the neural systems in my brain capable of forming the words 'cloud' and 'window' are normally inhibited and have become connected (associated). Once my neural system for 'cloud' is excited, it tends to activate my neural system for 'window' and conversely. But this does not happen always: it only happens when I try to remember either word, not when I am thinking of the physics of clouds or of the history of windows. The what and how of my memories depend on the clues present at the time I need to invoke them.

In any case, whatever the detailed mechanism of remembering, it does not seem to consist in the reactivation of some fixed neural circuit but "in the fresh production or reconstruction of an item" (Bindra, 1976, p. 330). If so, then instead of looking for special circuits, let alone individual neurons, recording specific experiences, one should look for changes in the patterns of activity of neural systems, fixed or itinerant (von Foerster, 1965; Young, 1973). And we should not look exclusively at the forgetting or weakening aspect (as Wickelgren, 1974, does) but also at the strengthening of synaptic connectivities (as Anderson, 1972, 1973, does). (In the latter models a memory equals the sum of the activities of all the neurons in a certain system of traces. A stimulus is recalled or recognized just in case it matches one of the ongoing activities of the system.)

Let us take a quick look at two phenomena involving memory. The first is comparison of current events with past ones. The mechanism for this comparison can be chemical—as is probably the case with bacterial chemotaxis—or neuronal. A possible mechanism of the latter kind for comparing events following one another quickly in time (i.e. short-term memory) is the following, summarized in Fig. 6.2 (Mountcastle, 1967). The interneuron C acts as a time delay: when A fires, B receives first the signal coming directly from A, and shortly thereafter (because synaptic transmission is slower than axonal transmission) the signal passing through C. Thus, at a given time t, B may receive two signals: one informing it about the state of A at time $t-1$, and the other informing it about the state of A at the previous time $t-2$. B can then compare the two events.

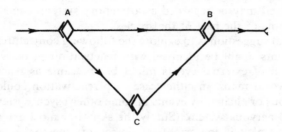

FIG. 6.2. Mountcastle's comparator memory system.

Our second example is the so-called *mind's eye*, or visual imagery. While normal vision consists in an activity of cells in the striate cortex stimulated by retinal signals, the visual images we form when closing the eyes is the same activity generated internally. The images in the visual cortex can be elicited by any of the neural systems connected with it—so much so that a visual image can be elicited by a sound or a pang of hunger, by a haptic sensation or an abstract idea, by a word or a smell. What holds for daydreaming holds also for dreaming during sleep and perhaps also for thinking in images. "The mechanism of imagery is an aberrant mechanism of exteroception, not a form of looking inward to observe the operations of the mind" (Hebb, 1968, p. 468). Finally, visual after-images may be just quickly fading visual memories (or memory images). The retina and the primary visual cortex may not work in these cases but the secondary does.

The upshot is of course that memory is not passive recording but a kind of activity of certain neural systems. This activity is creative in some respects and destructive in others rather than reproductive. And, like all other mental phenomena, memory must be studied at all levels, starting at the molecular level: while all memory systems are influenced by changes in the chemical composition of the brain, some of them may be chemosystems. After all, memory can be manipulated very efficiently by chemical means. (For example, intracranial injections of puromycin and actinomycin D, both inhibitors of RNA synthesis, block the establishment of long-term memory; and well-established memories can be erased with certain drugs, such as epinephrine, while other drugs, such as phenoxybenzamine, can counteract such amnestic action.) Besides, the genome itself may be regarded as a memory system, namely one that records some of the past of the species.

One final suggestion is to explore the following conjectures. Recall of bodily events might be identical with reactivation of body schemata, while recall of external events might be the same as reactivation of external world maps. In either case such reactivation could be either spontaneous or elicited by events in some other psychosystem or in the peripheral nervous system. (Surely the skin, our most extensive sense organ, must play an important role in sensory memory.)

Some memory systems have an ability that most do not possess, namely that of learning. The emergence of this ability was a huge evolutionary leap. Before that stage only mutation, recombination, and blind selection could bring about any improvements in the effectiveness of the nervous system. The learning organism, on the other hand, need not wait millions of years to make such improvements: it can add considerably to that genetic heritage and can do so within its own lifetime. But the subject of learning deserves a separate section.

2. Learning

Definition 2.8 identified learning as the acquisition of new neural functions, hence as involving plastic (not only wired-in) neural systems. (Plasticity is a neural disposition, learning its actualization.) In this sense all learning, even the humblest, is creative, for it consists in the emergence of patterns of neural activity that are not genetically programmed but are formed as the animal lives. What is programmed is the ability to learn.

Note that our definition differs from the usual behavioral definition of learning as modification of behavior in response to stimulation. (However, our definition does cover the acquisition of new behavior patterns, since every behavioral item is controlled by some neural system.) We have no use for the behavioristic definition of learning (hence of behavior!) for three reasons. The first is that, provided the environmental stimuli are strong enough, anything, from photon and atom to society, will adopt new behavior patterns. In particular, since organisms as simple as bacteria behave differently in media with different acidities, one might impute to them the capacity to learn. Being so accommodating, the behaviorist concept is useless. Secondly, not all the behavior changes occurring during development are imputable to learning: some are due to the sequential expression of certain genes (and therefore the synthesis of new proteins) and the resulting organization of the nervous system. Thirdly, in man learning may not be accompanied by any motor outputs or, when it is, such outputs may not be specific and therefore indicative of what has been learned. For example, learning set theory is behaviorally indistinguishable from learning philosophy.

To emphasize the idea that learning is a modification of neural activity, we make

DEFINITION 6.2. *Call E a kind of event or process in a neural system involving a plastic subsystem of an animal a, and S a kind of stimuli (external or internal) which a can sense or detect. Then a has* learned $e \in E$ *in the presence of $s \in S$ during the time interval $[t_1, t_2]$ iff*

(i) *e did not occur in a in the presence of s before t_1;*
(ii) *after t_2, e occurs in a whenever a senses s [i.e. a has memorized s].*

Since all behavior is controlled by some neural system (Postulate 5.1), this definition embraces the concept of behavioral learning, i.e. learning to perform a movement. Note also that we are not assuming that the learning stimulus is external, nor that what is learned concerns the environment. To be sure, making neural maps of pieces of one's surroundings is a kind of learning, but learning theories is a different kind.

According to the above definition, all learning is individual: there is no societal learning. The claim that a social group can learn can only mean that some of its members can learn to behave adaptively.

We shall also adopt

DEFINITION 6.3. *The* experience *of an animal at a given time is the set of all it has learned up until that time.*

In other words, the experience of an animal is its accumulated learning, i.e. the collection of changes in its plastic neural systems. That set does not include what the animal has learned at one time but forgotten ever since. On the other hand, it includes nonperceptual learning: i.e. experience is not just sensory experience but all learning. In particular it includes what we shall call 'knowledge'.

According to our definition, "learning" to avoid harmful stimuli is not learning proper, for it may well consist in a process involving no plastic neural systems: in fact, it consists in closing or blocking undesirable pathways, therefore in shrinking rather than expanding the state space of the nervous system. Since this, i.e. "learning" what *not* to do, is all that invertebrates seem capable of "learning" (cf. Young, 1973; Kandel, 1976; Hoyle, 1976), theirs is not learning according to our definition: it should therefore be rechristened—e.g. as screening or filtering.

(*A fortiori*, we have no use for the inhibition theory of learning, according to which "All learning and all thinking may be regarded as resulting from a single fundamental operation, the operation of inhibition of inappropriate responses or response tendencies" (Harlow, 1958, p. 282). If that hypothesis were true, then the humblest animal capable of learning would be no less than an uninhibited Einstein. Admittedly inhibition—as stressed by Mach and Pavlov—is as important as excitation, and yet it has been systematically neglected by behaviorism. Nevertheless, inhibition does not explain everything any more than excitation does.)

Nor is habituation a kind of learning proper, and this for the same reason, namely because it consists in the weakening of existing (wired-in) synaptic connections with repeated stimulation, which in turn results from a reduction of transmitter release in the synaptic cleft (cf. Kupferman, 1975; Kandel, 1976; Fentress, 1976). Nevertheless the study of habituation is of great importance for the understanding of learning: because it shows the dual of learning proper and thus suggests that learning consists in the strengthening of synaptic connections (Hebb's hypothesis), and because it can be conducted on relatively simple animals, namely invertebrates.

The upshot is that there seem to be three main kinds of synapse, or rather of synaptic connection, as far as learning is concerned (Groves and Thompson, 1970):

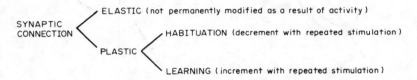

To say it more precisely, hence in a way that lends itself more easily to theoretical speculation: the probability of transmission of impulses from the presynaptic to the postsynaptic neuron across a synapse may be independent of the number of stimuli (*elastic*), may decrease with the number of stimuli (*habituating*), or may increase with it (*learning*) (Fig. 6.3).

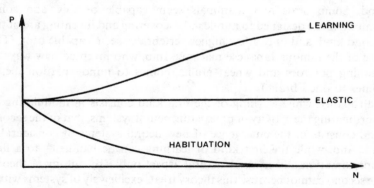

Fig. 6.3. Dependence of probability P of transmission of impulses across a synaptic gap on number N of trials.

An animal in the process of learning expands its neural state space. This expansion can be either quantitative (keeping the same axes) or qualitative (changing some axes) (Fig. 6.4). For example, when a baby

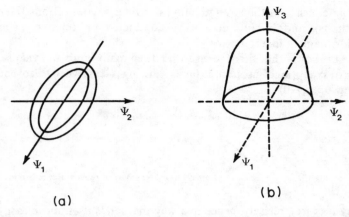

FIG. 6.4. (a) Quantitative growth of learning: more of the same. (b) Qualitative expansion of learning.

forms its first sentence, presumably it does the latter, whereas it does the former when it adds one more word to its verbal repertoire. Likewise learning instructions, as well as trial and error learning, are of the first kind. Some birds and mammals seem capable of this, and some computers are designed to mimic it. Discovering and inventing are of the second kind, and only a few higher vertebrates seem capable of it. (The case of the famous Japanese macaque Imo, who invented new ways of cleaning potatoes and wheat grains, comes to mind—pardon me, it comes to one's brain.)

Probably, while learning of the first kind consists in modulating or coordinating the activity of preexisting neural systems, that of the second kind consists in the emergence of new neural systems of considerable size. And, while the first kind of learning can be handled—to a first approximation and in its structural aspect only—by automata theory, the second cannot because this theory treats exclusively of systems with a fixed state space equipped with a fixed next-state function.

This distinction between two types of learning has yet to be established both experimentally and theoretically. If found true, it would be of some philosophical interest because it draws a line between routine tasks and creative acts, hence between computers (which are designed so that they cannot be creative) and human brains—which are the most creative systems we know of. However, the distinction is hardly of relevance to the mind–body issue, for in either case learning is assumed to be a change in some pattern of neural activity. And whether this change occurs at the cellular or even subcellular level (e.g. on the neuron membrane), or only at the supracellular one (e.g. in the connectivity among the components of a neural system), is a fascinating scientific question (cf. Dunn, 1976; Woollacott and Hoyle, 1977), but one with little ontological import. Indeed, in either case learning would be identical with some material change, not with a literal expansion of the mind. (Besides, there need be no conflict between the cellular and the supracellular models: learning might well be a change in both certain cell properties and synaptic connections.)

If we now disregard the neurophysiological mechanisms of learning and concentrate on the net result of a learning process, we find the following. Learning is a stochastic process, i.e. a sequence of events each with a definite probability. In the simple case where the animal is supposed to learn a list of N items, the process of learning item i may be regarded as a jump, with probability p_i, from a state I of innocence (ignorance) to a state F of fall (knowledge). More precisely, there will be four events for each item: $\langle I, I \rangle$ with probability $1 - p_i$, $\langle I, F \rangle$ with probability p_i, $\langle F, I \rangle$ with probability q_i, and $\langle F, F \rangle$ with probability $1 - q_i$. The transition matrix for item i is shown in Fig. 6.5. The total learning matrix for all N terms is the column matrix constituted by the N matrices L_i. This extremely simple model describes one-trial learning, i.e. all or none learning events. (Such learning events are more common than is usually realized. Thus a rat need not taste poisonous food, or a dog lick a flame, a hundred times before learning that stimuli of such kinds are

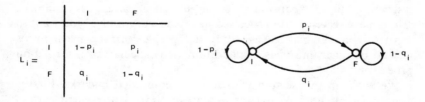

$$L_i = \begin{array}{c|cc} & I & F \\ \hline I & 1-p_i & p_i \\ F & q_i & 1-q_i \end{array}$$

FIG. 6.5. Learning as a stochastic process on the behavioral level: the learning matrix and the corresponding Moore graph.

noxious: a single experience may suffice them.) But of course the model can be generalized to multiple trial learning.

The stochastic learning models of the kind we have just looked at are quite adequate at the behavioral level, which is the one most mathematical psychologists are concerned with. However, those models have two severe shortcomings. One is that they are hardly explanatory theories: in fact they are essentially data summaries. Another is that they regard learning as a discrete process while, if learning is a modification of either membrane permeability or synaptic connectivity, then surely even quick learning is a continuous process at the physiological level. Even the so-called hypothesis theory of learning (Levine, 1974), which postulates the sudden formation and quick acceptance or rejection of hypotheses during learning tasks, is consistent with the hypothesis that such changes are swift neural processes rather than jumps. Therefore the behaviorist's thesis that all learning *must* be discrete (Estes, 1962; Greeno, 1974), just because behaviorists look only at the net behavioral manifestation of it, amounts to a wilful discarding of the very thing that does the learning, namely the plastic nervous system.

The information–theoretic treatments of learning do not fare better: not only do they ignore the physical, chemical, and biological specificity of the CNS, but these models can account at most for avoidance behavior, such as withdrawal. Indeed, they equate learning with information gain, i.e. with the "freezing" of some of the possible outputs of the system, so that it won't do certain "things". (The amount of information carried by a signal to a system equals the reduction in the number of options available to the system.) This is, indeed, what happens in the case of aversive behavior, but not when an animal learns to do new "things" for which it has not been programmed: in these cases not a restriction but an expansion of its outputs takes place, so it cannot be said to have received and processed information. Moral: If you want to learn how an animal learns, study its specific learning mechanisms instead of regarding it as a black box, in particular an information processor.

We wind up this section with some disconnected remarks. Firstly, although we do not have to learn to sense (detect), we do have to learn to perceive. In particular, we learn early in life to externalize or project the distant things we hear or see, and we do so by integrating information coming from the various senses and interpreting it. Secondly, we must also learn early on who or what to become attached to, what to eat, where to sleep, and so on. (This kind of early learning, which is quick and in general lasting—though it can be experimentally erased—is called *imprinting*.) Thirdly, the psychobiological approach to learning may suggest, but does not necessarily accompany, the attempt to reduce all kinds of learning to blind trial and error. While the latter is surely universal, it is not the only kind of learning: as we noted above, creative learning is of a different kind. Moreover, in human adults, and probably in other primates as well, even the solution to relatively simple tasks may proceed by way of forming and checking hypotheses (Levine, 1974)—a finding that should lay to rest the idea that human learners are passive. Fourthly, it seems that arousal of almost any kind suffices to motivate an animal to learn. Thus by merely applying a paper clip to the tail of a rat one facilitates its learning certain tasks (Koob *et al.*, 1976). This would seem to confirm the role of subcortical systems in learning. And this is not all: anticipation or foresight facilitates learning, particularly if attached a positive value, as we know from reinforcement schedules. But this point deserves a separate paragraph.

3. Expectation and purpose

All physical and chemical systems, and most biosystems, are *non-anticipatory*, i.e. they do not expect anything, so their behavior does not depend on the expected outcome of their actions. We now introduce anticipation, an ability only animals of some species have—in fact all and only those capable of learning to expect either reward or punishment when presented with certain stimuli or engaging in certain activities. A familiar example is the pet dog's joy at the sight of the leash: it looks forward to a walk.

We shall adopt

DEFINITION 6.4. *Animal b expects (or foresees) a future event of kind E when sensing an external or internal stimulus s while in state t, if and only if b has learned to associate s and t with an event of kind E.*

An alternative, somewhat more general, definition is the following one employing the notion of an internal map or model: "A system is an *anticipatory system* iff it is capable of building models of certain things." Such a model may be said to anticipate the evolution of a thing iff each model state corresponds to a thing state. (Note that, whereas the states of the thing change in the course of time, those of the model do not: the totality of model states are given the moment the model is completed.) Moreover, the model is true if it yields a correct (true) anticipation of the evolution in question. The advantage of this definition is that it is applicable to artificial systems. (For a similar definition, see Rosen, 1974.)

Because expectation depends on experience, casual observation of behavior, without any information on the learning history (experience) of the animal, does not allow one to foresee its behavior. Incidentally, this answers the old objection to the possibility of human psychology, that because no two persons react in the same way to the same stimulus, human behavior is unpredictable. Tell me the history and circumstances of a person, and give me a scientific theory of behavior, and I will be able to produce short-term forecasts of her behavior.

Because foresight depends on learning (and conversely), the lower animals, which have no learning ability, have no expectations either. But if an animal can learn, then it has expectations, and in turn expecting helps learning. In fact experiment shows that the level of performance of the higher animals is very sensitive to the value of the outcome (reward or punishment). Animals endowed with the ability to expect can regulate the effort they put into doing something.

The dual of expectation is of course surprise. If expectancy is quantitated, so is surprise, namely either as the reciprocal or the complement of the former. But both rest on learning: an animal incapable of learning is never surprised and never disappointed.

It seems that all vertebrates have organs serving an anticipatory or preparatory function. *Examples*: The salivary glands secrete saliva at the sight of food; the glucoreceptor cells in the intestine signal to the pancreas the intake of glucose and this stimulates it to release insulin; and the adrenal medulla, stimulated by the CNS, secretes epinephrine in preparation for flight or fight. In all these cases one subsystem alerts another. Moreover, in all these cases the anticipatory functions are autonomous or nearly so. No wonder that the mammalian brain too has anticipatory functions and more refined ones: that some animals can foresee and prepare themselves for what may come. They can be said to behave in a goal-seeking or purposive way.

Although much, perhaps most, of what an animal does is biologically valuable or at least indifferent—or it would soon be dead—much of it is genetically programmed rather than directed towards goals. Watch an ant carrying a leaf to its ant-hill: it surmounts or dodges obstacles so formidable, and acts in such a persistent way, that one is tempted to attribute it purposiveness and even doggedness. Moreover, its behavior satisfies a rather popular criterion of goal-directedness proposed long ago by William McDougall, namely this: "An action is goal-directed iff its outcome is invariant—within bounds—under changes in the circumstances under which it is performed" (cf. Ackoff and Emery, 1972). However, an ant has no choice but to behave the way it does: it is genetically programmed to act that way, and its nervous system is far too primitive to be able to expect anything, let alone to guide its owner by the expectation of any goals. (See Hoyle, 1976, for the "motor tapes" controlling insect behavior.) Consequently the above-mentioned criterion of goal-directedness is inadequate, so much so that it is satisfied by the flow of a river towards the sea. In this case, too, the flow persists under changing circumstances, to the point that the water dodges obstacles and can even change the course of flow from source to mouth.

Inborn or stereotyped behavior cannot be goal-seeking because the animal cannot help but perform it. Only learned behavior *can* be purposive, and this because expectation presupposes learning (Definition 6.4). To be sure once an animal has learned the right actions conducive to a goal it can automatize them to such an extent that they look innate. But if a behavior pattern is genuinely purposive, the animal, far from being its prisoner, must be able to correct it in case of failure.

In sum, all purposive behavior is learned and, being learned, it is also motivated: the outcome brings a reduction in drive. (We are not requiring that the goal be biovaluable in all respects, for in the case of man we must make room for vices, which are self-destructive.) Also, the action must be anticipatory: the animal must be able to foresee the outcome to some extent. We summarize all this in

DEFINITION 6.5. *An action X of an animal b has the* purpose *or goal Y iff*

(i) *b may choose not to do X;*

(ii) *b has learned that doing X brings about, or increases the chances of attaining, Y;*
(iii) *b expects the possible occurrence of Y upon doing X;*
(iv) *b values Y.*

Note the conditions for purposiveness: freedom, learning, expectation, and valuation. Obviously machines, no matter how sophisticated, do not fulfill all four conditions, hence they cannot be goal-seeking. Most animal behavior is nonpurposive: it only looks goal-seeking because it is so often efficient, but this efficiency is the result of a long and wasteful evolutionary process resulting in control mechanisms that work auto-nomously, i.e. without the intervention of any plastic neural systems, hence without learning or expectation. For example, most animals mate and rear their young in a spontaneous or nonlearned manner—as a result of obscure hormonal changes, not because they are anxious to perpetuate their species. Primates, on the other hand, must learn to perform adequately: although their sexual drive is innate, their courtship and copulation behavior are learned and goal-seeking.

The biovalue of purposive action cannot be overrated: it is almost as effective as stereotyped (rigidly programmed) behavior, and much more so than behavior that is either input-caused (like the knee jerk reflex) or input-modulated like the ant walk or the crawling of a snake. (Interestingly enough the two extremes of this scale of behavior are generated endogenously: the first is independent of environmental stimuli and the fourth is modulated or trimmed but not caused by them.) However, biovalue or efficiency is not a faithful indicator of purposiveness—nor is the presence of control mechanisms. Indeed, every multicellular animal has a number of molecular and cellular control mechanisms that regulate the production of biovaluable events and yet cannot be graced with the property of purposiveness. Goal-seeking behavior implies control, which in turn implies biovalue, but the converse implications are false.

Dualists claim that purposive behavior confirms their doctrine, for purposes cannot possibly be physical entities or events. This view, though still popular, was downed by cyberneticians, who suggested a concrete general mechanism of purposeful action, namely the negative feedback loop (Rosenblueth *et al.*, 1943, 1950). Since then neural modelers have been able to explain a number of purposive behavior patterns (cf. Milner, 1977). According to such models purposes are not states or entities in an immaterial mind but certain patterns of neural activities. This view, rather than the mentalistic conception of purpose, agrees with evolutionary biology, which is concerned with explaining the emergence of goal-seeking behavior as a latecomer that has nothing to do with supernatural design.

Having defined the notion of a goal we can now define that of a means:

DEFINITION 6.6. *An action X of an animal b is a* suitable means *for attaining a goal Y of b iff in fact b's performing X brings about, or increases the probability of occurrence of, Y.*

4. Nature and nurture

The experience (accumulated learning) of an animal depends on both its genetic make-up and environment(s). Heredity supplies the potential, and the environment the chances to actualize some of it. (Henry Fielding said so much in *Tom Jones* more than two centuries ago.) (Fig. 6.6.) A rich heredity is useless in a poor environment, and a rich environment does not compensate for a poor inheritance. (Hence cloning won't suffice to mass-produce geniuses.)

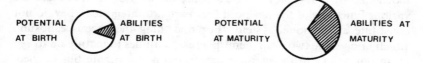

POTENTIAL AT BIRTH — ABILITIES AT BIRTH   POTENTIAL AT MATURITY — ABILITIES AT MATURITY

FIG. 6.6. Experience rides on heredity. Potential at maturity is generally greater than at birth because some genes are "expressed" late, hence new chemical reactions can occur at maturity which were impossible at birth.

The intertwining of heredity and environment—hence the failure of both nativism and environmentalism—is nowhere as obvious as in the development of the mammalian brain from infancy to senility. Consider just the following findings. (a) It is useless to try to teach advanced subjects to either very young or retarded children; (b) development is severely slowed down in a substandard environment incapable of providing the required nourishment (Provence and Lipton, 1962) or varied stimulation; (c) rearing has observable chemical and anatomical effects on brain structure, particularly on cortex thickness, dendritic branching, and number of glial cells (see Bennett, 1976; Diamond *et al.*, 1976, Rosenzweig *et al.*, 1976); (d) even a genius will become senile if he lives long enough.

The organization of the brain of an adult animal, hence its behavioral repertoire, depends then, both on its genic blueprint and on the opportunities and challenges presented by its environment, particularly in early life. (The primate brain is so plastic that its sensory cortex can learn to see correctly when the animal is equipped with image-inverting goggles. And it is so creative that it can deliberately alter its environment to suit its purposes.) The psychoneural monist has no difficulty in understanding the development and the involution of mental abilities, namely in terms of the emergence and (functional) breakdown of neural systems. On the other hand, the psychophysical dualist has no clue about the maturation and decay of the immaterial mind.

The newborn human is mindless (Delgado, 1969)—*pace* the psychoanalytic myths. Firstly, because many neurons form only after birth. Secondly, because many (perhaps most) dendritic connections between neurons develop after birth. Thirdly, because the neurons in the sensory areas are initially poor in RNA and proteins, and so do not develop biochemically unless they receive sensory inputs. Fourthly, because the various functions of the newborn brain are not integrated: they do not constitute a functional system. (For one thing the corpus callosum, which bridges the two brain hemispheres, continues to mature up to age 10 in humans.) Fifthly, because perception is not innate but learned. Hence a human being reared in an extremely poor environment does not even learn to perceive correctly. Remember the case of the rain forest pygmy who, when taken to the prairie, mistook a herd of buffaloes for insects. And forget about chickens and many other animals which, unlike humans, perceive correctly no sooner than they are born: we are presently concerned with humans, and extrapolations from other species won't always do.

In short, the uneducated human brain has hardly a human mind, as Kant himself remarked in spite of his innatism. The practical consequences of this developmental view of mind are numerous and momentous—e.g. for the importance of a well-timed education and for the groundlessness of the fantasies about intrauterine and infantile mental life. In short, the mental functions are the most changeable of all bodily functions—which is a way of saying that the human brain is the most versatile and self-organizing of all systems in the known world (Luria, 1973).

To affirm that the newborn is mindless amounts to holding that there are no innate ideas, no *a priori* intuitions, no inherited world views. There is only an inherited CNS with a definite circuitry—part of which is hard-wired or rigid, part soft-wired or plastic—and an inherited natural and social environment. So, some ideas are easier to acquire than others. Therefore our image of the external world is a result not only of external stimuli and of active mentation (in particular conjecturing) but also of our genetic make-up and our social heritage. Hence no matter how much and how varied the information impinging upon an animal, it won't absorb it unless it is prepared to do so by both its inherited CNS and its experience.

Every newborn human has a unique set of potentialities. Given the suitable environment, he or she will develop into a farmer, an administrator, or an interpreter. Not that he or she is biologically destined or predetermined to become either: there are no genes for farming, managing, or interpreting. The genic potentialities are more general than that: the potentiality to learn to do *any* manual work, to transact *any* business, to talk *any* language. The circumstances, which are always specific, channel the actualization of such general inborn potentialities. It is not that the environment chooses or selects a specific inborn potentiality such as that of being able to learn Chinese. Rather than filtering out special potentialities, the environment renders them specific by supplying or curtailing opportunities for development. As with the case of biological development, the environment controls mental development but does not produce it—which is not surprising since mental development is an aspect of biological development. (With one difference though: human mental development is controlled by an environment which is social as well as natural.)

Our mental functions are moulded from birth in a variety of more or less subtle ways. They are moulded by our relatives and neighbors; by our peers and pets; by our teachers and bosses; and, above all after a certain age, by ourselves: by our active search for certain stimuli and things to do, and avoidance of others. In addition there are of course more brutal and quicker ways of effecting radical changes in our mental functions, such as brain injury and surgery; concussion and electrical stimulation; and drugs of various strengths, from tea to heroin. Some of these stimuli, in particular gentle electric stimulation, can elicit or block brain processes of all kinds—perception, imagination, remembering, emotion, pain, pleasure, etc. (cf. Penfield, 1958).

If the mental were immaterial it would be impossible to influence it by physical, chemical, or surgical means. Since it can be so influenced, even to the point of total destruction, it follows that the mental is not immaterial—a simple exercise in logic. Moreover, since what the physical, chemical, and surgical means modify are certain brain functions (processes), it is obvious that the mind is a certain system of functions of the CNS. The only way the dualist can evade this conclusion is either by ignoring the huge heap of experimental evidence or by claiming that the working brain is governed by an unworldly spirit. In either way he oversteps the boundaries of science. One neuroscientist who has taken this step is Eccles (1978, p. 7): "Beyond science are the existential problems of the existence of the cosmos on the one hand, and of one's own conscious existence on the other [. . .] These existential problems require a supernatural explanation to be admitted by we [sic] scientists in all humility."

CHAPTER 7

Thinking and Knowing

1. Thinking

Forming concepts, propositions, problems, and directions are examples of thinking; so are comparing and transforming concepts, propositions, problems, and directions. Thinking can be visual (in pictures), verbal (in words), or abstract (in formulas). It can be chaotic or orderly, creative or routine. Thinking of any kind is, we assume, an activity of some plastic neural systems. (Moreover, in right-handed humans rational thinking is done chiefly by the left association neocortex.)

Of all mental activities, thinking is probably the one most affected by chemical changes and changes in basic properties of neurons. For example, humans unable to oxydize the amino acid phenylalanine cannot think; thyroid hypofunction (insufficient production of thyroid hormones) produces cretinism; and normal subjects cannot think straight when in states of extreme stress, which are often states of hormonal imbalance, or when under the action of psychotropic drugs. Believers in the immateriality of the mind must ignore the mounting evidence for the hypothesis that the content and level of performance of thinking depend upon such physiological variables. And, to be consistent, they should never resort to such stimulants as caffeine and nicotine.

We shall deal here only with two basic thought processes, namely concept attainment and proposition formation. Let us begin with the former, i.e. the process of forming kinds, such as the class of cats or that of triangles. There is some evidence that this process is a function of neuron systems. Thus Hubel and Wiesel (1962) discovered that the striate visual cortex of the cat and the monkey contains neurons of two kinds: "simple" ones, which respond only to very specific retinal stimulation, and "complex" neurons—generalists—which respond to a far greater range of variation of retinal stimulation. There is no difficulty in conjecturing that elsewhere in the cortex there are still more general purpose neural units.

Such generality or poor discrimination can be increased by multiplying the number of units or by connecting them in such a way that the target unit will respond to any stimulus of a given kind, regardless of individual differences. We shall assume this to be the case for higher vertebrates, i.e. that the associative cortices of these animals contain psychons, whether spatially fixed or itinerant, capable of disregarding differences among (external or internal) stimuli of some kind—such as differences in the feathering of birds. In other words, we hypothesize that an animal is capable of forming a certain concept just in case it is equipped with a plastic neural system (psychon) whose function or activity is roughly the same when stimulated by any member of a certain set of stimuli. Obviously, this assumption covers only "concrete" concepts, i.e. classes of real things or events. One way of spelling it out is this.

POSTULATE 7.1. *Let C be a set of (simultaneous or successive) things or events. There are animals equipped with psychons whose activity is caused or triggered, directly or indirectly, by any member of C, and is independent of the particular member that activates them.*

DEFINITION 7.1. *Let C be a class of things or events and b an animal satisfying Postulate 7.1, i.e. possessing a psychon that can be activated uniformly by any member of C. Then b attains a concept $\theta_b(C)$ of C (or conceives C, or thinks up C) iff the activity (process, function) stimulated by a C in the corresponding psychon of b equals $\theta_b(C)$.*

Example: According to our hypothesis each color concept is in charge of a given psychon and the psychon for the general concept "colored" should be one activated by either of the specific color psychons.

Consider next the formation of propositions, problems, or instructions. We conjecture that in each of these cases the operation involved is that of *psychon pairing* or neural association—the "material basis" of psychological association. Consider:

"Children are helpless" pairs "children" to "are helpless".

"Why are children helpless?" pairs the previous statement to one or
    more psychons capable of searching for an answer, such as
    "because they are weak and inexperienced".

"Protect children!" pairs the concept of protective duty to that of
    children.

In each of these cases two psychons—possibly cortical columns—are
activated, one for each concept (or concept cluster). The sequential
activity of the two-component system consists in thinking the corresponding proposition, problem, or directive. This schema is easily
generalizable to complex propositions, problems, and instructions. The
idea is encapsulated in

POSTULATE 7.2. *Thinking up a proposition (or problem or instruction) is
(identical with) the sequential activation of the psychons whose activities
are the concepts occurring in the proposition in the given order.*

Note the difference between a proposition and a sentence. One and the
same proposition, such as "I love you", may be expressed by many
sentences, such as 'You are loved by me', 'Je t'aime', and 'Ich liebe Dich'.
Presumably upon hearing such sentences the thinking part of the brain
discards those it does not understand and conflates all others into a
single proposition. Note also the difference between propositions (which
are conceptual objects) and propositional thoughts: while the former are
fictions the latter are brain processes. Thus 'Her lips are red and moist',
'Her lips are moist and red', 'Red and moist are her lips', and 'Moist and
red are her lips' are different sentences and also different propositional
thoughts. But they are all lumped into the same proposition—i.e. we
choose to ignore their (material) differences and so feign that they are
one (proposition).

Upon hearing an ambiguous phrase, such as 'Loving mothers.', our
brain presumably oscillates between two thoughts—i.e. two different
psychons are activated alternatively. This oscillation (doubt) may
continue until an additional clue (located in the context) allows the brain
to disambiguate the phrase, i.e. to block the activity of the unwanted
psychon. We assume that the formation and dissolution of beliefs is
parallel, i.e. we make

POSTULATE 7.3. *Let b be an animal, p and q propositions, and τ a time interval. Then*

    (i) *b* believes *p during τ iff b has a psychon for p that can be activated during τ;*

    (ii) *b* entertains *p during τ iff b has psychons for p, and other propositions related to p, that can be activated during τ;*

    (iii) *b* is undecided *between p and q during τ iff b has psychons for p and q during τ, such that the activation of the psychon for p inhibits that for q and conversely (i.e. cyclically);*

    (iv) *b* believes *p* more than *q during τ iff b doubts between p and q during τ, and the activity of the psychon for p is more intense during τ than the activity of the psychon for q.*

Note that all this has nothing to do with either probability or truth: belief matters are psychological hence subject to experimental investigation—*pace* the philosophers who advocate *a priori* theories of belief. Indeed, it is perfectly possible to evaluate the degrees of belief or credence that a human subject assigns certain propositions, and thus establish her belief system. In any case, here is a possible definition of the concept:

DEFINITION 7.2. *Let P_{bt} be a set of propositions thinkable by animal b at time t and let $w_{bt}: P_{bt} \to [-1, 1]$ be a partial function from P_{bt} to the double real unit interval, such that $w_{bt}(p)$, for p in P_{bt}, is the value or weight that b assigns to p at time t. Then the* belief system *of b at time t is the structure $B_{bt} = \langle P_{bt}, w_{bt} \rangle$.*

The weight function w_{bt} can change in the course of time; in fact it changes dramatically at certain stages. And it is a partial not total function, because some propositions in P_{bt} are neither believed nor disbelieved.

Now that we have sketched models of concept attainment, proposition formation, and the assignment of credence to propositions, we can envisage the problem of forming complex constructs such as the intersection of sets and the thinking of sequences of propositions. We assume that these are cases of sequential activation of psychons—not of simultaneous association of ideas in an immaterial mind, the way British empiricism had it. In other words, we assume

POSTULATE 7.4. *A sequence of thoughts about propositions is (identical with) the sequential activation of the psychons whose activities are the propositions in the sequence.*

This holds for "trains of thought", in particular inferences. It also holds for conjunctions, in particular inductions (or inductive generalizations). The ability to form some such propositions must be granted all higher animals. Moreover, the induction mechanism must be such that it allows for generalization from a single instance. (Only the *test* for the truth of such generalizations calls for the examination of all or at least a sizable sample of the set of conjuncts.)

(Admittedly, mental transformations or operations are poorly understood in psychobiological terms. However, it is plausible that there is a minimal system of mental transformations. Piaget has conjectured that this system has group structure. However, he did not specify the set whose structure the group is. We assume that it is the set of concrete neural activities of the mental kind, and that the minimal structure of this set is richer than a group. We make bold and postulate that the event space of the adult human associative cortex has the structure of a uniquely complemented lattice, where infima are conjunctions and suprema disjunctions. Additional structures can be built upon this basic structure. In particular, deductive inference can be construed as climbing up certain branches of such a lattice, i.e. as the sequential activation of psychons along filters built on the lattice. This allows us to define a particular kind of intelligence that can be termed *logical intelligence*, namely thus: An animal possesses *logical intelligence* iff it is capable of thinking, and some of its thoughts have the structure of a uniquely complemented lattice.)

This model of thinking is compatible with the models of Hebb (1949) and Bindra (1976). All three have a precedent in the famous McCulloch and Pitts (1943) model (in McCulloch, 1965), perhaps the first neuronal model of ideation. However, this older model does not work for the following reasons: (a) it attributes to individual neurons the ability of thinking up propositions, and does not face the problem of the formation of propositions; (b) it identifies the negation of a proposition with the inhibition of the neuron "embodying" the proposition, rather than with the activation of the unit that thinks up the denial of the given proposition—i.e. it identifies negating a proposition with nonthinking instead of with a particular kind of thinking; (c) it lacks the flexibility that must be attributed to psychons to account for erratic thinking, errors, and effects of emotion.

Rational thought is thought controlled by certain master thoughts, such as "Abhor contradiction", "Check what follows", and "Supply evidence". Such rational control of thinking seems to be peculiar to humans, and even rather recent and still not very widespread. (Moreover, these controls do not work most of the time. Particularly, they are inactive in dreaming, which is low grade, pictorial, and unbridled thinking.) However, what is relevant to the mind–body issue is that thought, whether rational or nonrational, is an operation of the "enchanted loom"—Sherrington's description of the living brain. Moreover, it is an operation that engages not only psychons but also motor centers, sensory areas, and endocrine glands. Therefore pure thought, or pure reason, seems to be biologically impossible. A thought experiment will render this plausible.

Imagine that the associative cortex were cut off from the rest of the world except for an adequate supply of oxygen and nutrients. Suppose, that is, that all the afferent and efferent nerve fibers connecting the associative cortex to the rest of the brain, as well as to the sense organs, were cut off or blocked. If this were possible then we would find that the cortex is asleep all the time, for the reticular formation (in the brain stem) regulates the cortical tone (cf. Magoun, 1958). Even restoring the connection with the brain stem would not do much good: the cortex might be able to hallucinate but, because of the absence of sensory inflow, it would not be very active, and in any case it would do anything but engage in pure rational thinking. As a matter of fact there is no need to imagine such a switching off of the cortex, since the so-called transcendental meditation does just that, for it is nothing but sleeping— whence the therapeutic value of transcendental meditation (Pagano et al., 1976). To summarize in classical terms: (a) pure reason is impossible; (b) reason and emotion are activities of distinct but interacting systems. This being so, rather than wishing to suppress emotion (as rationalists demand), or else reason (as irrationalists wish), we should try to balance them. This is the neurophysiological critique of pure reason as well as pure emotion.

We have distinguished constructs from thoughts about them—e.g.

propositions from (propositional) thoughts about them. Unlike constructs, thoughts are brain processes. Therefore no two thoughts can be exactly identical. Nobody thinks twice of the number 5, or of the Moon, in exactly the same way, if only because we never go through the same states. However, we can assume that all the processes of thinking of the number 5 (or of any other construct) fit the same neural pattern, i.e. are equivalent in an essential respect. This notion is elucidated by

DEFINITION 7.3. *Two thoughts are* equivalent *iff they consist in thinking of the same constructs. That is,*

$$\vartheta_a(\mathrm{C}) \sim \vartheta_b(\mathrm{C}') \quad iff \quad \mathrm{C} = \mathrm{C}' \quad for \ any \ animals \ a \ and \ b.$$

It would be desirable to define a construct as a set of equivalent neural events instead of presupposing the concept of a construct. This would be desirable because it would root constructs on neural events while preserving their abstract quality (in particular their being nonspatiotemporal). However, we have not found the proper equivalence relation that would allow one to construct such a definition.

To sum up, thought is a brain process. This thesis has a number of consequences. Firstly, the laws of thought are neurophysiological laws, not logical ones. Secondly, since thought is a natural process, it is false that "we can think about nature without thinking about thought" (Whitehead, 1920, p. 4). Thirdly, while there is no way propositions can be assigned probabilities (Bunge, 1974b), there is no objection to assigning probabilities to thoughts, in particular to thoughts about hypotheses. For example, within a stochastic theory of thought processes, such as the so-called hypothesis theory of concept identification (Restle, 1971), one can speak of the probability that a person may think, under given circumstances, of the concept of a mammal, or of the psychobiological conception of mind.

The dualist might complain that, by assuming that what does the thinking is the brain, we beg the question. But then what is it that does the thinking? His answer is that the mind does it. But in turn he defines the mind as that which thinks (and feels, imagines, wills, etc.). So, he is the one who runs in circles. Worse, he removes thinking from experimental inquiry, and thus blocks scientific research.

Let us finally deal briefly with the problem of artificial intelligence. According to our definitions computers do not think, for only animals endowed with plastic neural systems can think. But this definition could be too narrow. Why should thought be a function of certain neural systems only? Why could not man bypass the evolutionary process and design and put together thinking machines? After all, do not computers compute, and is not computation a mental function? Wrong. Computers do not compute. Only the total system programmer-computer is capable of computing—provided the first component does not make some fatal mistake. "A small and irrelevant error in the program of instructions . . . can send the machines spinning merrily through realms of utter nonsense. The machine does not care, for it looks only *at* the symbols; it never looks *through* them to see what they might mean" (Miller, 1964, p. 290).

The computer does not think but can mimic thought—provided it is of the rule-directed or algorithmic type, i.e. provided it is not creative. Like chimpanzees, computers can imitate some human actions; unlike chimpanzees, they do not initiate such imitations. Computers are information processors. As such they are not supposed to either discard information (which the primate brain does all the time) or originate information (which the primate brain does often). If they were censors and creators we would not rely on them. In other words, whereas in computers we always value reliability, in brains we often value unreliability, i.e. connections that may or may not conduct sensory messages, and connections that may or may not repeat the old routine. And whereas we value motivation and valuation in the case of natural intelligence, we eschew it in artificial intelligence: imagine using a computer with its own motivation and value system. In sum, artificial intelligence is admirable to the extent that it supplements natural intelligence, ridiculous if proposed as a realistic model of it, dangerous if proposed as a substitute for it. (See Weizenbaum, 1976, for some of the dangers of the computer cult.)

2. Cognition

All cognition is learned but not every learned item is of a cognitive nature. For example, we learn to see and hear, yet we do not count seeing and hearing as cognitive activities but rather as ancillary to cognition. All cognition is cognition of some object, concrete or conceptual, and it consists in some information about its object—complete or partial, true or false.

Cognition can be *behavioral* (e.g. knowing how to ski), *perceptual* (e.g. knowing the song of the mockingbird), or *conceptual* (e.g. knowing that the mockingbird can imitate the call of other birds). There is also self-knowledge, or cognition of (some of the) processes in our own brains, but we shall postpone its consideration to Ch. 8, Sec. 1, for it requires the concept of consciousness, which is not yet at hand.

If behavioral, cognition is the ability of the motor system to steer motions of a certain kind; if perceptual, cognition is a network of percepts, and if conceptual, a system of concepts. Conceptual cognition can in turn be either of real objects (things or events) or of conceptual items such as sets and doctrines. But whether behavioral, perceptual, or conceptual, and whether concerned with concrete objects or with constructs, every cognition will be assumed to be a brain process—hence a subject for neuroscience as well as for psychology.

We summarize the preceding in

DEFINITION 7.4. *Let a be an animal. Then*

   (i) *if b is a learned behavior type (pattern), a knows how to do (or perform) b if and only if b is in the behavioral repertoire of a;*
   (ii) *if c is a construct, then a knows c iff a can think up (or conceive) c;*
   (iii) *if e is an event external to the brain of a, then a has* knowledge of *e iff a can feel or perceive e or think of e.*

We take it for granted that animals of several species know how to perform certain actions, know some constructs, and have some knowledge of events. We include among the latter the empathic knowledge of other animals. Empathy, extolled by intuitionists and mistrusted by rationalists, is admittedly fallible—but it is also indispensable. There is nothing mysterious about empathy, for all animals of the same species have similar CNSs and experiences.

We may also assume, with Pavlov, that all higher vertebrates have an inborn investigative or exploratory drive or instinct: they all want to know certain things because knowledge is biovaluable. (In the higher evolutionary rungs knowing becomes its own reward quite apart from its possible adaptive value.)

Note that having *knowledge of x* is not the same as *knowing x*, or having true (or certain) knowledge of x: the latter is a very special kind of cognition. We shall define it only for the special case in which the object of knowledge is a binary relation between events, e.g. that of precedence:

DEFINITION 7.5. *Let e_1 and e_2 be two members of an event space E of some thing, and let e_1 be R-related to e_2, i.e. Re_1e_2. Further, call e_1^* and e_2^* the corresponding (perceptual or conceptual) representations of e_1 and e_2 respectively, in the brain of an animal b. Then b has* true *knowledge of the fact that Re_1e_2 iff*

(i) *b recognizes e_1 and e_2 as members of E (i.e. as changes in the thing concerned), and*

(ii) *b perceives or conceives of e_1 and e_2 as being R-related, i.e. iff b experiences $Re_1^*e_2^*$.*

Example: Let e_1 and e_2 be two events in either an animal or its surroundings such that e_1 precedes e_2 in time. Then the animal has true (or adequate) knowledge of the temporal order in which e_1 and e_2 occur just in case e_1^* precedes e_2^* in time. If the animal happens to be an educated human adult, he will probably say that the proposition Re_1e_2 (is factually true) iff $Re_1^*e_2^*$ (is the case in his brain). And if he is a philosopher, he may suggest that the only feasible way of formulating the correspondence (or adequation) theory of truth—so far just a program—is within the context of physiological psychology and along the lines of the preceding example. (In general the relation R^* between e^*s will not be the same as the relation R between es, so the subject will know Re_1e_2 iff she experiences $R^*e_1^*e_2^*$.) And, needless to say, all such knowledge is fallible.

To what do we humans owe our superior cognitive power? Why does it exceed by far that of the bottle-nose dolphin even though the brain : body size is roughly the same for both species? A first possible answer is that man's neural plasticity is greater than the dolphin's. A second possibility, compatible with the former, is that the dendritic arborization of human neurons is far richer than that of the dolphin. A third possibility, compatible with the former two, has been suggested recently, namely that man makes full use of all his nervous tissue instead of wasting half of it in duplicating functions. Let us hear the author of this hypothesis concerning the function of cerebral lateralization or asymmetry: "The asymmetry of the human brain seems to be a recent evolutionary attempt at 'de-duplication' of function, an attempt to utilize all 1300 cm^3 of the brain mass, instead of half that much, to construct our spatiotemporal worlds. The cost we pay in minor perceptual and motoric biases and in the loss of a safety circuit in case of cerebral injury is minor in comparison with the cognitive power we gain" (Levy, 1977, p. 169). All three and perhaps additional hypotheses seem worth investigating, but they are unlikely to be as long as evolutionary thinking does not make a decisive inroad in psychobiology.

We can now use the concept of knowledge to elucidate that of decision:

DEFINITION 7.6. *Let a be an arbitrary member of a set A of alternatives accessible to an animal b with value system* $\mathscr{V}_b = \langle S, \gtrsim_b \rangle$. *Then b decides to choose a iff*

  (i) *b can have knowledge of every member of A;*
  (ii) $A \subseteq S$ *(i.e. b prefers some members of A to others); and*
  (iii) *b in fact chooses a.*

A possible decision mechanism is this. If the subject perceives or thinks of a number of objects, and is motivated to choose among them, then she will start by comparing them. Presumably each object will be apprehended by one psychon at a time, and the excitation levels of the various psychons will be different. If one of them is greater than the others, that one will prevail and will send the strongest (or the only) signal to a volition psychon. Alternative neural models are of course possible. (For electrophysiological indicators of decisions, see Ritter *et al.*, 1979.)

The ability to make decisions is restricted to animals capable of gaining knowledge. But not all knowledge is of the same grade, nor is all valuation correct. When both are, they constitute the basis of rational decisions:

DEFINITION 7.7. *A decision made by an animal is rational iff it involves*

  (i) *adequate knowledge and correct valuations;*
  (ii) *foresight of the possible outcomes of the corresponding action.*

DEFINITION 7.8. *A rational animal* is one capable of making rational *decisions*.

Can reasons be causes? In ordinary language we often exchange 'reason' and 'cause'. In science and philosophy we must distinguish them, for a reason is a premise in an argument whereas a cause is an event. Yet, although reasons cannot be causes, reason*ings*—the brain processes consisting in thinking up reasons—cannot help having causal efficacy, particularly if they occur in the elaboration of decisions.

It is possible that rational decisions are not the exclusive property of man: apes seem capable of making them. And it is certain that no animal is rational all the time. Besides, there are degrees of rationality, and one and the same individual is often capable of improving his rationality score. A full-fledged theory of rationality should define the degree of rationality of a decision as a function of the degree of truth of both the instrumental knowledge and the foresight, as well as of the correctness of the valuation that goes into the decision. As long as no such theory is forthcoming we must make do with measuring the degree of rationality of an animal as a fraction of his rational decisions.

Finally, a word on the influence of knowledge on emotion and behavior, particularly since the converse influence is usually emphasized. One and the same (external or internal) stimulus will evoke different responses if joined to different cognitive states. Thus the sight of a wild animal may elicit fear if the subject believes it to be dangerous, and curiosity if he believes it to be harmless. Even bodily states are "interpreted" differently—e.g. now as euphoria, later as anger—in different cognitive and environmental situations by subjects in "the same physiological state" (Schachter, 1964). In short, knowledge has a considerable impact on feeling and behaving. This is sometimes interpreted as refuting the claim that there is some correspondence (or even identity) between physiological and psychological states. However, this interpretation is incorrect, for according to psychoneural monism the phrase 'The cognitive state of a subject influences her feelings and behavior' is short for 'The associative cortex of a subject is linked to her limbic system and motor centres, so that interactions among these subsystems of the brain are bound to occur'.

3. Creativity

All higher vertebrates are creative, and man is so superlatively. This may be conceded while at the same time doubting whether the notion of creativity is clear. It is if construed as neural novelty, i.e. the emergence of new neural systems or new functions of existing neural systems—due e.g. to new connections. Such neural novelties may or may not have behavioral manifestations. If they do, one speaks of *adaptive behavior*, in particular imitation and invention, according as the novelty is in the particular animal or in the entire species; otherwise one speaks of *mental creativity*.

We may define creativity in terms of the concepts introduced previously:

DEFINITION 7.9. *Let a be an animal of species K with behavioral repertoire B(K) at time t. Then*

  (i) *a invents behavior type (or pattern) b at time t iff a does b for the first time, and b has not belonged in B(K) up until t;*
 (ii) *a invents construct c at time t iff a knows c for the first time at time t and no other animal of the same species knew c before t;*
(iii) *a discovers event e at time t iff a has knowledge of e for the first time at time t and no other animal of the same species had such knowledge before t;*
 (iv) *a is creative iff a invents a behavior type or a construct, or discovers an event before any other members of its species;*
  (v) *a is absolutely creative (or original) iff a creates something before any other animal of any species.*

And now the hypothesis:

POSTULATE 7.5. *Every creative act is the activity, or an effect of the activity, of a newly formed neural system.*

This view of creativity as genuine novelty is at variance with the two most widespread doctrines on the matter. One is the religious view that only a deity can be creative. The other is associationism, according to which all novelty is just a recombination or redistribution of preexisting units (cf. James, 1890). The first view is empirically false and the second cannot even be stated in the case of mental events or processes. What are the mental atoms and what their mode of composition? Was creating the bow or the incest taboo, the first song or the first theory, just a "rearrangement of original unchanging materials"? No such myth is necessary if the mental is seen as the specific function of an enormously complex and quickly changing neural system. In any event creativity has been the subject of numerous scientific investigations. (See the extensive bibliographies of Aratesh and Aratesh, 1976 and Rothenberg and Greenberg, 1976.)

All thinking proceeds on the basis of some previous learning, where the "elements" or "raw materials" are laid out. But creative thinking requires, in addition, a pinch of randomness. If you let your habitual associations take over, you are unlikely to do or think anything radically new. But if you manage to inhibit or forget some such connections, or else allow some new connections to be strengthened by fresh experience—even if initially unrelated to your problem—"the right elements may fall into place". This is why interrupting one's routine and going for a walk, or listening to music, or even taking up a new problem, is so often more productive than continuing to sweat over a problem: because such diversions give the brain a chance to reorganize itself, in particular to form new connections, some of them at random. In contrast, rule-directed thinking follows preformed grooves.

The behavior of both the routine and the creative worker can be modeled by black boxes. Assume, for the sake of simplicity, that there is just one stimulus, e.g. a request or demand, and only one response, e.g. the balancing of a ledger or the writing of a symphony. Let 1 symbolize the stimulus and 0 its absence, and a the activity and $\bar{a}$ its absence. Then the function $f: \{0, 1\} \rightarrow \{a, \bar{a}\}$ representing the behavior of the reliable routine worker is such that $f(0) = \bar{a}$ and $f(1) = a$—i.e. he performs only on demand and uniformly. On the other hand, the creative worker sometimes responds satisfactorily, at other times does not respond at all, and sometimes acts under no stimulus. This other kind of creator can be modeled by a stochastic black box with transition probabilities

$$p(0 \mid 0) = p \qquad \text{spontaneous inactivity}$$
$$p(1 \mid 0) = 1 - p \qquad \text{spontaneous activity}$$
$$p(0 \mid 1) = q \qquad \text{elicited inactivity}$$
$$p(1 \mid 1) = 1 - q \qquad \text{elicited activity}$$

What is characteristic about this system is not so much that the stimulus–response relation is stochastic but that it exhibits spontaneity, i.e. that it is not passive. What such a model cannot represent is the creative nature of such spontaneous activity. Only a mechanismic model (i.e. a translucid box) could do so. Such a model would include a state space with untrodden regions or even axes (representing properties) unused by the animal before the start of certain creative processes. And these processes, being neural changes (Postulate 7.5), must be presumed to be lawful even if we have not succeeded in discovering their laws, hence in predicting the corresponding creations.

Although creativity is maximal in humans, it is likely to be found among all mammals and birds—if only the prejudice against the very concept of creation is overcome and the phenomenon is investigated, particularly among young animals placed in unusual circumstances. We make bold and assume that all higher vertebrates are creative. More precisely, we lay down

POSTULATE 7.6. *All animals endowed with plastic neural systems are creative.*

However, so far as we know, only humans are absolutely creative, i.e. capable of inventing or discovering certain "things" before any other animals. In particular, man is the only known animal capable of inventing myths and theories, of arguing about them, of designing new behavior patterns and rebelling against others. We shall make use of this assumption of absolute creativity (or originality) in defining humanness in Ch. 9, Sec. 5. We shall therefore be accused of miscreance by those who believe that only the deity has the power to create, and of idealism by those for whom all novelty is but the rearrangement of preexisting units. So much the worse for them.

4. The "world" of the creations of the human mind

We have asserted that feeling, imagining, and thinking are brain processes. Does it follow that symphonies, novels, technological inventions, scientific theories, and other cultural objects are "just" neural processes, hence material ones? Do not they deserve a higher place? The traditional answer is of course that such "products of the human mind" do belong to a higher "sphere" or "world" placed higher than the "material basis". The latest version of this doctrine is Popper's view on what he calls "world 3" (Popper, 1972, 1974; Popper and Eccles, 1977). This "world", Popper claims, is a creation of the human mind, yet once created it enjoys autonomy and reacts back on the mind (world 2) and, through it, on the physical world, or world 1. (For example, the design of a dam, when implemented, modifies the geography of a region.) Let us examine this doctrine and then expound our own view on the matter of the ontological status of human creations.

To begin with there is uncertainty as to what exactly inhabits world 3. At one time this was "*the world of objective contents of thought*, especially of scientific and poetic thoughts and of works of art" (Popper, 1968, p. 333). Later it became a mixed bag: "the world of statements in themselves" (1974, p. 144), and also that of books, journals, letters, and the like (1974, p. 145). The latest list of products of the human mind is this: human language, theories of self and of death, works of art and of science, including technology (Popper and Eccles, 1977, p. 16). From these writings of Popper's we do not know for sure what a "product of the human mind" is, let alone what its "objective content" may be. Hence it is not clear whether a sculpture (or musical score, or poem, or machine) belongs to world 3, or whether only the equivalence class of the original sculpture (i.e. itself and all of its copies) belongs in it. We are told that, unlike the members of the first two worlds, those of the third are, or come close to being, above corruption—hence similar to the ideas or eternal objects of Plato, Hegel, and Whitehead. In fact some of them (at other places all of them) are "unembodied" or "abstract".

So, we do not really know what world 3 might be, because we are offered neither a theory nor a definition of it. We only know what it is not. In particular it cannot be a *set*, for its membership is not well defined: we are only given a partial list of its "inmates". (Besides, if "the world of possible objects of thought" is conceived of as a set, a contradiction results: see Keuth, 1974.) Nor is it a *system*, because there is no way totally heterogeneous objects, such as statements and drawings, can combine to form a system. At any rate we are not offered a calculus containing the operation(s) whereby any two such heterogeneous objects could combine to form a third member of the alleged "world". So, world 3 is not a *world* at all—not a whole composed of mutually coupled components and exhibiting properties of its own (i.e. emergent properties), except for its putative autonomy.

This autonomy of the "world" of the "creations of the human mind" is supposed to be relative to the latter as well as to the physical world. Thus the laws of logic are neither psychological nor physiological (granted)—and, moreover, they are supposed to be "objective" in some unspecified sense. The idea is probably that the formulas of logic (and mathematics), once guessed and proved, hold come what may. However, this does not prove that conceptual (e.g. mathematical) objects, or any other members of "world 3", lead autonomous existences. It only shows that, since they do not represent the real world, their truth does not depend upon it and, therefore, we can *feign* that they are autonomous objects. However, this is not what Popper claims: he assigns his "world 3" reality and causal efficacy. Unfortunately he makes no attempt to substantiate this claim, let alone refute it. So it does not comply with Popper's own methodology of conjecture and refutation, let alone with the ontology of changing things adopted by science.

So much for the idealist fantasy of a self-existent world of ideas, objective mind, or absolute spirit.

Let us now sketch our own view about the ontological status of the so-called creations of the human mind. We begin by distinguishing the creative process—whether in science, technology, art, or any other field—from its public materializations, such as books, works of art, and machines. Every creative process is a process in some brain or other. In a few cases such mental processes are externalized as physical things or processes which, when perceived by competent observers, elicit in their brains processes similar to those underwent by the creators. Thus a musical piece can be whistled, performed on musical instruments, and listened to, or written down and read. Novels and theories, artifacts and constitutions are similar.

What becomes of a musical piece between performances or listenings, or after everybody has forgotten it? It does not exist. If the memories of the piece have faded in all brains, and if all its scores and records have been destroyed, the music itself is no more and has no chance of resurrection—except for the most unlikely chance of being reinvented. But if some traces of it do remain—either in brains or on paper or records or tapes—then the musical piece has the possibility of "coming alive" again. Something that cannot be played on an instrument or a record player or something similar, and cannot even be hummed, is not a musical piece.

We submit that the same holds, *mutatis mutandis*, for all cultural objects. Thus a sculpture that nobody looks at is just a chunk of matter and so is a philosophical treatise that nobody reads. There is no immortality in cultural creations just because they can be externalized and catalogued. Only that which is being re-created—re-perceived, re-felt, re-thought, re-enacted endures. Deserted libraries, museums, art galleries, and laboratories are just cultural cemeteries. Nothing is more dependent and vulnerable—less autonomous—than the "world" of culture. (Let the current contempt for basic science prevail, and soon there will be no scientific culture left.) Culture lives neither in cultural artifacts, such as books, nor in an immaterial and autonomous world of ghosts: it lives in the brains of those who care about it—who cultivate it. (After all, this is the original signification of the word: *cultivation*.)

Ideas, then, do not exist by themselves any more than pleasures and pains, memories and flashes of insight. All these are brain processes. However, nothing prevents us from *feigning* that there are ideas, that they are "there" for grabs—which is what we do when saying that someone "discovered" such and such an idea. We pretend that there are infinitely many integers even though we can think of only finitely many of them—and this because we assign the infinite set of all integers definite properties, such as that of being included in the set of rational numbers. Likewise we make believe that every deductive system contains infinitely many theorems—and this because, if pressed, we can prove any of them. All such fictions are mental creations and, far from being idle, or merely entertaining, are an essential part of modern culture. But it would be sheer animism to endow such fictions with real autonomous existence and causal efficacy. A differential equation does not exist by itself and therefore is harmless; only thinking of it can have some effect. In short, ideas in themselves are fictions and as such have no physical existence: only the brain processes of thinking them up are real.

But what about the force of ideas? Do not ideas move mountains? Has it not been in the names of ideas, and particularly ideals, that entire societies have been built or destroyed, nations subjugated or liberated, families formed or wiped out, individuals exalted or crushed? Surely even the crassest of materialists must recognize the power of ideas, particularly those our grandparents used to call *idées-forces*, such as those of fatherland and freedom. Answer: Certainly, ideation—a brain process—can be powerful. Moreover, ideation is powerful when it consists in imagining and planning a course of action engaging the cooperation of vast masses of individuals. But ideas in themselves, being fictions, are impotent. The power of ideation stems from its materiality, not from its ideality.

CHAPTER 8

Consciousness and Personality

1. Awareness and consciousness

Behaviorism has no use for the pet concept of mentalism, namely that of consciousness. However, there is no escaping it. For one thing the experimental neurophysiologist uses it when he deals with a "conscious" animal in contrast to an anesthetized or sleeping one. The psychologist too uses the concept, e.g. when describing the gradual automation or "mechanization" of learned tasks—as when he states that performing movement X was initially accompanied by consciousness but X became gradually automatic or unconscious. The description of the functioning of the split brain also requires the concept of consciousness—as when one says that each hemisphere can be independently conscious. Finally, the mere description of yoga experiences, such as the voluntary control of heartbeats, uses the concept of initial conscious control. Hence the comeback of this concept, first banned by reflexologists, behaviorists, and even James (1912). Even ethologists are starting to appreciate the need for it (Griffin, 1976).

Mentalists, on the other hand, have made much of consciousness— too much in fact—and have equated it with mentation or ideation. But, as everyone knows, much mentation is unconscious (or subconscious). Hence we cannot accept the mentalist definition. Besides, we want to distinguish consciousness from awareness: we shall say that an animal is (or fails to be) *aware* of what goes on in its environment or in itself (in particular, of what it does or is done to it); and if the animal is aware of some of its own brain processes (not necessarily mental) we shall say that it is *conscious*. This distinction has a neurophysiological basis: whichever the "seat" of consciousness may be, that of awareness seems to be the reticular activating system in the brain stem.

Our definitions are:

DEFINITION 8.1. *Let b be an animal. Then*

(*i*) *b is aware of (or* notices) *stimulus x (internal or external) iff b feels or perceives x—otherwise b is* unaware *of x;*
(*ii*) *b is* conscious *of brain process x in b iff b thinks of x—otherwise b is* unconscious *of x.*

(We could also have defined awareness in terms of attention.) Awareness requires only sensors—not even a perceptual system— whereas consciousness requires also intelligence, i.e. the ability to think. The lower animals can be aware but not conscious. And a subject may be conscious yet unaware of external stimuli (i.e. "absent-minded" or "oblivious of his surroundings"). Hence awareness and consciousness, though often conflated—particularly by neurophysiologists—are mutually independent. (And the expression 'conscious awareness' is hardly intelligible.) Hence we assume

POSTULATE 8.1. *The consciousness of an animal b is the set of all the states of the CNS of b in which b is conscious of some neural process or other in b.*

In other words our consciousness of mental event *x* is direct knowledge of *x*. This is what introspection is all about: inward "looking" in a way—not at the immaterial mind, though, because the mind is a set and therefore imperceptible. Likewise consciousness (or the conscious mind) has been defined as a set, so it is not an entity.

We shall postulate that a conscious event is a brain activity consisting in monitoring (recording, analyzing, controlling, or keeping track of) some other brain activity, much as a voltmeter measures the electromotive force between two points of an electric network (Fig. 8.1). Conscious events are then activities of certain (probably rather large) neural systems. We do not know yet for sure which these systems are: we only know that, unless the higher brain stem and the thalamus are active, the brain can be in no conscious state (Penfield, 1966). Some investigators have "implicated" the brain stem – left medial – frontal cingulate axis (Flor-Henry, 1976). Still other investigations "implicate" the parietal lobes (Mountcastle, 1978). However, the empirical evidence for either

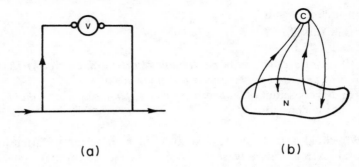

FIG. 8.1 (a) The voltmeter as the "consciousness" of an electric circuit. (b) The hypothetical neural system C monitoring the activity of neural system N: subject is aware of activity in N iff N stimulates C or C controls N.

hypothesis is just that the blocking or the dysfunction of either system suffices for the loss of consciousness. This only shows that such systems are *necessary* for conscious activity, not that they are the "seat" or "organ" of consciousness—i.e. the dashboard of the higher mammalian brain.

Whether or not there is a specialized organ of consciousness, and if so whichever it may turn out to be, we assume that consciousness is a set of neural functions:

POSTULATE 8.2. *Let P be a plastic subsystem of the CNS of an animal b engaged in a mental process p. Then the CNS of b contains a plastic neural system Q, other than P and connected with P, whose activity q equals b's being conscious (thinking) of p.*

This hypothesis is far from outlandish: after all, every biosystem is a control biosystem, i.e. it monitors (watches and checks) its own activity. By sensing and correcting its own functioning, the biosystem assures normality or the return to it. So, it should come as no surprise that the brain, the most complex of biosystems and the supreme control of the animal, is capable of controlling its own activity.

Conscious events seem intuitively to be continuous, but this impression won't persuade a mathematician. There is probably no continuous "stream of consciousness" (or sequence of conscious events). Instead, what may happen is an alternate sequence of discrete though quick tradeoffs between neural systems capable of thinking, and their neural monitors—e.g., $N_1-C_1-N_2-C_2-\ldots$ When N_1 is "on", it activates C_1, which in turn inhibits N_1. This is a chance for N_2, which activates C_2, which in turn inhibits N_2—and so on (Fig. 8.2).

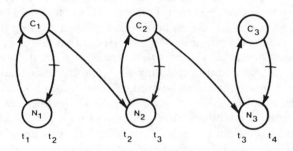

FIG. 8.2. Sequence of conscious mental events: psychon N_1 at time t_1 excites control C_1, which inhibits N_1 at time t_2 and at the same time stimulates psychon N_2, etc.

Since by hypothesis two distinct and interconnected neural systems are involved in all conscious states, it is perfectly possible for them to interact. Thus if a subject is conscious of a routine mental task, he or she may bungle it: the monitoring interferes with the execution of the well-learned task. (Paying too much attention to the dashboard may cause an accident.) If, on the other hand, the subject is beginning to learn a task, he had better have a sharp awareness and consciousness of it: the monitoring system will guide the establishing of the psychon. To account for such phenomena there is no need to invoke an immaterial consciousness and "downward causation" (as Sperry, 1969, Popper and Eccles, 1977, and so many others have done). If one wishes to speculate on the causal efficiency of conscious events (not of Consciousness), then he ought to do so within the scientific framework of changing things instead of the mythical framework of nonembodied entities. Consciousness, in short, far from being in the realm of the supernatural and therefore bound to remain a mystery (Eccles, 1978), should be regarded as a subject for scientific inquiry (Doty, 1975; Dimond, 1976, Fernández-Guardiola, 1979b).

2. Degrees of consciousness

Since, according to psychoneural monism, awareness and consciousness are activities of a biosystem, they can be dimmed or heightened by appropriately inhibiting or stimulating the neural components involved. Such degrees are nothing but the intensities of the activities of the corresponding neural control systems. Hence it should be possible to measure such levels of consciousness, e.g. by measuring the flow of blood into the brain "structures" (subsystems) that do the monitoring.

Piaget and others have shown that there is a gradual sharpening of awareness and consciousness during development in normal children. Moreover, consciousness can be awakened, as in the cure of idiocy due to thyroid malfunction; or reawakened, as in the remission of Parkinsonianism after decades of inactivity. And it can be dimmed and even extinguished altogether in deep sleep, or because of a marked oxygen deficit (anoxia), or sugar deficit (hypoglycemia). If consciousness were a separate entity we would not know how to explain or produce such variations and, in particular, the daily obliteration and resurgence of consciousness.

We equate consciousness with self-knowledge, hence degree of consciousness with degree (or level) of self-knowledge. Like all knowledge, self-knowledge is partial and fallible: we never have the complete picture of what goes on in our brains, and even such partial pictures as we have are often wrong. Yet from Descartes on, philosophers have insisted that, if there is something about which we do have direct (immediate), full, and certain knowledge, it is ourselves—meaning our mind (cf. Chisholm, 1976). Surely we do have some immediate knowledge of some of our mental processes. But is it as profound, exact, and certain as claimed by those philosophers? The writers on the unconscious, particularly Freud, have taught us long ago that that is a delusion: that we often ignore our strongest desires and the real motives of our actions. (Accepting this does not commit us to admitting Freud's mythical explanations.) The ancient philosopher who admonished us to know ourselves, i.e. to *gain* some knowledge of our own mind instead of taking it for granted, knew that such knowledge is hard to come by. Mistrust those under 30: they seldom know themselves. And mistrust those over 30: they seldom know themselves as well as they should. But trust science to find out, by and by, more about ourselves.

Being conscious helps the learning of new tasks but may hinder performing routine tasks: we want the latter automated as fully as possible. Fortunately we do not have to do much about this: it is a law that, as learned tasks are repeated (successfully), they tend to become automated, i.e. unconscious. That is, we can adopt

POSTULATE 8.3. *In the course of the life of an animal capable of learning, learned behavior, if initially conscious, becomes gradually nonconscious.*

When automatisms prove insufficient to solve a problem or execute a task, we need to become conscious of it: when facing new problems, attempting to devise new strategies for coping with them or to evaluate the outcome of unusual actions. Monkeys learn ideas and habits and, if they retain the latter, they fail to make use of their concepts: "a trained monkey is a cognitive machine but, like human cognitive machines, employs ideas only if a problem it must solve cannot be solved in any other manner" (Meyer, 1971).

In general, novelty is best faced when conscious. A conscious animal can know and evaluate itself, hence examine and correct its own thinking and behavior, thus adapting itself, or modifying its environment, in time to survive. (More on the adaptive value of consciousness in Griffin, 1976.) Given the enormous biovalue of consciousness as a device for quick adaptation, it is no wonder that man has been so successful on the whole, for his CNS is the one capable of (a) best detecting novelty, and (b) being in the clearest focused conscious states.

In any event consciousness is not an entity but a set of brain states. Therefore to speak of "states of consciousness" is sheer reification: there are only conscious (and nonconscious) states of the brain—or rather brain states of different consciousness level. Likewise it is mistaken to speak of the Unconscious (or the Subconscious) as an entity, in particular one capable of influencing Consciousness (another entity). There are only conscious and unconscious states and events, and the latter can have causal efficacy only in so far as they are changes of state of concrete things, if only because the causal relation is defined only for events in concrete things.

What holds for consciousness and unconsciousness holds also for

Freud's Id and Superego. There can be no mental entities within mental entities because mental entities are nonentities. To be sure there are controls, e.g. feedback systems, in the brain. And some such controls may "censor" (inhibit or dim) certain brain activities, e.g. block the flow of information to the system doing the thinking. For example, one may have learned an item A and, in the course of mental (brain) work, think up an item B incompatible with A. If A is deeply ingrained, it may "repress" or "suppress" B altogether, i.e. inhibit the psychon that does B. But if B is as vivid as A, further psychons may be activated until "the contradiction is resolved" in favor of one of the original options—or of a third one. Physiologically this is nothing but an interplay of competing feedback neural circuits.

In short, many animals can be in conscious states as well as in unconscious states, and they can experience both conscious and unconscious events. Moreover, since such events are brain events they have causal efficacy: they modulate, control, or even trigger other bodily events. In particular, unconscious mental events were suspected of playing some role in the inner life of humans long before Freud proposed his mentalistic and untestable hypothesis of an immaterial Unconscious. Hume (1739) had spoken of unconscious mental states, and Eduard von Hartmann devoted to them his monumental *Die Philosophie des Unbewussten* (1870), which was quite influential one century ago. And, of course, the brothers Karamazov were not always conscious of their motives. So, the idea is pre-Freudian and it is plausible—but it has yet to be investigated scientifically. (For an amusing criticism of Freud's mythical Unconscious, see Russell, 1921.)

We wind up this section with three remarks on consciousness and society. Firstly, self-consciousness is a brain process but cannot be understood in neurophysiological terms alone. Indeed, it seems that preliterate people do not engage in self-analysis and are likely to evaluate themselves in terms of social behavior. An active participation in cultural and political activities can elicit dramatic changes in a short lapse: it can lead to "the formation of a new inner world" (Luria, 1976, p. 159).

Secondly, since both conscious and unconscious states have been defined above as brain states, in our framework it makes no sense to speak of *collective consciousness* or *collective unconscious*, two favorites with certain ideologists and even some political scientists. It does make sense, on the other hand, to speak of *shared* beliefs and valuations as well as of *shared* though unconsciously held attitudes.

Thirdly and lastly, dualists contend that moral consciousness—or conscience—cannot be accounted for in psychobiological terms, on the grounds that duty is an ethical category, not a biological one, and ethics is concerned with *ought* rather than *is*. Yet consider for a moment the hermit and the outcast: neither of them has occasion to use whatever conscience he may be left with, for conscience—like speech and social graces—is eminently social. You may feel empathy for your neighbor in trouble, or feel inclined to help him, or at least abstain from harming him, provided you have got a neighbor to begin with. That "inner voice" suggesting that you go to his rescue, or reproaching you for not having done so, is the "voice" of society, not that of an immaterial watchman. Unlike the mythical lone wolf, the normal human being has been moulded by society ("encultured", "socialized") into a minimally cooperative animal.

So, conscience does have to do with our material circumstances rather than with a God-given list of duties. And such material circumstances include our genetic make-up: it may well be that some individuals are genetically more prone than others to come to the rescue of fellow human beings in distress. If so, such inborn propensities must have been strengthened (selected) in certain societies and weakened (weeded out) in others. Thus morality must have a biological root as well as a social one. Therefore sociobiology does have something to say about it—though probably less than its enthusiasts proclaim and more than its detractors imagine. In any event the development of morality has ceased to be a matter of philosophical speculation to become a subject of scientific research. A result of recent research into the possible mechanism of acquisition of moral rules is that conditioning (by reward and punishment) and imitation (of peers and adults) are the most important ones. (See the contributions of J. Aronfred, A. Bandura, and L. Kohlberg to Goslan, 1969.)

3. Will

Only some conscious behavior is intentional. Indeed, what began as a voluntary act may, if learned, become automatic, i.e. still goal-striving but no longer intentional; (b) conscious behavior may be aimless, as in daydreaming and loafing. Volition involves expectation but it need not involve foresight. In fact one may engage voluntarily in a certain action just to see what happens—i.e. expecting that it will have some interesting outcome although one may have no clue as to what precisely it will be. This is exploratory behavior. All one expects in this case is some utility, such as the reduction of curiosity. Hence it is mistaken to hold that an animal does something voluntarily just in case it can foresee the outcome of its action and evaluate it. In sum, we propose

DEFINITION 8.2. *An animal act is* voluntary (*or* intentional) *iff it is a conscious purposeful act—otherwise it is* involuntary.

The will is not an entity but a neural activity: x wills y iff x forms consciously the purpose of doing y. Nor is it a mysterious faculty of an immaterial mind but a capacity of highly evolved CNSs, namely "a control of behavior by the thought process" (Hebb, 1968, p. 75). Moreover, the neural activity called 'intention' is localized in the anterior cortices (Pribram, 1960); so, when the forebrain is damaged, intentions are dimmed or destroyed (Luria, 1966).

When you pick a fruit from a tree or a book from a shelf, and are aware of what you are doing and, moreover, have a definite purpose in doing so, what happens is that certain psychons in your associative cortex—most likely psychons containing neurons in the frontal lobes—activate certain motor centers, which in turn control the behavior of actually picking the fruit or the book. But, once triggered by "the will" (the willing psychon), this behavior is largely automatic (Fig. 8.3).

Volition is one of the spin-offs of consciousness. Voluntary acts, being conscious and purposeful, can make the most of knowledge and valuation, particularly in facing emergencies, and so have the greatest chance of being effective—or disastrous if the knowledge is fictitious and the valuation wrong.

Now voluntary acts can be free or compelled. The general who decides to launch an attack may act freely, but those of his soldiers who

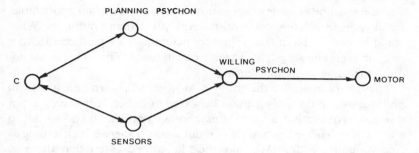

FIG. 8.3. The planning or scheming psychon activates the willing psychon, which in turn controls the motor system. The whole is controlled by consciousness and sensory inflow.

go unwillingly to battle act voluntarily though under compulsion. (Hence the term 'volunteer' is inadequate, for it covers both 'free volunteer' and 'forced volunteer'.) Free will is volition with a free choice of goal, with or without foresight of possible outcome. We make then

DEFINITION 8.3. *An animal acts of its own* free will *iff*

   (*i*) *its action is voluntary; and*
   (*ii*) *it has free choice of its goal(s)* (*i.e. is under no programmed or external compulsion to attain the chosen goal*).

This notion of free will is not Spinozistic because it does not involve knowledge. Nor is it, consequently, identical with rational decision making.

Free will is usually regarded as impossible, hence its very notion as nonscientific. By vulgar materalists (in particular mechanists, such as behaviorists and reflexologists) because it cannot possibly be exerted by a physical–chemical system. By positivists and behaviorists because it is unobservable. Most spiritualists accept free will but deny it a scientific status because they regard the free voluntary act as lawless ("spontaneous"), "gratuitous" (not conditioned by any goal), and original (nonrepetitive), hence unpredictable. None of these characteristics is implied by our definition.

Since free volition is assumed to be a neural process, it must be lawful. To be sure, it is not causal: no spontaneous or self-started process is. But causality is just one mode of lawfulness (Bunge, 1959). Being lawful, free volition must be capable of repetition (*ceteris paribus*) and predictable. Finally, being voluntary it is purposeful rather than gratuitous. What could be said is that a free voluntary action may be performed under risk, or even knowing that it won't be effective. (This is heroism, not quite the same as foolhardiness.)

Thus, paradoxically, the problem of free will, born and grown in philosophy and theology, cannot be solved by either. However, it is not a pseudoproblem but a task for psychology (individual and social) to study volition in general and to find out whether there is such a thing as free voluntary action. We take the plunge and assert that there is. Actually this hypothesis follows from Postulates 8.2 and Definitions 8.3 and 8.4:

THEOREM 8.1. *All animals capable of being in conscious states are able to perform free voluntary acts.*

Since consciousness is not exclusively human, neither is free will.

The upshot of the preceding is the following classification of animal acts.

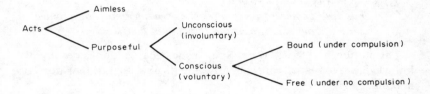

Finally, let me insist that there is nothing unscientific about the above notion of free will or self-started (spontaneous) volition processes. Admittedly this notion is inconsistent with S–R psychology and reflexology, but these in turn presuppose Aristotelian physics, where no thing moves unless it is moved from the outside. According to modern science, on the other hand, self-movement (or self-determination) is no less real than other-movement (or other-determination). *Examples*: inertial motion, wave propagation in a vacuum, spontaneous nuclear disintegration, self-assembly of molecules and of larger systems. In all these cases the forces either do not exist or are internal to the system concerned. Why should psychobiologists reject the notion of spontaneity (or self-starting) if physicists, chemists, and biologists have tamed it?

4. Self

There seem to be at least two notions of a subject, self or ego. One is the clear notion used in ordinary knowledge and in psychology, the other is the obscure notion (or rather family of obscure notions) of self that occurs in traditional philosophy. You and I understand the sentence "I am happy", but I suspect that neither of us understands what Fichte and Hegel wrote about the self, particularly about "the absolute I".

The concept of I needs no more a definition than the concept of Earth. The concept of I is just an instance of the concept of animal endowed with consciousness, just as the concept of Earth is an instance of the concept of a planet. Being concrete systems, both the Earth and I want descriptions, explanations, and predictions rather than definitions. (Only concepts are definable.)

The concept of I occurs tacitly in all general statements concerning primate perception, feeling, mood, thought, and the like. In fact I am just a particular case of the subject occurring in the general statements of human pscyhology. The whole of human psychology concerns me, you, and others like us, in fact billions of us. Therefore to hold that the notion of ego is unlawful, hence beyond the reach of science, is groundless.

To be sure I am unique—as well as very similar to all other humans. But to claim that I cannot be an object of scientific inquiry because I am unique and opaque to the public is no more convincing than holding that geophysics and geology are impossible because our favorite planet is unique and inaccessible for the most part. Actually no two things are identical, and every complex system has idiosyncrasies that escape every single general law—by defintion of "general law". Terra and I are no exception to this (meta)law. That philosopher X finds it difficult (or puzzling, or impossible, or scandalous) to think that his precious me be understandable in scientific terms, is a piece of information about X's world view but not an argument worth our time.

What am I but a human being—not a mindless body nor a

disembodied soul I hope, nor a mysterious compound of body and mind—i.e. an animal endowed with a brain capable of being occasionally aware and conscious. I do not *have* a body and I do not *have* mental states in the same way that I have (own) a typewriter. My body is not an instrument of my immaterial mind, nor is my mind a helper of my body. As long as I am awake I am a *minding animal*—and of course also a digesting, walking, typing, etc., one—and just one out of four billion similar contemporary animals. I shall cease to exist the moment my brain ceases to function.

I am not unknowable. I know myself pretty well, though in some respects not as well as my family, my friends, my students, or my physicians. Each of us has some knowledge of me, I directly, they through my behavior. Admittedly this knowledge is not all scientific. However, if I were to become a subject of psychological and neurophysiological study, the scientific knowledge of me would expand quickly. Science has access to me, to you, to all human subjects. It is not concerned with eliminating subjectivity but with explaining it objectively.

So much for the ordinary and scientific concept of I. Our philosophical concept of self can be introduced by

DEFINITION 8.4. *An animal*

    (*i*) *has (or is in a state of)* self-awareness *iff it is aware of itself (i.e. of events occurring in itself) as different from all other entities;*

    (*ii*) *has (or is in a state of)* self-consciousness *iff it is conscious of some of its own past conscious states;*

    (*iii*) *has a* self *at a given time iff it is self-aware or self-conscious at that time.*

According to this definition, the self is not an entity but a state of an entity, namely an advanced brain. Therefore to say that "the self has a brain" (Popper and Eccles, 1977) amounts in our view to saying that certain brain states have a brain.

Not only humans have self-awareness but, so far as we know, only humans have self-consciousness, at least if normal and from a certain age on. The young child is self-aware but not self-conscious. Self-consciousness is believed to appear at about seven years of age (Piaget) and to originate in internalized speech (Vigotskii). It is probably as old a human attribute as language, and both have evolved (and continue to evolve) together with society. (Jaynes, 1976, claims that self-consciousness—which he identifies with consciousness—is no older than a couple of millennia, on the ground that *mention* of soul-searching, doubts, fears, and the like, does not appear earlier in the literature. But this is like conjecturing that the Britons of the Victorian era did not enjoy sex just because their novelists never mentioned it.)

The self-awareness and self-consciousness of animal X is the way X "sees" (feels and thinks) himself: it is the subjective image or representation of X by X. This self-image of the subject is bound to differ from all the other images of it. Everyone of us believes himself to be more (or less) charming, clever, or good than others "perceive" him to be. Moreover, this image changes with age, as everyone knows except the philosophers who insist that the self is immutable.

5. Person

There are a number of concepts of a person: as many as there are personality theories (or pseudotheories). We need consider only two. According to spiritualists and dualists a person is identical with a mind. Such an equation is acceptable also to a materialist provided he construes the mind as a system of neural functions. However, such a construal might be unacceptable to most psychologists since they include a number of nonmental characteristics among the personality traits. For example, the intensity of biological drives, inherited preferences, gait, posture, and reaction velocities often count as personality traits.

A second concept of a person is that of an animal endowed with a personality, where in turn "personality" is defined as the union of mind and behavioral repertoire. This definition agrees with the current usage among personality theorists, except that it extends personality to some nonhumans. But ethologists might welcome this extension, for they seem to agree that certain animals—namely those with mental abilities—have definite personality traits. (Hence they should be prepared to admit the existence of nonhuman persons. But they should also be wary of attributing to all animals all human personality traits. It would not advance ethology to say that, while moles are introverts, sparrows are extroverts.) At any rate we propose the following

DEFINITION 8.5. *Let b be animal endowed with a plastic neural system capable of mentation (i.e. with a nonvoid mind). Then*

(i) *the* personality *of b is the functional system composed of all the motor and mental functions of b*;
(ii) *a* person *is an animal endowed with a personality.*

Our definitions have the following consequences. Firstly, since personality is defined as the union of behavior and mentation, it is a whole-body property. (That is, there can be no personality organ, nor even localized personality traits such as the "philoprogenitive bump" imagined by the phrenologists.) Secondly, for the same reason the destruction or ablation of large regions of the CNS, as well as the paralysis or amputation of limbs, are bound to produce significant personality changes. (For example, lobotomy divests people of initiative and foresight.) Similar personality changes, though often reversible ones, can be induced by certain drugs, such as LSD and alcohol. Irreversible and massive destruction of the brain destroys personality altogether, in which case the animal ceases to be a person both psychologically and legally.

Thirdly, learning shapes and often enriches personality, though not always in a manner approved by society. (Original persons are bound to rebel against what they consider absurd or unfair, and rebels are not treated as kindly as well-adjusted persons.) Fourthly, people who undergo shattering experiences (bereavement, war, concentration camp, prison, or ideological conversion) may acquire whole new personalities. Fifthly, in deep sleep or in coma we lose much if not all our personality; we become nonpersons or nearly so. (But of course when reawakening we "recover", or rather reconstruct, our personality.)

Sixthly, since the behavior and mentation of animals equipped with plastic neural systems depend partly upon their environment, one and the same animal is bound to exhibit different personalities in different environments—e.g. tyrannical at home and meek at work or conversely (Fig. 8.4).

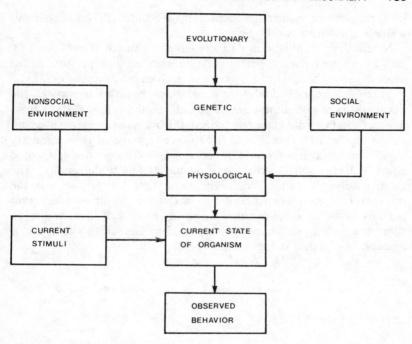

FIG. 8.4. The determinants of personality (From Gray, 1972b). All the various causal factors converge on the box labeled 'physiological' because they act by way of physiological pathways. For alternative views, see Cartwright (1979).

Seventhly, there is no *personal identity* or enduring personality any more than there is digestive or cardiovascular identity: the behavior and mentation of a higher vertebrate are more changeable and vulnerable than any other bodily function. (For an early criticism of the idea of personal identity, see Hume, 1739, Part IV, Sec. VI.) There is no *identity* of the human person but, at most, *continuity* of the "personing" (behaving and mentating) body.

Eighthly, since mind is not incorporeal stuff but a collection of brain functions, and since there are no two identical brains, "identical" twins reared in the same environment have different minds, hence are different persons, instead of constituting (as Shaffer, 1977, has claimed) a single mind with two bodies.

Ninthly, since split brain patients have two minds (Corollary 3.7), they also have a double personality, i.e. they are two persons united anatomically (though not for the reason given by Puccetti, 1973).

Tenthly, if an individual were to get a new brain by transplant, the personalities of both donor and recipient would disappear, and a third new personality would emerge. Indeed, the brain in its new encasement would receive new stimuli and fail to receive some of the customary stimuli; and, because it would be controlling a different body, it would effect different movements, so it would function differently. The original selves would be lost. The same holds, *a fortiori*, for the transplant of each hemisphere into a different skull: two different persons would be manufactured—possibly neither of them viable. In short, tampering with a minding body involves tampering with its mind. Enough of ghoulish thought experiments.

CHAPTER 9

Sociality

1. Social behavior

A bird's territorial call and a criminal's "antisocial" action are no less social than a bee's dance or a baboon's scouting on behalf of its troop, even though the former tend to reinforce solitude whereas the latter strengthen gregariousness (cf. Hinde, 1974). The notion in question is elucidated by

DEFINITION 9.1. *An animal engages in* social behavior *iff it acts on, or is acted upon by, other individuals of the same species.*

The condition of conspecificity excludes preying and flight from predators from the social behavioral repertoire. On the other hand, according to our definition sexual behavior (courting and mating) and parental care do qualify as social. Note also that social behavior does not require purposefulness or consciousness: it may be automatic—in particular genetically programmed—as in insects.

Although not all animals are gregarious or social (i.e. live in communities), all are social in the above sense, if not actually at least potentially. We assume, therefore,

POSTULATE 9.1. *The behavioral repertoire of every animal includes types (patterns) of social behavior.*

Whereas in social insects most of social behavior is inherited, in mammals it is the other way around—i.e. mostly learned, largely by imitation from parents and peers. (Consequently extrapolations from insect societies to human society must be treated with caution if not derision.) And, because populations of the same species differ, social behavior is bound to differ from group to group. (An anthropologist would say that no two social groups of animals of the same species are culturally identical.)

191

Social behavior, like all behavior, is controlled both internally—in particular by the NES—and externally. For example, aggressiveness depends upon endogenous variables such as certain hormones (in particular testosterones) and the excitation of certain brain systems (e.g. the anterior hypothalamus), as well as upon exogenous variables, such as scarcity of food, crowding, and cold. (Because aggressiveness is not an irrepressible instinct *à la* Freud or Lorenz, but a temporary organic state related to environmental events, it can be controlled in various ways: with aggression—inhibition hormones, electrical stimulation, surgery, and the modification of certain environmental features.) Another example of the generalization that all social behavior is controlled by both endogenous and exogenous variables is this: if the serotonin level in a monkey is lowered to 30 percent of normal, the animal loses interest in its surroundings, becomes introvert, and as a consequence loses social rank (Redmond, Jr. *et al.*, 1971).

A further example: animals stake out territories only in moderately rich environments. If the food is either vastly dispersed or densely concentrated, no territories are likely to be set up—in the former case because vigilance does not pay, in the latter because there is no competition. Hence individuals of different species may behave similarly under similar environmental conditions, whereas conspecifics will show different social behavior in different environments—e.g. while some will be fiercely individualistic others will be gregarious, depending on the distribution of food, availability of breeding grounds, danger from predators, etc. For example, the familiar blue jay forms only sexual pairs in some territories, extended families in others, and flocks in still others. Likewise the anubis baboon inhabiting the forests of Uganda has a single-level social organization, whereas the baboon that roams the savannas of Kenya exhibits a rigid social hierarchy subserving the defense against predators (cf. Wilson, 1975).

For the above reasons biological determinism holds only for animals whose social behavior repertoire is inherited, hence stereotyped. The social behavior of bees and ants, the ritualized courtship of birds, and the patterns of aggression and submission of wild dogs, seem to be of that kind. (But a social animal "inherits" not only through the genome: it is born into an existing society that conditions its life style, even its mode of perceiving.) On the other hand, primates seem to inherit only those patterns of social behavior that concern reproduction and the care of the young. The remaining social behavior patterns are learned. What primates do inherit is (a) the *need* for social intercourse, and (b) the *capacity* to form and change rules of social behavior, and to form and undo social groups.

Animals get together forming families or communities, temporary or permanent, loosely or tightly knit, when such behavior improves their lot. The simplest such system is the family, and the simplest family is the mother–infant couple. The root or basis of such a system is of course the care of the young. More precisely: a family is a system (normally of conspecifics) whose structure includes the relation of rearing. One may postulate that all families are composed of animals whose young are born without fully developed behavior repertoires—i.e. that need caring for if they are to survive.

Note that, although families are formed naturally, i.e. on the strength of natural bonds only, they are not biosystems. In fact only the components of a family are alive, i.e. metabolize, are capable of reproducing, etc. A family is a social system, not a "living whole"—*pace* the social organicists or holists.

We give now a definition of a social system in tune with our general qualitative definition of a system:

DEFINITION 9.2. *A system* σ *is a* sociosystem *(or* social system, *or* social group*) iff*

(i) *the* composition *of* σ *is a set of animals of the same order;*
(ii) *the* environment *of* σ *is the set of things, other than the components of* σ, *that act on or are acted on by the latter;*
(iii) *the* structure *of* σ *is the social behavior repertoire of the members of* σ.

In the vast majority of cases social systems are composed of conspecifics. Among the exceptions are the bird families that include one or two chicks of a different species, and the ant societies including slave ants belonging to a different species.

Note that a sociosystem, to be such, must be a system to begin with, i.e. its components must be held together by some bonds or other. And note also that not every social system is a society or community: only a self-reliant or autonomous sociosystem is a society. Thus a group of beggars and thieves, even if well organized like those of Brecht's *Threepenny Opera*, is a subsystem of a society but not a society. The definition we want is

DEFINITION 9.3. *A sociosystem is a society iff it is self-sufficient* [*i.e. does not depend entirely upon other sociosystems*].

2. The cement of social groups

What elicits the formation of a social system and keeps it together despite the somewhat divergent interests of its members? Our answer is this: rearing of the young in the case of the family, sharing (or participating) in the case of other social systems, and social pressure (peaceful or forceful) in all. Neither biological bonds (like the mother–infant bond) nor force are difficult to explain. What is puzzling is that social bonds of other kinds should exist; therefore we shall spend some time explaining how cooperation (sharing and participating) forms the cement of society, even in conditions of competition.

Cooperation need not be conscious: it can be automatic, as in social insects. Animals can cooperate either in their own individual interest (as is the case with sexual partners and with partners in a foraging expedition) or in the interest of their group—be it a family, band, colony, or some other social system. The cooperation among members of an ant colony, or a pack of wolves, are good examples of cooperation beneficial to a supraindividual whole.

The general concept is elucidated by

DEFINITION 9.4. *Let a and b be animals. Then a and b cooperate with one another iff the social behavior of each is valuable to the other or to a third animal.*

When cooperation concerns things (e.g. goods) of some kind, it is called sharing, and participation when it concerns activities. More explicitly:

DEFINITION 9.5. *Let* σ *be a social system with composition* $\mathscr{C}(\sigma)$, *environment* $\mathscr{E}(\sigma)$, *and structure* $\mathscr{S}(\sigma)$, *and let* $T \subset \mathscr{C}(\sigma) \cup \mathscr{E}(\sigma)$ *be a set of members of* σ *or of items in the environment of* σ, *and* $A \subset \mathscr{S}(\sigma)$ *a kind of activity in σ. Then for any component x of σ,*

(i) *x* shares *in T iff x cooperates with other member(s) of σ in acting on items in T;*

(ii) *x* participates *in A iff x cooperates with other member(s) of σ in doing A.*

Now two examples of cooperative social behavior. One: the defense of feeding or breeding grounds, or of the weaker members of the social group. Two: play, which seems common to all higher birds and mammals with a family or social organization (Thorpe, 1966). Note that play may involve both cooperation and competition.

Now we make explicit our assumption that association is based on cooperation:

POSTULATE 9.2. *A set of conspecific animals forms a social system if and only if each of them cooperates with some other members of the same set [i.e. shares in the resources of the society or participates in some of its activities].*

The early evolutionists stressed competition at the expense of cooperation. We have learned since that the struggle for life involves both. For example, flocking and the formation of colonies are effective defenses against predation (Hamilton, 1971). Group grazing, hunting in packs, and active defense involve cooperation—not to speak of higher forms of sociality such as division of labor and games.

Most cooperative behavior is unconscious and much of it inborn rather than learned. However, not all of it is utilitarian in a narrow-sighted way: there seems to be friendship and even love among birds and mammals of certain species. For example, among cormorants, court-ship and nest building are relatively independent of sexual activity and may begin before there are any physiological changes related to the reproductive cycle (Kortland, 1955). Also, there are examples of altruism (or solidarity) and of compassion among subhuman animals: of sharing food with nonrelatives, of helping others extricate themselves from difficult situations, of abstaining from harming conspecifics, etc. (Cruelty and vandalism seem to be human inventions. But so are the institutions designed to protect the weak and help the needy.) Since there is not much clarity about these notions, let us define them:

DEFINITION 9.6. *For any animals a and b,*

  (*i*) *a behaves* altruistically (*or* solidarily) *towards b iff a engages in purposeful social behavior that may be of value to b though not directly or immediately to a;*
  (*ii*) *a and b are* reciprocally altruistic (*or* solidary) *iff a is altruistic towards b and conversely.*

Note that only social behavior can be altruistic. This condition excludes behavior that is valuable by accident, such as defecation, which can be beneficial to beetles, or nest building, which can be exploited by birds that use alien nests.

A coarse measure of solidarity is this. Let a and b be animals, and $N(b)$ the set of needs of b (e.g. food, shelter, or care), and $G(a, b)$ the set of items a is prepared to give b. (Both $N(b)$ and $G(a, b)$ are supposed to be reckoned during the same period of time.) Then the *solidarity* of a towards b is $G(a, b) \cap N(b)$. A quantitation of this concept is this. The *degree of solidarity* of a towards b (over the given period) is

$$s(a, b) = |G(a, b) \cap N(b)| / |N(b)|$$

where '$|X|$' designates the numerocity of X.
(The more you give needed items the more solidary your behavior. Items that are not needed do not count.) The reciprocal solidarity between a and b is of course $s(a, b) + s(b, a)$. This measures the total number of items exchanged between a and b without regard to their value.

A more precise concept is easily constructed by assigning a value to each item needed and got. Such value need not be biological: in the case of higher animals it can be social, i.e. the items being traded off may benefit society as a whole. If only for this reason one can hardly subscribe to the cost–benefit analysis of altruism (cf. Wilson, 1975), which rests on the premise that genes are so smart and species-conscious that they know it is good business for an individual to lay down its life for three or more siblings, for in this case the chances are that its full genetic equipment (or rather a replica of it) will be saved for the benefit of posterity. Genuine altruism requires a highly developed CNS capable of becoming aware that a conspecific is in need. Skipping levels, the way some sociobiologists do, won't do.

In addition to the inter-individual actions that keep sociosystems going, there are the group influences on the individual that prevent it from rending the social fabric. Some of them have significant physiological effects—hence the justification for the new discipline of social physiology. *Example 1*: Young female mice attain sexual maturity earlier if reared in the company of male mice than either in isolation or in the company of females. (Male mice secrete a pheromone that stimulates the ovary.) *Example 2*: An injection of epinephrine produces friendly feelings in human subjects immersed in a friendly environment, and hostile feelings in individuals placed in a hostile environment (Schachter and Singer, 1962). *Example 3*: Exacting social tasks and embroiled social relations can cause stress, which in turn can cause dramatic physiological and even anatomical changes (ulcers, enlarged or deformed organs, etc.), which in turn can deteriorate the brain functioning.

So, the state of the social system depends on the physiological state of its components—and conversely. Social pressure is felt most acutely in the brain, hence it is likely to be manifested in behavior. (The precursor here again is Hippocrates, who in his treatise *Airs, Waters, Places* discussed the influence of institutions on character, claiming among other things that "where there are kings, there must be the greatest cowards".) Of course social pressure is not a mysterious action of the whole on the part but rather the action (direct or indirect) of the various components of a social group on those who deviate from the norm or mode. As in the case of an elastic spring, the force to conform is the greater, the greater the deviation. We need not attempt to reformulate this metaphorical statement in exact terms, but it will be convenient to clarify the notion of deviance because we shall use it. Here is one elucidation:

DEFINITION 9.7. *Let F be a function representing a property of members of a social system* σ, *and assume that the distribution of F in* $\mathscr{C}(\sigma)$ *is bell-shaped, with average* $\overline{F}$ *and scatter d. Then, for any member x of* σ,

(i) *x* conforms *with respect to F iff* $|F(x) - \overline{F}| \leq d$;
(ii) *x* deviates *with respect to F iff x does not conform with respect to F.*

We assume the obvious, namely that every social group contains some deviants, and that the group pressure on an individual increases with its deviance:

POSTULATE 9.3. *In every social system (i) there are deviants in some respects, and (ii) some of their fellow members subject them to a pressure that is a monotonically increasing function of their deviance.*

In most vertebrate societies social structure has a rather weak reaction on individual behavior. Indeed, flocks and troops of various kinds split and even dissolve altogether under altered environmental conditions. In nierarchical primate societies, on the other hand, the overall social structure seems to be overpowering as long as the social system lasts. This makes for social stability—as well as for the occasional rebellion. The deviant, underprivileged, or just young, are often outcast. In a few cases they may find a more favorable habitat offering new opportunities and challenges. If so, their offspring will be subjected to pressures (both external and internal) different from those operating in their community of origin—and so a new race, or even species, may evolve in time (Christian, 1970).

3. Communication

All social animals, and many which are not, can exchange information of some kind (cf. Sebeok, 1977). There is a great variety of kinds of animal communication:

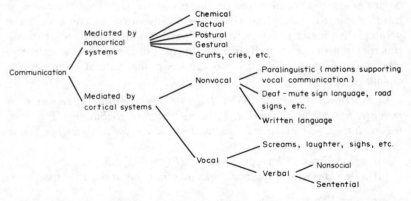

We shall adopt the standard distinction between a signal, the message it carries, and its significance to a recipient (cf. Morris, 1938; Smith, 1965). These will be our conventions:

DEFINITION 9.8.

(i) *An* animal signal *is a physical process executed or controlled by an animal, perceptible by other animals and capable of altering their behavior;*

(ii) *the* message *carried by an animal signal is an encoded representation of events in the CNS of the signaling individual;*

(iii) *the* significance *of a message to a recipient is the change in the latter's CNS caused by the signal carrying the message;*

(iv) *an animal* understands *a message iff the events triggered by the carrier signal in its CNS are similar to those in the animal that emitted the signal;*

(v) *two animals* communicate *with one another iff they understand the messages of the signals they exchange.*

Note the following points. Firstly, an animal signal may be blunt—as in pushing, or subtle—as in singing. Secondly, communication is always among animals—of the same or different species—though it is not always direct. For example, we do not talk to a self-instruction computer but rather to its programmer(s). And computers do not communicate among each other: their programmers do. (One of the programmers might be a person in a previous state, e.g. when he committed some data to the computer memory.) Thirdly, although communication can be valuable (or disvaluable), it is not necessarily purposeful. For example, the signals exchanged by ants and bees, being genetically programmed, are not purposeful even though they are functional (biovaluable). Also men can betray mental states involuntarily, e.g. by grimaces, sighs, or expletives. Fourthly, the psychoneural concept of significance (Definition 9.9 (iii)) differs from both the behavioral notion (cf. Paivio, 1971) and the semantical one (cf. Bunge, 1974b). The former is more powerful than the behavioral concept of significance as the set of behavioral changes brought about by the message: uninteresting messages may leave one cold, and frightening ones frozen. Fifthly, a great many kinds of signal are inheritable; courtship and fight displays are among them.

It is fashionable to speak of *animal languages*. However, not every set of signals is a language; for example, the set of human gestures is not a language. A language is a *system* of *learned* signals such that (a) each signal is either simple or a concatenate of two or more simple signals (i.e. a language has a syntax), and (b) it allows an animal to compose an unlimited number of distinct messages—it can grow together with the animal's experience. A single basic signal, such as a distinct sound or light flash, suffices to build a language, since that unit can concatenate with itself as many times as desired, thus forming infinitely many words. On the other hand, the "language" of the bees, for all its complexity, does not satisfy our conditions, for bees do not learn their signals from scratch, do not form complex messages out of simple ones, and their signals are finite in number.

The following convention captures the above idea:

DEFINITION 9.9. *Let S be a finite nonempty set, and o a binary operation in S. Further, call $\mathscr{L} = \langle S^*, o \rangle$ the free semigroup on S, i.e. the set of concatenates of members of S. Then $\mathscr{L}$ is a language iff*

   (*i*) *S is a set of learned animal signals;*
   (*ii*) *there is at least one animal capable of understanding some of the messages carried by members of S^*.*

This definition allows for private languages such as those discussed (and denied) by Wittgenstein and his followers, and found to be invented by deaf children (Goldin-Meadow *et al.*, 1977). This is interesting because sign languages are reputed to have the same expressive power as natural spoken languages, and because they can be learned by apes such as the famous chimpanzee Washoe (Gardner and Gardner, 1969) and the gorilla Koko (Patterson, 1978). Here is a protocol of the conversation conducted about a biting accident between Koko and her trainer, Penny:

"ME: 'What did you do to Penny?'
"KOKO: 'Bite.'
   [KOKO, *at the time of the incident, called it a scratch.*]
"ME: 'You admit it?'
"KOKO: 'Sorry bite scratch.'
   [*At this point I showed KOKO the mark on my hand—it really did look like a scratch.*]

"Koko: 'Wrong bite.'
"Me: 'Why bite?'
"Koko: 'Because mad.'
"Me: 'Why mad?'
"Koko: 'Don't know.' "

These findings have weakened the hypothesis that language is exclusively human—weakened rather than refuted, for the apes in question were taught a manmade language, namely the American Sign Language, whereas humans *create* languages. (Likewise chimpanzees can be taught to ride bicycles and gorillas to operate photographic cameras, but they have invented neither of these tools.) In any event these experiments have refuted conclusively the hypothesis that man is the only animal capable of learning and developing languages. Chimpanzees and gorillas not only learn phrases taught them but can construct new ones. Moreover, they can learn to communicate amongst themselves using sign language as well as by means of geometric symbols representing words (see Savage-Rumbaugh *et al.*, 1978).

Of course apes make a limited use of language because they are incapable of thinking most of the ideas that could be expressed by means of sign language or some other artificial language. Even so, it is clear that, by using borrowed languages, apes *express thoughts* of their own. Thus they refute the linguistic philosopher's contention that it is "really senseless to conjecture that animals *may* have thoughts" (Malcolm, 1973). We can now be sure, on the strength of experiments with teaching languages to anthropoid apes, that animals can think, which is more than can be said about certain philosophers. (See also Premack *et al.*, 1978.)

Because chimpanzees and gorillas can be trained to communicate with their trainers and among themselves, not only by means of sign language (Gardner and Gardner, 1969) but also with the help of plastic chips (Premack, 1971) and via computers (Rumbaugh *et al.*, 1973), man can no longer be defined as *the language user*. On the other hand, we can obviously postulate that humans, and anthropoid apes and possibly other animals as well, have an inborn linguistic ability. However, this is not to say that man is born with a *knowledge* of certain basic structural features common to all natural languages (Chomsky's thesis). What we are born with is the vocal tract, the Wernicke and Broca areas, and subsidiary neural systems, as well as a social environment (the carrier of a tradition) that stimulates the acquisition and development of verbal languages. (Feral or wild children are mute.) This anatomical and social legacy allows us to mobilize whatever neural systems may be needed to produce or understand speech. Needless to say, such a legacy is not constant. The brain and the vocal tract must have evolved in harmony with each other, and the two in harmony with society: anatomical evolution could have no selective advantage in this case unless society set a premium on it (Lieberman, 1976). Such symbiosis would certainly stop, and the resulting evolution would turn into an involution, if all men were to enter the order of Trappist monks.

Human language is not only a communication tool but also, and perhaps even mainly, a thinking tool. Not that thought is impossible without language: figurative thought is not linguistic, and mathematical thought can be largely nonlinguistic, as pointed out by Piaget. Besides, deaf mutes can think and so can many subjects afflicted with severe aphasia following stroke or brain injury. Besides, some subhuman animals incapable of using a language unless taught can be assumed to think—as Darwin supposed.

Coherent speech implies understanding but not conversely—i.e. correct thinking is necessary for correct speech. However, (a) thinking is considerably expedited by (inner) speech to such an extent that it is often described as "speaking to oneself" (and coherent speech as "thinking aloud"); (b) once thoughts have been verbalized, language may take the lead—sentences become readymade thoughts, which is an asset in routine situations and a liability in novel situations; (c) the speech and thought "centers" are very close to each other—they probably encroach on each other—so that "almost anything that is bad [or good] for brain function may be bad [or good] for language" (Lenneberg, 1970, p. 366); (d) learning is considerably facilitated by language, which in turn is enriched by knowledge, so that language can be regarded as an aspect of cognition as well as an aspect of sociality.

4. Protoeconomy, protoculture, protopolity

Every human society, no matter how primitive or evolved, is composed of four main subsystems: kinship, economy, culture, and polity (Bunge, 1979a). All four are already found in some prehuman societies.

That prehuman societies have a kinship system—i.e. a social network based on reproduction—seems obvious. Two clear examples are insect and bird societies. Nor is there any doubt that some prehuman societies have an economic system, i.e. a social network based on work. (In insect societies the kinship and economic systems have the same membership.) As for politics in the wide sense of management of social activities, it is well known that in certain animal societies law and order, as well as defense, are well organized. A striking example is that of the Japanese macaque society, which is divided into five social classes, every one of which has a definite role or function, i.e. membership in a social class is equivalent to role in the troop. Thus the alpha male is the supreme strategist; the subleader males police the troop and defend it against predators; the adult females raise and protect the offspring; the juveniles groom the adults; and the peripheral males warn the troop against predators, fight them, and train and discipline the juvenile males (Gray Eaton, 1976).

Less well known, but no less true, is that some prehuman societies have a culture of sorts, i.e. a system whose members engage in activities that are chiefly mental rather than biological, productive, or managerial. The patterns of such activities can, moreover, be transmitted throughout the community as well as handed over to the next generation—i.e. traditions form, spread, and are kept. Such a transmission is effected by imitation and occasionally also by teaching, hence with the help of signals. Again, the Japanese macaques are exemplary in this regard (Kawai, 1965). However, the formation of a protoculture with its tradition has also been found among chimpanzees (Menzel et al., 1972). In both cases the initiation of new traditions called for some bold individuals that sought novelty rather than fearing it.

Because economic, cultural, and political systems are already found *in nuce* in prehuman societies, we should characterize the corresponding concepts. The following characterization will suffice:

DEFINITION 9.10. *Let σ be an animal society. Then*:

(i) *the economy of σ is the subsystem of σ whose members engage in the active and organized transformation of the environment of σ;*

(ii) *the* culture *of σ is the subsystem of σ whose members engage in mental activities that control (or are controlled by) some of the activities or other members of σ;*

(iii) *the* polity *of σ is the subsystem of σ whose members control (or are controlled by) the social behavior of other members of σ.*

The extreme cases are those in which all three subsystems are void, and all three have the same membership. The most interesting case is that of tripartite societies, particularly those composed of absolutely creative animals, i.e. animals capable of discovering and inventing certain things before any other animals. We submit that this is the case with all humans, from *Homo erectus* through *habilis* and *sapiens* to *sapiens sapiens*. That is, we assume

POSTULATE 9.4. *An animal society is* human *iff*:

(i) *some of its members, or their ancestors or descendants, are absolutely creative (original);*

(ii) *it is composed of an economy, a culture, and a polity.*

DEFINITION 9.11. *An animal is a* human being *iff it is a component of a human society or descends from members of such.*

5. Humanness

We have defined humanness in psychological and sociological terms rather than in purely biological ones. In this we follow the tradition of anthropology and prehistory. Note also that clause (i) of Postulate 9.4 suggests that the economy, the culture, and the polity, far from being rigid, are plastic—as plastic as their members. Man is not only an economic, cultural, and political animal, but also one that can alter very quickly almost any feature of this triad without having to wait for genic mutations or environmental cataclysms: *man is the supreme creator and destroyer of social organizations and functions.* This wonderful potential for creation and destruction characterizes man better than any of the popular formulas, such as "Man is the smartest (or sexiest, or most adaptable, or most aggressive, or most acquisitive, or what have you) of all apes". Although we share common ancestors with anthropoid apes we are not apes—period (Table 9.1).

Table 9.1. *Comparison between man and ape (mainly chimpanzee)*

Trait	Ape	Man
Female receptiveness	During estrus	At most times
Growth rate	Slow	Slowest
Canines in male	Large	Small
Thumbs	Small	Large and much used
Brain : body ratio	Large	Largest
Neural plasticity	Fair	Largest
Locomotion	Brachiating	Bipedal
Sounds	Few	Speech (syntax)
Food consumption	*In situ*	At camp or home
Ecological niche	Narrow	Largest
Migratory capacity	Small	Greatest
Adaptability	Small	Greatest
Learning capacity	Fair	Greatest
Specialization	Fair	Nil
Creativity	Fair	Greatest
Imagination	Small	Unlimited
Curiosity	Fair	Greatest
Model of reality	Superficial	Unlimited depth
Purposefulness	Fair	Greatest
Foresight	Small	Greatest
Self-control	None	Greatest
Sensitivity	Fair	Greatest
Self-consciousness	Dim	Acute
Wickedness	None	Greatest
Goodness	None	Greatest
Solidarity	Small	Greatest
Tool manufacture	Occasional	Systematic
Teamwork	In hunting	In many activities
Social group size	Small	Unlimited
Economy	Rudimentary	Unlimited complexity
Culture	Rudimentary	Unlimited richness
Polity	Rudimentary	Unlimited complexity
Social plasticity	Small	Greatest

When drawing up lists of human peculiarities one must not forget that man does not evolve certain traits except in certain societies. In particular the much-vaunted rationality of man—accepted since Aristotle as defining humanness—is not conspicuous in preliterate societies, where generalization and abstraction are nearly unknown. Thus consider the following protocol from a famous field study conducted in Central Asia during the period of transition to socialism, i.e. in 1931–2 (Luria, 1976, p. 108).

Subject: Abdurakhm, age thirty-seven, from remote Kashgar village, illiterate.

"*Cotton can grow only where it is hot and dry. In England it is cold and damp. Can cotton grow there?*"

"I've only been in the Kashgar country; I don't know beyond that . . ."

"*But on the basis of what I said to you, can cotton grow there?*"

"If the land is good, cotton will grow there, but if it is damp and poor, it won't grow. If it's like the Kashgar country, it will grow there too. If the soil is loose, it can grow there too, of course."

The syllogism is repeated. "*What can you conclude from my words?*"

"If it's cold there it won't grow; if the soil is loose and good, it will."

"*But what do my words suggest?*"

"Well, we Moslems, we Kashgars, we're ignorant people; we've never been anywhere, so we don't know if it's hot or cold there."

This subject proved to be typical: preliterate peasants find it hard if not impossible to rise above immediate practical concerns. On the other hand, people with some schooling, though living in the same villages, experienced no difficulty in performing the required logical operations. "The significance of schooling lies not just in the acquisition of new knowledge, but in the creation of new motives and formal modes of discursive verbal and logical thinking divorced from immediate practical experience" (Luria, 1976, p. 133). In other words, learning can be more than just "information processing and storage": it can modify some brain functions to the extent of transforming its owner from a quasi-rational animal into a rational one. (See also Goody, 1977.)

When did mankind start to think rationally in general and abstract terms? Perhaps as recently as 2500 years ago, i.e. the last one-fortieth of the history of *Homo sapiens*. And how much longer may we enjoy this newly acquired privilege? Not much if we continue to refuse applying it to the solution of the current apocalyptic world problems—the excess of people, weapons, and power, and the shortage of energy, food, and cooperation.

6. Upshot

Man is unique but is not uniquely characterized by this or that biological, psychological, or social trait. What makes man human is a whole *functional system* of biological, psychological, and social properties that cannot be understood apart from one another (cf. Table 9.1). This unique functional system, far from giving him permanence, ensures his relentless, often fast, and largely self-controlled social (i.e. economic, cultural, and political) evolution. An intelligent brain controls skillful hands that reshape the natural environment, as well as an efficient tongue that, by acting on other brains, can reshape the social milieu. In turn, such changed natural and social circumstances contribute to the molding of new individuals capable of effecting further changes in the natural and social environments.

Human sociality has come to be unique if only because of its variability. However, it has rather firm genetic, physiological, and ecological roots: the family is necessary for the rearing of helpless infants, and the community for subsistence and defense. And, just as the family is held together by caring for the young, society is held together by sharing resources and participating in social activities. Even communication and politics—in the general sense of management of social behavior—are primarily means to regulate cooperation. In particular they serve to keep competition within bounds, preventing it from rending the social fabric. Therefore, to emphasize conflict, in particular individual aggression and war, at the expense of cooperation, is to abandon all hope of understanding the very emergence and continuation of society. Communities break down precisely because of acute conflict, either internal or with other societies or with nature.

To be sure there is conflict within every society and even every sociosystem of nonstereotyped animals. Sometimes the conflict arises from the limitation of resources, at other times from the diversity of goals of the various members. However, conflict need not result in destruction. Every successful society has—by definition—checks and balances that avoid the resolution of conflict by fight, i.e. it possesses mechanisms capable of preserving the wholeness of the society though not necessarily all of its properties. War is the stigma of unsuccessful society. The good society is the one that optimizes cooperation (sharing and participation) and puts a premium on kindliness, fairness, responsibility, industry, and creativity (Fig. 9.1).

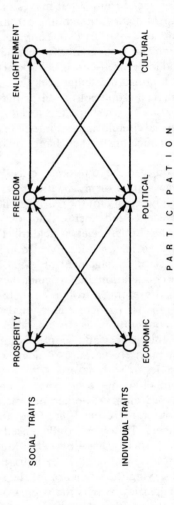

FIG. 9.1. The good society is based on the sharing of economic, political, and cultural tasks and goods. Replace participation with greed or exclusivism, and you get the corresponding social consequences: poverty, oppression, and ignorance—the hallmarks of the evil society. Note that, just as psychological traits surface as social ones, so the latter favor or inhibit the former.

CHAPTER 10

Conclusion: Towards Understanding Mind

1. Types of psychological explanation

Psychology is supposed to explain behavior and mentation, and to do so scientifically, i.e. in terms of laws and data. The object of an explanation can be a property, a fact, or a generalization. To give a scientific explanation of a property is to equate the corresponding concept ("variable") with another concept, usually a complex one. (For example, equating a certain mental state with the activity of a certain plastic neural system is explaining the former, a psychological item, in terms of the latter, a neurophysiological one.) To give a scientific explanation of a fact is to deduce the corresponding proposition (or formula) representing the fact from a set of law statements and a set of data that can be plugged into such laws. And to propose a scientific explanation of a generalization is to deduce it from wider scope generalizations together with subsidiary assumptions and data. In all three cases the key to explanation is some law statement or set of such. In the simplest case (property explanation) a single premise, namely the law itself, is required. In the other two cases at least one law statement occurs among the premises of a deductive argument.

The laws involved in the explanation of behavior or mentation may involve biological (e.g. neurophysiological) concepts, psychological (in particular psychosociological) concepts, or concepts of both types. Traditional mentalist psychology and behaviorism reject alike any attempt to link concepts of both types. Psychobiology, in particular physiological psychology, attempts to relate the two sets of concepts by equating certain psychological and biological items, and by deducing psychological facts and generalizations from biological ones. In particular psychobiology is concerned with fleshing out the hyphen in stimulus–response psychology with neural mechanisms. (*Example*: psychobiological explanations of withdrawal and habituation behavior in invertebrates.) But of course explaining stimulus–response generalizations is the least of the worries of the psychobiologist: his main ambition is to explain subjective experience—not in terms of myths but of laws concerning the central nervous system.

Now, unlike the generalizations of ordinary knowledge, scientific laws are supposed to belong to theories, i.e. logically organized systems of propositions. Moreover, scientific laws, though conjectural, are also supposed to have a solid empirical backing in observation, measurement, or experiment. Finally, they are also supposed to be compatible with the laws in adjoining fields. In short, law statements are systematic, well corroborated, and in harmony with the rest of science (see Bunge, 1967, Vol. 1).

Unfortunately there are but few well-built and well-corroborated theories in psychology. Those which are neatly built and satisfactorily tested are often superficial: they hardly reach the nervous system; and those which are deep are often underdeveloped: in particular they are rarely mathematized. We need far more and better psychological theories if we are to attain a better understanding of behavior and mentation. And, since every effort at theory construction is stimulated or inhibited by some philosophy or other, we had better become aware of the philosophies of mind underlying the various psychological theories: recall Table 1.1 in Ch. 1, Sec. 1. Table 10.1 exhibits the types of explanation suggested by the various philosophies of mind.

The differences in explanation types are most marked with regard to subjective experience, for many dualists are willing to leave behavior in the hands of physiology. (They err of course because what is typical of primate behavior cannot be explained without the help of psychological categories such as those of purpose and creativity. That these attributes are in turn explicable in neurophysiological terms is another matter.)

The greatest divergence in the explanation of mentation is that existing between the various schools of materialism, on the one hand, and those of mentalism, on the other. (We lump into "mentalism" all the philosophies of mind that postulate mind as a separate entity. Thus not only the various versions of dualism but also idealistic monism, or

Table 10.1. *Ten types of explanation of behavior and mentation*

	Philosophy of mind	Explanation of behavior	Explanation of mentation
$\mathscr{M}1$	Idealism, panpsychism, phenomenalism	Manifestation of the workings of a spirit (individual or world-wide). No precise laws	Autonomous and spontaneous activity of the mind coverable by laws containing only mentalist predicates
$\mathscr{M}2$	Neutral monism, double aspect view	Behavior and mentation manifestations of the workings of a being neither material nor mental, explainable with a single set of laws with two projections or translations (behavioral and mentalist)	
$\mathscr{M}3$	Eliminative materialism, behaviorism	Outcome of stimuli, hence describable by S—R laws (no intervention of the CNS)	Mentation nonexistent, hence not to be explained
$\mathscr{M}4$	Reductive Materialism	Motor outcome of physical CNS events, hence explainable in physical terms	Physical activity of the CNS
$\mathscr{M}5$	Emergent materialism	Motor outcome of biological CNS events, explainable with the help of biological laws, some of which contain new predicates	Biological activity of plastic subsystems of CNS, explainable with the help of biological laws containing new predicates
$\mathscr{D}1$	Mutual independence of body and mind	Biological events explainable in purely physiological terms plus possibly theological ones	Mental events explainable in purely mentalist terms plus possibly theological ones
$\mathscr{D}2$	Psychophysical parallelism, preestablished harmony		
$\mathscr{D}3$	Epiphenomenalism	Motor outcome of CNS events	Non-motor effect of CNS activity
$\mathscr{D}4$	Animism	Motor outcome of mental events (e.g. intending and wishing)	Unexplainable except possibly in supernatural terms
$\mathscr{D}5$	Interactionism	Under dual control of body and mind. Only partially explainable	Autonomous though influenced by bodily events. Unexplainable by science

Table 10.2. *Sketchy hypothetical accounts of some mental properties, events, and processes in man. Two rival views: mentalism and psychobiology*

Problem	Mentalist account	Psychobiological account
What is learning?	Enrichment of the mind	Formation or reinforcement of synaptic connections
What is vision?	A mental process triggered by visual sensory inputs	An activity of the visual system involving its cortical areas in the occipital lobe
What is experienced (felt or judged) stimulus magnitude?	The mind's evaluation of the stimulus	Frenquency of firing of the corresponding neural system (including the sensory areas of the cerebral cortex)
What is thinking?	The highest activity of the mind	The activity of certain plastic neural systems
What is self-consciousness?	Inward looking	The monitoring, by certain plastic neural systems, of activity in other neural systems
What is a drive?	A mental conation	A physiological imbalance
What are dreams?	Processes in a part of the mind	Rudimentary and mainly pictorial thinking (a type of brain process)
What is initiative?	Spontaneous movement of the mind	Self-started forebrain process
Why is Z in a happy mood?	Because her mind is in a state of happiness	Because her brain is brimming with biogenic amines
Why is he in pain?	No explanation	Because he got a cut, and the affected nerves activated his brain stem
Why is he so irritable?	Because his wife's naggings have hurt his ego	Because his wife's naggings have overworked his neuroendocrine system
Why is it so hard to express emotions in words?	No explanation	Because emotion is an activity of the right hemisphere, which is mute
Why is human sexuality rather insensitive to level of hormones in blood?	Because it is more psychological than biological	Because sexual arousal and pleasure are hypothalamic activities more strongly influenced by the cerebral cortex than by the endocrine glands

212

Table 10.2. (*contd.*)

Problem	Mentalist account	Psychobiological account
Why do overprotected children grow into helpless adults?	Because their minds are not prepared to face problems	Because they get smaller adrenal glands and are less motivated to face obstacles
Why can we be in conscious states?	Because we are endowed with a mind, part of which is Consciousness	Because our ancestors evolved neural systems capable of being in conscious states, which have a survival value
Why do we sometimes hallucinate?	Either because our mind is fed the wrong information or because it is sick	Either through the activation of the wrong neural systems or because of sick nervous tissue (e.g. excess or defect of some neurotransmitter)
How does voluntary movement come about?	It is caused by the mind ordering the body to move	A plastic neural system in the forebrain (the "seat" of will) activates a motor neural system in the precentral cortex
How did Z recover from his depression?	No explanation	Z was given an antidepressant drug which prevents the breakdown of norepinephrine
Why did our remote ancestors become humanized?	Because they were given a soul	Because some of them were endowed with exceptionally large and plastic associative areas, which enabled them to think up new ideas and to create new things and new ways of life
How did the incest taboo evolve?	Either by grace or by the decree of a wise ruler who acted on moral grounds	Imbreeding amplifies abnormalities, so those human groups that prohibited incest (for whatever reason) had an edge over those which practised it
How do you account for ghosts, telepathy, etc.?	In terms of immaterial and disembodied minds and the like	We do not explain nonexistents, but are ready to explain belief in them

$\mathcal{M}$ 1 in Table 10.1, are mentalist.) The difference boils down to this: whereas mentalism has (simple) explanations for everything mental in mental terms alone, materialism gropes for (usually complex) explanations of the mental in terms of brain processes and possibly social circumstances as well. In order to best appreciate such differences we have taken a nearly random sample of psychological problems and the solutions—sketchy and hypothetical—to them offered by mentalism and by psychobiology (Table 10.2).

Note that the psychobiological accounts do not deny the existence of psychological problems, i.e. they do not eliminate all of the psychological categories but only those without neurophysiological roots. The reduction of psychology to neurophysiology does not involve the denial of the mental and is only partial. (Recall Ch. 3, Sec. 6.) Given the enormous impact of the social milieu on ideation and behavior, the explanation of the latter often calls for the cooperation of social science. This applies in particular to the so-called psychosomatic disorders, such as certain duodenal ulcers. In this case the social behavior of other people acts on the subject's brain, which in turn acts on his stomach. (On the other hand, according to animism, e.g. psychoanalysis, other minds act directly on the subject's mind, which in turn acts on his body.) Ignoring the social level, which is what every good reductionist does, won't do in such cases.

We have been preaching the reduction of psychology to neurophysiology, but have also warned that such reduction can only be partial or weak, and this for two reasons. One reason is that psychology contains certain concepts and statements that are not to be found in today's neuroscience. Consequently neuroscience must be enriched with some such constructs if it is to yield the known psychological regularities and, *a fortiori*, the new ones we would like to know. The second reason for the incomplete reducibility of psychology to neurophysiology is that neuroscience does not handle sociological variables, which are essential to account for the behavior and mentation of the social higher vertebrates. For these reasons the reductionistic effort should be supplemented by an integrative one. Let me explain.

Behavior and mentation are activities of systems that cross a number of real (not just cognitive) levels, from the physical level to the societal one. Hence they cannot be handled by any one-level science. Whenever the object of study is a multilevel system, only a multidisciplinary approach—one covering all of the intervening levels—holds promise. In such cases pig-headed reductionism is bound to fail for insisting on *ab initio* procedures that cannot be implemented for want of the necessary cross-level assumptions. (Take into account that it has not been possible to write down, let alone solve, the Schrödinger equation for a biomolecule, let alone for a neuron, even less for a neuronal system.) In such cases, pressing for reduction is quixotic: it is not a fruitful research strategy. In such cases only the opportunistic (or catch-as-catch-can) strategy suggested by systemism and a multilevel worldview can bring success, for it is the one that integrates the physical, the chemical, the biological, and the sociological approaches, and the one that builds bridges among them (see Bunge, 1980a).

Finally, what about teleological explanation? Some philosophers, notably Taylor (1964) and von Wright (1971), have claimed that, unlike the other sciences, psychology needs teleological explanations, as when we say that so-and-so did that because he wanted to attain this goal. To be sure the psychology of higher vertebrates must reckon with goals. However, (a) goal-seeking behavior can be explained in a scientific fashion, and yet (b) this explanation may be regarded as a special case of causal explanation rather than as a case of empathic understanding (*Verstehen*). Let me explain.

Admittedly, teleological explanations are noncausal if goals are attributed causal efficacy, i.e. are conceived of as future situations pulling on the present. But this is not only teleology: it is nonscience. Not goals but their *brain representation*—i.e. states of expectation—may have causal efficacy. Such current representations (images or thoughts, in particular plans) may be counted among the causal factors leading to behavior seeking to attain them because they are brain events, and every event is bound to have some effect. The schema is neither "Response because cause" (neglect of goal) nor "Response because goal" (neglect of cause) but rather "Response because cause—including brain representation of goal". In sum, although goals *are* peculiar to some vertebrate behavior, they do not call for teleological explanations. Moreover, there are no teleological explanations but, instead, explanations of purposes (not in terms of them). And such explanations can be, nay ought to be, scientific.

2. The threat of dualism and the promise of monism

Motion is change of place of some concrete thing—body, field, or what have you. There is no motion separate from moving things, and things are not the "basis" or "substrate" of motion, nor do they "mediate" motion or are "responsible" for it. Things just move. Likewise there is no chemical reaction aside from what reactants and reaction products do, nor metabolism beyond metabolizing systems, nor social change over and above changing communities. In every science states are states *of* concrete (material) entities, and events are changes of state *of* concrete entities. There is one scandalous exception, though.

The exception is of course mentalist psychology and psychiatry: it is only here (and in idealist philosophies of mind) that talk of mentation alongside or above the brain is tolerated, nay encouraged by a prescientific ideology. This separation between mind and that which does the minding—between function and organ—has kept psychology, psychiatry, and the philosophy of mind estranged from biology (in particular neuroscience and the theory of evolution) and has prevented a full utilization of the scientific approach to the mind–body problem. (In particular "The study of mental evolution has been handicapped by a metaphysical [mind–body] dualism" (Lashley, 1949).) It is not that the mental is beyond the reach of science, but that it has only rarely been approached in a scientific manner. In particular, psychophysical dualism is not a possible scientific hypothesis concerning the mental but an unscientific myth that can be upheld only for ideological reasons.

Our rejecting psychophysical dualism does not force us to adopt eliminative or vulgar materialism in either of its versions—i.e the theses that mind and brain are identical, that there is no mind, or that the capacities for perception, imagination, and even reasoning are inherent in all animals or even in all things. (This last version is of course indistinguishable from panpsychism or primitive animism.) Psychobiology suggests not just psychoneural monism but also emergentism, i.e. the thesis that mentality is an emergent property possessed only by animals endowed with an extremely complex and plastic nervous system. This ability confers on their owners such decisive adaptive advantages, and is related to so many other properties and laws (physiological, psychological, and social), that one is justified in asserting that the organisms endowed with it constitute a level of their own, namely that of psychosystems. However, this is not saying that minds constitute a level of their own, and this simply because there are no disembodied (or even embodied) minds, but only minding brains or, rather, minding animals. In short, minds do not constitute a supra-organic level, because they form no level at all. But psychosystems do.

To repeat the same idea in different words: one can hold that the mental is emergent relative to the merely physical without reifying the former. That is, one can maintain that the mind is not a thing composed of lower level things—let alone a thing composed of no things whatever—but a collection of functions or activities of certain neural systems that individual neurons presumably do not possess. (The primate brain and some of its subsystems can mentate, i.e. be in mental states, but the mind cannot even mind its own business because it has no more independent existence than does mass alongside bodies or history apart from people. Only the functioning—controlling and mentating—brain can mind its own business or rather that of the whole animal.) And so emergentist (or systemic) materialism—unlike eliminative materialism—is seen to be compatible with overall pluralism, or the world view that proclaims the qualitative variety and mutability of reality (see Bunge, 1977a) as well as its level structure (see Bunge, 1979a).

Our espousing emergentist (or systemic) materialism does not entail claiming that it has already solved the mind–body problem. It hasn't and it won't, because emergentist materialism is a philosophy providing only a scaffolding for the detailed scientific investigation of the many problems one carelessly lumps under the rubric "the mind–body problem". It behoves neuroscientists, psychologists, and neurologists to attack these problems—as scientists, not as amateur philosophers or theologians.

However, philosophers are far from behaving as nonparticipant spectators of the scientific investigation of the mind–body problem. (No wonder, for this problem is both scientific and philosophic.) The dualist philosophy of mind has actively blocked for centuries the scientific approach to the problem by denying that brain research could help solve the "mystery" of mind. On the other hand, emergentist materialism contributes to the scientific investigation of the problem by (a) dispelling confusions, (b) exposing myths, and (c) suggesting that all problems traditionally labeled 'mental' be construed as problems concerning brain functions of animals living in natural and possibly also social environments. To be sure emergentist materialism is too new in the science of mind to be anything other than a faith and a program, but it is a reasonable faith rather than a groundless dogma, and it is a promising program rather than a device for discouraging research.

As a matter of fact emergentist materialism has been quite successful: witness the advances of neurophysiology, psychochemistry, psychopharmacology, neurology, and physiological psychology over the past

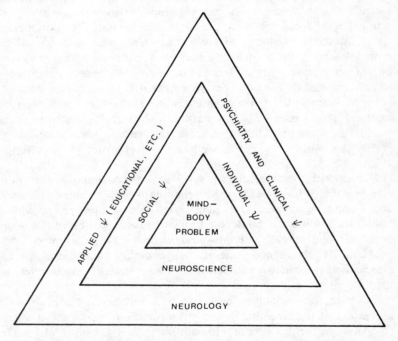

FIG. 10.1. The sciences that grow around the mind–body problem, itself a scientific and philosophical problem. Neuroscience, the basis of all of them, is composed of neuroanatomy and neurophysiology, and their tributaries, neurobiophysics, and neurochemistry.

two decades—all of them inspired by the thesis that perception, emotion, and mentation are brain functions, and their disturbances brain dysfunctions. Admittedly most investigators do not give credit to any philosophy of mind, either because they are unware of their debt or because it is not good form to be seen in the company of a lady of ill repute. But the philosopher of science will not fail to discern the heuristic role of emergentist materialism in the recent advances of the above-mentioned sciences of the brain, as well as in the tendency towards their unification (Fig. 10.1).

Moreover, emergentist materialism is the only philosophy that enjoys the support of all the sciences, has not been concocted *ad hoc* for the mind–body problem, does not promote a quixotic reductionism, and defends neuroscience and psychology against obstruction by obsolete and barren philosophies and ideologies. By so doing it defends the freedom and creativity of man: neither machine to be programmed nor pigeon to be conditioned at will, but the only absolutely creative animal, the one capable of creating a science of the mental and of shaping his own life—for better or worse—in the light of his knowledge and prejudice.

Epilogue: *A Behavioral Approach*
by DONALD O. HEBB

I AM fundamentally in agreement with Professor Bunge's conclusions about the nature of mind. Still, I may venture to suggest some modification of how he sees the contribution made by behavioral science. Psychology may be more sophisticated in a scientific sense, and in more vigorous health, than it appears here (and in most philosophic discussions in this field).

Like Bunge, I am a psychoneural monist. His treatment of the mind–body problem is stimulating and clarifying for me, but he and I have arrived at our similar conclusions from different directions and it is of interest to me to see how the situation looks to one whose background is in physical instead of biological science. Obviously for the monist it must ultimately be possible to find that the mechanisms of thought and consciousness in the activities of the brain are capable of being formulated in neurological terms. And that, fundamentally, is a psychological task. How is psychology progressing with it? In Bunge's eyes, it is evident, psychology does not come off too well. "Behaviorism" looks like an unmitigated mistake; mind and consciousness, though at the heart of the problem, were nevertheless lost to psychology in the modern period, until their recent rediscovery; and theory has been and is ineffectual for lack of being both mathematical in form and neurological in substance. What reply can a psychologist make to such a negative appraisal?

First behaviorism, with a look at the historical record. Behaviorism was founded in 1913 by John B. Watson, and it is absolutely essential to see that he was doing two things, not one. His main contribution was a fundamental reorientation of psychological method. A subsidiary attempt, logically distinct, was to devise a theory compatible with the new method. It was this theory that made the trouble, the only thing for which Watson seems known today. That the theory turned out eventually to be unsatisfactory should not make us forget that Watson almost singlehandedly transformed psychology into an objective bio-logical science, denying the validity of introspective report and showing by example how to work with behavior instead. K. S. Lashley spent the main part of his career refuting Watson's theory of behavior, but nevertheless held that all of modern psychology is deeply in Watson's debt in respect of fundamental method.

The Theory was eventually demolished, but not easily, for it was much stronger logically than one might guess. Even its denial of mind and mental process, its proposal that these are illusory, was not an obvious denial of revealed truth. Mind and mentation are not primary data, immediately given phenomena. As C. S. Peirce first observed, they are known not directly but by inference. Therefore they are theoretical things or events. Further, therefore, it was not nonsense to propose an alternative theory, and when it is considered that the neurology of the day, with great unanimity, made the brain a one-way transmitter of sensory information to muscle and gland with no independent internal activity that might constitute thought, one must see that Watson had good grounds for proposing an exclusively stimulus–response theory of behavior. The theory was wrong, but showing that it was wrong added greatly to our understanding of the mind and mental processes.

I count myself a behaviorist, being convinced especially by George Humphrey (*Thinking*, 1951) that introspective knowledge is illusory at best, and I point out that there are behaviorists and behaviorists. I am glad to align myself with Lashley and E. C. Tolman, both of whom called themselves behaviorists and fought behaviorism in its narrow sense. The terms "mind" and "consciousness" disappeared, more or less, from psychology for 20 or 30 years for their connotation of dualism at that earlier time; but the corresponding conception of controlling cognitive processes remained vigorously active. Lashley himself was prepared to use the terms, but others preferred to talk about "interven-ing variables", "surrogate responses", or "mediating processes". The *problem* did not disappear. The thirties and forties saw the long-drawn-out "continuity–noncontinuity" controversy between those who, still following Watson, denied any role to insight or thought in animal learning (continuity theory), and their opponents, led by Tolman and Lashley. The issue was whether cognitive activity could be shown to affect the shape of the learning curve (discontinuity). The debate ended in effect with a paper by Paul Meehl and Kenneth MacCorquodale in 1951, a peace-making demonstration that expectancy (a mental variable) was not really incompatible with C. L. Hull's neo-Watsonian position.

The neo-Watsonians during this period were a relatively small but energetic minority. Their views became widely known. Those of the great majority were less exciting, but the fact is that mind and thought and consciousness were present in the thought of most psychologists during that period—but *incognito*.

The rapid development of psychological knowledge that began in the fifties, therefore, was not really because psychologists had changed their "ontological presuppositions concerning the mental" but because of new data and new techniques. My book, *The Organization of Behavior*, brought some of these to the attention of psychologists in 1949: Adrian on spontaneous firing by neural cells, for example, or Lorente de Nó on closed circuits in the brain and the importance of summation at the synapse. These were developments of the thirties but because of the war it was only toward the end of the forties that their impact was felt and only then that the new electronic technology became available for experimental use. Once more, the development of biological science was contingent on the prior development of physical science.

As for the idea that psychological theory would be in better shape if it became more neurological and more mathematical, I am myself somewhat skeptical. Ultimately, nonneurological "black-box" formulations must be capable of translation into neurological terms, if consciousness and thought are, as I believe, a state or activity of the brain; but in the present state of knowledge black-box theory can in some situations be the most effective way of making progress. When Tolman 30 years ago proposed the idea of what he called a cognitive map, he added significantly to our understanding of animal intelligence—at a time when there was simply no way of pointing to a neurological mechanism. Now John O'Keefe and Lynn Nadel in *The Hippocampus as a Cognitive Map* (Oxford University Press, 1978) utilize the behavioral relations embodied in Tolman's theoretical idea in establishing a neurological basis for that idea. Its existence, as a black-box formulation, certainly facilitated their neurophysiological research. There are other examples. Indeed, one may repeatedly find in this book such examples of formulations that historically preceded their later translation into specific neurological knowledge. Almost by necessity, the mathematical formulation is an abstraction that must function in this way. Psychology has not been lacking in quantification of its behavioral variables—i.e. quantification with respect to data—but theory has been another matter.

My argument in short is that psychology is not in bad shape, and cell-assembly theory—e.g. in Dalbir Bindra's *Theory of Intelligent Behavior*—is developing considerable explanatory power. It is neurologically based but not mathematical, and I would have said that this is the line that further development would have to take. However, I am impressed by the effectiveness of the more formal propositional style of the present book, as I am also by Alwyn C. Scott's *Neurophysics* (Wiley, 1977). There is more than one path leading to salvation! The dualist-interactionist one cannot lead there; as Professor Bunge argues, it removes the essential problem from the purview of scientific method. But the mathematicizer and the nonmathematicizer within the monistic universe of thought can support one another, and even the black-box theorist has an effective part to play.

Glossary of Technical Terms

Cartesian product. The cartesian product $A \times B$ of sets A and B is the set formed by all the ordered pairs of the form $\langle a, b \rangle$, where a is in A and b is in B. Note that, unless $a = b$, $\langle a, b \rangle \neq \langle b, a \rangle$.

Concept. In philosophy, the unit construct, or indecomposable constituent of a proposition. *Examples*: sets, relations, functions (in particular predicates). In psychology, whatever is conceived rather than just perceived.

Definition. The identification of two concepts. *Examples*: "2 is the successor of 1", "A neural system is *plastic* if and only if its connectivity is variable in time".

Emergence. The appearance of a new quality or of a thing possessing qualitatively new traits. In particular, the emergent properties of a system are those possessed by the system as a whole and lacking in every component of it.

Epistemology. The branch of philosophy concerned with the nature, sources, and reach of human knowledge.

Explanation. The deduction of a given proposition from a set of premises containing laws and data.

Function. In mathematics, a relation between two sets, that assigns each member of the first exactly one of the second. *Standard notation*: $f: A \to B$. The *value* of f at a, where a is a member of A, is designated $f(a)$, a member of B. In biology and technology, a function of a thing is what the thing does. *Example*: a function of the primate brain is to think. Note that, although every purposeful activity is a function of some animal, the converse is false.

Hypothesis. A proposition going beyond the data at hand and subject to correction. *Example*: every law statement is a hypothesis.

Idealism. The set of ontologies (*q.v.*) according to which ideas are autonomous or self-existent. Varieties of idealism: subjective and objective.

Intersection. See *Set-theoretic operations*.

Map. See *Function*.

Materialism. The class of ontologies (*q.v.*) according to which reality is composed exclusively of material or concrete things. *Examples*: physicalism, dialectical materialism, emergentist materialism.

Ontology. The branch of philosophy concerned with the nature of reality. It studies, in particular, the general concepts of thing, change, space, law, causation, life, mind, and society.

Postulate. A hypothesis justified by its logical consequences (theorems, corollaries). Synonym: axiom. The *foundation* of a theory is a set of postulates from which all the formulas of the theory follow.

Predicate. A function (*q.v.*) from some set to a set of propositions. *Example*: "plasticity" is a predicate representing a property of certain subsystems of the brain.

Reduction. A concept is reduced to another if the former is defined (*q.v.*) in terms of the latter. A proposition is reduced to another if the former is explained (*q.v.*) with the help of the latter. *Example*: psychobiology reduces psychological predicates and propositions to biological ones.

Set theoretic operations. The *union* $A \cup B$ of sets A and B is the set containing all As and all Bs. The *intersection* $A \cap B$ contains all and only the elements shared by A and B. The *complement* of A (in a given universe or class) is the set of all elements (of the universe) that are not members of A. The *difference* between sets A and B is the set formed by the members of A that fail to be in B. Notation: $A - B$, or $A \cap \overline{B}$. In general $A - B \neq B - A$. The *symmetric difference* between A and B, or $A \Delta B$, is the set of elements that are not common to A and B, i.e. $A - B \cup B - A$.

Set theoretic relations. The *membership* relation: a belongs to (is in) set A. Notation: $a \in A$. The *inclusion* relation: set A is included in (or is part of) set B if every member of A is also a member of B. Notation: $A \subset B$.

State space. The state space of a thing is the set of all the states a thing can be in. Each species of thing is characterized by one state space. Typically, a state space for a thing is an n-dimensional space formed by the ranges of the functions representing the n properties of the thing. A state of a thing is representable by a point in its state space.

System. A complex object composed of interdependent items. A *conceptual* system, such as a theory, is composed of propositions. A *concrete* (or *material*) system, such as a brain, is composed of material modules, such as molecules or fields. A system σ can be characterized by its composition $\mathscr{C}(\sigma)$, environment $\mathscr{E}(\sigma)$, and structure $\mathscr{S}(\sigma)$ (*q.v.*).

System composition. The composition of a system σ is the set $\mathscr{C}(\sigma)$ of its parts. The A-composition of σ is the set of parts of σ that are kind A, i.e. $\mathscr{C}(\sigma) \cap A$. For example, the cellular composition of the nervous system is the set of its neurons and glial cells.

System environment. The environment of a system σ is the set $\mathscr{E}(\sigma)$ of concrete items not in the composition of σ, that act on, or are acted upon by, components of σ.

System structure. The set of relations among the components of a system or among them and environmental items. The structure of a system includes the connections or bonds among its components. Notation: $\mathscr{S}(\sigma)$.

Theory. A system of logically related propositions.

Bibliography

ACKOFF, R. L., and F. E. EMERY (1972) *On Purposeful Systems*. Chicago: Aldine.

AGASSI, J. (1977) *Towards a Rational Philosophical Anthropology*. The Hague: Martinus Nijhoff.

ALSTON, W. P. (1974) Conceptual prolegomena to a psychological theory of intentional action. In Brown (1974), pp. 71–101.

AMARI, SHUN-ICHI (1977) A mathematical approach to neural systems. In Metzler, pp. 67–117.

ANDERSON, A. R. (ed.) (1964) *Minds and Machines*. Englewood Cliffs, NJ: Prentice-Hall.

ANDERSON, J. A. (1972) A simple neural network generating an interactive memory. *Math. Biosci.* **14**: 197–220.

ANDERSON, J. A. (1973) A theory for the recognition of items from short memorized lists. *Psychol. Rev.* **80**: 417–438.

APTER, M. (1970) *The Computer Simulation of Behavior*. New York: Harper & Row.

ARATESH, A. R., and J. D. ARATESH (1976) *Creativity in Human Development*. New York: Schenkman.

ARBIB, M. A., W. L. KILMER, and D. N. SPINELLI (1976) Neural models and memory. In Rosenzweig and Bennett, pp. 109–132.

ARMSTRONG, D. (1968) *A Materialist Theory of the Mind*. London: Routledge & Kegan Paul.

AYER, A. J. (1963) *The Concept of a Person and Other Essays*. London: Macmillan.

BANDURA, A. (1969) *Principles of Behavior Modification*. New York: Holt, Rinehart & Winston.

BARBER, T. X. (1978) Hypnosis, suggestions, and psychosomatic phenomena. *Am. J. Clin. Hypnosis* **21**: 13–27.

BARTLETT, F., and E. R. JOHN (1973) Equipotentiality quantified: the anatomical distribution of the engram. *Science* **181**: 764–767.

BARTLETT, F. C. (1932) *Remembering: A Study in Experimental and Social Psychology*. Cambridge: Cambridge University Press.

BECHTEREVA, N. P. (1978) *The Neurophysiological Aspects of Human Mental Activity*, 2nd edn. New York: Oxford University Press.

BÉKÉSY, G. VON (1967) *Sensory Inhibition*. Princeton: Princeton University Press.

BELOFF, J. (1962) *The Existence of Mind*. London: MacGibbon & Kee.

BENNETT, E. L. (1976) Cerebral effects of differential experience and training. In Rosenzweig and Bennett, pp. 279–287.

226

BERGSTRÖM, R. M. (1967) Neural macrostates. *Synthese* **17:** 425–443.
BERKOVITZ, L. (ed.) (1964) *Advances in Experimental Social Psychology*, Vol. 1. New York: Academic Press.
BINDRA, D. (1970) The problem of subjective experience. *Psychol. Rev.* **77:** 581–584.
BINDRA, D. (1976) *A Theory of Intelligent Behavior*. New York: Wiley Interscience.
BINDRA, D. (1978) How adaptive behavior is produced: a perceptual–motivational alternative to response–reinforcement. *Behav. Brain Sci.* **1:** 41–52.
BINDRA, D. (ed.) (1980) *The Brain's Mind: A Neuroscience Perspective on the Mind–Body Problem*. New York: Gardner Press.
BISHOP, G. (1956) Natural history of the nerve impulse. *Physiol. Rev.* **36:** 376–399.
BLAKEMORE, C. (1973) The baffled brain. In Gregory and Gombrich, pp. 9–48.
BLAKEMORE, C. (1977) *Mechanics of the Mind*. Cambridge: Cambridge University Press.
BLAKEMORE, C., and F. W. CAMPBELL (1969) Adaptation to spatial stimuli. *J. Physiol.* **200:** 11–13.
BLAKEMORE, C., S. D. IVERSEN, and O. L. ZANGWILL (1972) Brain functions. *A. Rev. Psychol.* **23:** 413–456.
BOGEN, J. E. (1969) The other side of the brain: an appositional mind. *Bull. Los Angeles Neurol. Soc.* **34** (3) 135–162.
BORING, E. G. (1932) The physiology of consciousness. *Science* **75:** 32–39.
BORNSTEIN, M. H. (1975) The influence of visual perception on culture. *Am. Anthropol.* **77:** 744–798.
BORST, C. V. (ed.) (1970) *The Mind–Brain Identity Theory*. London: Macmillan; New York: St. Martin's Press.
BRAIN, LORD (1965) Some aspects of the brain–mind relationship. In Smythies (1965a), pp. 63–79.
BRANDT, R., and J. KIM (1967) The logic of the identity theory. *J. Phil.* **64:** 515–537.
BROAD, C. D. (1949) The relevance of psychical research to philosophy. *Philosophy* **24:** 291–309.
BROAD, C. D. (1962) *Lectures on Psychical Research*. London: Routledge & Kegan Paul; New York: Humanities Press.
BRONOWSKI, J., and U. BELLUGI (1970) Language, name, and concept. *Science* **168:** 669–673.
BROWN, J. (1977) *Mind, Brain, and Consciousness: the Neuropsychology of Cognition*. New York: Academic Press.
BROWN, S. C. (ed.) (1974) *Philosophy of Psychology*. London: Macmillan.
BULLOCK, T. H. (1958) Evolution of neurophysiological mechanisms. In A. Roe and G. G. Simpson (eds.), *Behavior and Evolution*, pp. 165–177. New Haven: Yale University Press.
BULLOCK, T. H. (1977) Identifiable and addressed neurons in the vertebrates. In D. Faber and H. Korn (eds.), *Neurobiology of the Mauthner Cell*, pp. 1–12. New York: Raven Press.
BUNGE, M. (1956) Do computers think? *Br. J. Phil. Sci.* **7:** 139–148; **7:** 212–219.
BUNGE, M. (1959) *Causality*. Cambridge, Mass.: Harvard University Press. Rev. edn.: Dover, 1979.
BUNGE, M. (1963) *The Myth of Simplicity*. Englewood Cliffs, NJ: Prentice-Hall.
BUNGE, M (1967) *Scientific Research*. Berlin, Heidelberg, and New York: Springer-Verlag.
BUNGE, M. (1973a) *Method, Model and Matter*. Dordrecht: Reidel.
BUNGE, M. (1973b) *Philosophy of Physics*. Dordrecht: Reidel.

BUNGE, M. (1974a) *Sense and Reference*. Treatise, Vol. 1. Dordrecht and Boston: Reidel.
BUNGE, M. (1974b) *Interpretation and Truth*. Treatise, Vol. 2. Dordrecht and Boston: Reidel.
BUNGE, M. (1977a) *The Furniture of the World*. Treatise, Vol. 3. Boston: Reidel.
BUNGE, M. (1977b) States and events. In W. E. Hartnett (ed.), *Systems: Approaches, Theories, Applications*. Boston: Reidel.
BUNGE, M. (1977c) Emergence and the mind. *Neuroscience* 2: 501–509.
BUNGE, M. (1977d) General systems and holism. *General Systems* XXII: 87–90.
BUNGE, M. (1979a) *A World of Systems*. Treatise, Vol. 4. Dordrecht and Boston: Reidel.
BUNGE, M. (1979b) The mind–body problem in an evolutionary perspective. In G. Wolstenholme and M. O'Connor (eds.), *Brain and Mind*. Amsterdam and New York: Elsevier, Excerpta Medica, North-Holland.
BUNGE, M. (1979c) Cytoarchitectonic similarity does not entail functional identity. *Behav. Brain Sci.* 1: 350.
BUNGE, M. (1979d) The mind–body problem, information theory, and Christian dogma. *Neurosci.* 4: 453–4.
BUNGE, M. (1980a) From neuron to behavior and mentation: an exercise in levelmanship. In H. Pinsker (ed.), *Information Processing in the Nervous System*. New York: Raven Press.
BUNGE, M. (1980b) The psychoneural identity theory. In Bindra.
BUNGE, M. and R. LLINÁS (1978) The mind–body problem in the light of contemporary neurobiology. *16th World Congress of Philosophy, Section Papers*, pp. 131–133.
BUSER, P. A., and A. ROUGEUL-BUSER (eds.) (1978) *Cerebral Correlates of Conscious Experience*. Amsterdam: North-Holland.
BYNUM, W. F. (1976) Varieties of cartesian experience in early nineteenth century neurophysiology. In S. F. Spicker and H. T. Engelhardt (eds.), *Philosophical Dimensions of the Neuro-medical Sciences*, pp. 15–33. Dordrecht and Boston: Reidel.

CARTWRIGHT, D. S. (1979) *Theories and Models of Personality*. Dubuque: Wm. C. Brown.
CHENG, CHUNG-YING (ed.) (1975) *Philosophical Aspects of the Mind–Body Problem*. Honolulu: University Press of Hawaii.
CHISHOLM, R. M. (1976) *Person and Object: A Metaphysical Study*. La Salle, Ill.: Open Court.
CHOMSKY, N. (1968) *Language and Mind*. New York: Harcourt, Brace & World.
CHRISTIAN, J. J. (1970) Mammalian evolution: is it due to social subordination? *Science* 170: 344–346.
CLARKE, W. N. (1967) Cybernetics and the uniqueness of man. *Proceedings of the 7th Inter-American Congress of Philosophy*, Vol. II, pp. 49–54. Québec: Presses de l'Université Laval.
COLE, M., and I. MALTZMAN (eds.) (1969) *A Handbook of Contemporary Soviet Psychology*. New York: Basic Books.
COOPER, L. (1973) A possible organization of animal memory and learning. In B. Lundqvist and S. Lundqvist (eds.), *Collective Properties of Physical Systems*. New York: Academic Press.
CORNING, W., and M. BALABAN (1968) *The Mind: Biological Approaches to its Functions*. New York: Wiley.

CORNMAN, J. W. (1971) *Materialism and Sensations*. New Haven: Yale University Press.
COTMAN, C. W. (ed.) (1978) *Neuronal Plasticity*. New York: Raven.
COWAN, J. (1976) Are there modifiable synapses in the visual cortex? In Rosenzweig and Bennett, pp. 133–143.
CRAIK, K. J. W. (1943) *The Nature of Explanation*. Cambridge: Cambridge University Press.
CRAIK, K. J. W. (1966) *The Nature of Psychology*. Stephen L. Sherwood (ed.). Cambridge: Cambridge University Press.
CRAVIOTO, J., E. R. DELICARDIE, and H. G. BIRCH (1966) Nutrition, growth and neurointegrative development: an experimental and ecologic study. *Pediatrics* **38** (No. 2, Part II) 319–372.
CULBERTSON, J. T. (1976) *Sensations, Memories and the Flow of Time*. Santa Margarita,. Calif.: The Cromwel Press.

DAVIDSON, D. (1970) Mental events. In L. Foster and J. W. Swanson (eds.), *Experience and Theory*, pp. 79–101. Amherst: University of Massachusetts Press.
DAVIS, W. J. (1976) Plasticity in the invertebrates. In Rosenzweig and Bennett, pp. 430–462.
DELGADO, J. M. R. (1969) *Physical Control of the Mind*. New York: Harper & Row.
DENENBERG, V. H. (1970) The mother as a motivator. In W. J. Arnold and M. M. Page (eds.), *Nebraska Symposium on Motivation*, pp. 69–93. Lincoln: University of Nebraska Press.
DENENBERG, V. H., J. GARBANATI, G. SHERMAN, D. YUTZEY, and R. KAPLAN (1978) Infantile stimulation induces brain lateralization in rats. *Science* **201**: 1150–51.
DESCARTES, *Oeuvres* (C. ADAM and P. TANNERY, eds.) (1909). Paris: Cerf.
DIAMOND, M. C. *et al.* (1976) Effects of environment on morphology of rat cerebral cortex and hippocampus. *J. Neurobiol.* **7**: 75–85.
DIMOND, S. J. (1976) Brain circuits for consciousness. *Brain Behav. Evol.* **13**: 376–395.
DOTY, R. W., Sr. (1965) Philosophy and the brain. *Perspect. Biol. Med.* **9**: 23–34.
DOTY, R. W., Sr. (1975) Consciousness from neurons. *Acta Neurobiol. Exp.* **35**: 791–804.
DREYFUS, H. (1972) *What Computers Can't Do*. New York: Harper & Row.
DUCASSE, C. J. (1951) *Nature, Mind and Death*. La Salle, Ill.: Open Court.
DUNN, A. J. (1976) Biochemical correlates of training experiences: a discussion of the evidence. In Rosenzweig and Bennett, pp. 311–320.

ECCLES, J. C. (1951) Hypotheses relating to the brain–mind problem. *Nature* **168**: 53–64.
ECCLES, J. C. (1965) *The Brain and Unity of Conscious Experience*. Cambridge: Cambridge University Press.
ECCLES, J. C. (ed.) (1966) *Brain and Conscious Experience*. Berlin, Heidelberg and New York: Springer-Verlag.
ECCLES, J. C. (1977) *The Understanding of the Brain*, 2nd edn. New York: McGraw-Hill.
ECCLES, J. C. (1978a) Keynote address to the 4th annual meeting of the ICUS. In *What ICUS Is*. New York: International Cultural Foundation.
ECCLES, J. C. (1978b) *The Human Mystery*. New York: Springer-Verlag.
EDELMAN, G. M., and V. B. MOUNTCASTLE (1978) *The Mindful Brain*. Cambridge, Mass.: MIT Press.
EISDORFER, C., J. NOWLIN, and F. WILKIE (1971) Improvement of learning in the aged by modification of autonomic nervous system activity. *Science* **170**: 1327–1329.

ELLIS, B. (1967) Physical monism. *Synthese* **17**: 141–161.
ERICKSON, C. J., and D. S. LEHRMAN (1964) Effect of castration of male ring doves upon ovarian activity of females. *J. Comp. Physiol. Psychol.* **58**: 164–166.
ESTES, W. K. (1962) Learning theory. In P. R. Farnsworth, O. McNemar, and Q. McNemar (eds.), *Annual Review of Psychology*, Vol. 13. Palo Alto, Calif.: Annual Reviews.

FEIGL, H. (1958) The 'mental' and the 'physical'. In H. Feigl, M. Scriven and G. Maxwell (eds.), *Minnesota Studies in the Philosophy of Science*, Vol. II, pp. 370–497. Minneapolis: University of Minnesota Press.
FEIGL, H. (1960) Mind–body, not a pseudo-problem. In Hoòk, pp. 33–44.
FEIGL, H. (1971) Some crucial issues of mind–body monism. *Synthese* **22**: 295–312.
FENTRESS, J. C. (ed.) (1976) *Simpler Networks and Behavior*. Sunderland, Mass.: Sinauer Associates.
FERNÁNDEZ-GUARDIOLA, A. (ed.) (1979a) *La conciencia*. México: Trillas.
FERNÁNDEZ-GUARDIOLA, A. (1979b) El problema mente-cuerpo. In Fernández-Guardiola, 1979a, pp. 89–105.
FEUERBACH, L. (1843) Grundsätze der Philosophie der Zukunft. In *Kleine philosophische Schriften*. Leipzig: Meiner 1950.
FLOR-HENRY, P. (1976) Lateralized temporal-limbic dysfunction and psychopathology. *Ann. NY Acad. Sci.* **280**: 777–795.
FREEMAN, R. D., and L. N. THIBOS (1973) Electrophysiological evidence that abnormally early visual experience can modify the human brain. *Science* **180**: 876–878.
FREEMAN, W. J. (1973) A model of the olfactory system. In M. A. B. Brazier, D. O. Walter, and D. Schneider (eds.), *Neural Modeling*, pp. 41–72. Los Angeles: UCLA Brain Research Institute, Brain Research Information Service.
FREEMAN, W. J. (1975) *Mass Action in the Nervous System*. New York: Academic Press.
FRONDIZI, R. (1953) *The Nature of the Self: A Functional Interpretation*. New Haven: Yale University Press. Repr. Carbondale, Ill.: Southern Illinois Press, 1971.

GANDELMAN, R., M. X. ZARROW, V. H. DENENBERG, and M. MEYERS (1971) Olfactory bulb removal eliminates maternal behavior. *Science* **171**: 210–211.
GARDNER, R. A., and B. T. GARDNER (1969) Teaching sign language to a chimpanzee. *Science* **165**: 664–672.
GARDNER, B. T., and R. A. GARDNER (1971) Two-way communication with an infant chimpanzee. In A. M. Schrier and F. Stollnitz (eds.), *Behavior of Non-human Primates*, Vol. I, pp. 117–184. New York: Academic Press.
GAZZANIGA, M. S. (1967) The split brain in man. *Sci. Am.* **217** (2): 24–29.
GAZZANIGA, M. S., and J. E. LEDOUX (1978) *The Integrated Mind*. New York and London: Plenum Press.
GHISELIN, M. T. (1973) Darwin and evolutionary psychology. *Science* **179**: 964–968.
GIACOBINI, E. (1971) Molecular mechanisms of nervous transmission and synaptic plasticity. *Prog. Brain Res.* **34**: 243–258.
GIBSON, E. J. (1969) *Principles of Perceptual Learning and Development*. New York: Appleton–Century–Crofts.
GIBSON, J. J. (1966) *The Senses Considered as Perceptual Systems*. Boston: Houghton Mifflin.

GLOBUS, G. G., G. MAXWELL, and I. SAVODNIK (eds.) (1976) *Consciousness and the Brain.* New York and London: Plenum Press.

GLOVER, J. (ed.) (1976) *The Philosophy of Mind.* Oxford: Oxford University Press.

GOLDIN-MEADOW, S., and H. FELDMAN (1977) The development of language-like communication without a language model. *Science* 197: 401–403.

GOLDMAN, P. S., and J. H. NAUTA (1977) Columnar distribution of cortico–cortico fibres, etc. *Brain Res.* 122: 393–413.

GOODY, J. (1977) *The Domestication of the Savage Mind.* Cambridge: Cambridge University Press.

GOSLAN, D. A. (1969) *Handbook of Socialization Theory and Research.* Chicago: Rand McNally.

GRAY, J. A. (1972a) The psychophysiological nature of introversion–extroversion. In Nebylitsyn and Gray, pp. 182–205.

GRAY, J. A. (1972b) Learning theory, the conceptual nervous system, and personality. In Nebylitsyn and Gray, 372–399.

GRAY EATON, G. (1976) The social order of Japanese macaques. *Sci. Am.* 235 (4): 96–106.

GREENO, J. G. (1974) Representation of learning as discrete transition in a finite state space. In D. Krantz, R. Duncan Luce, and P. Suppes (eds.), *Learning, Memory, and Thinking,* pp. 1–43. San Francisco: W. H. Freeman.

GREENOUGH, W. T., R. W. WEST, and T. J. DeVOOGD (1978) Subsynaptic plate perforations: changes with age and experience in the rat. *Science* 202: 1096–1098.

GREGORY, F. (1977) *Scientific Materialism in Nineteenth Century Germany.* Dordrecht and Boston: Reidel.

GREGORY, R. L. (1970) *The Intelligent Eye.* London: Weidenfeld & Nicolson; New York: McGraw-Hill.

GREGORY, R. L. (1973) The confounded eye. In Gregory and Gombrich, pp. 49–98.

GREGORY, R. L., and E. H. GOMBRICH (eds.) (1973) *Illusion in Nature and Art.* London: Duckworth.

GRENE, M. (ed.) (1971) *Interpretations of Life and Mind.* London: Routledge & Kegan Paul.

GRIFFIN, D. R. (1976) *The Question of Animal Awareness.* New York: Rockefeller University Press.

GRIFFITH, J. S. (1967) *A View of the Brain.* Oxford: Clarendon Press.

GROSS, C. G., and H. P. ZEIGLER (eds.) (1969) *Readings in Physiological Psychology. Motivation.* New York: Harper & Row.

GROVES, P. M., and R. F. THOMPSON (1970) Habituation: a dual-process theory. *Psych. Rev.* 77: 419–450.

GROVES, P. M., and G. V. REBEC (1976) Biochemistry and behavior. *A. Rev. Psychol.* 27: 91–127.

GRUBER, H., and P. H. BARRETT (1974) *Darwin on Man: A Psychological Study of Scientific Creativity, together with Darwin's Early and Unpublished Notebooks.* New York: E. P. Dutton.

GUNDERSON, K. (1970) Asymmetries and mind–body perplexities. In M. Radner and S. Winokur (eds.), *Minnesota Studies in the Philosophy of Science,* Vol. IV, pp. 207–309. Minneapolis: University of Minnesota Press.

HAMILTON, W. D. (1971) Geometry of the selfish herd. *J. Theoret. Biol.* 31: 295–311.

HAMPSHIRE, S. (ed.) (1966) *Philosophy of Mind.* New York: Harper & Row.
HARLOW, H. F. (1958) The evolution of learning. In Roe and Simpson, pp. 269–290.
HARTLEY, D. (1749) *Observations on Man,* 2 vols. London: J. Leake & W. Frederick.
HEATH, R. G. (1977) Subcortical brain function correlates of psychopathology and epilepsy. In C. Shagass, S. Gershon and A. Friedhoff (eds.), *Psychopathology and Brain Dysfunction,* pp. 51–67. New York: Raven Press.
HEBB, D. O. (1949) *The Organization of Behavior.* New York: Wiley.
HEBB, D. O. (1959a) Intelligence, brain function and the theory of mind. *Brain* **82:** 260–275.
HEBB, D. O. (1959b) A neuropsychological theory. In S. Koch (ed.), *Psychology: The Study of a Science,* Vol. I, pp. 622–643. New York: McGraw-Hill.
HEBB, D. O. (1966) *A Textbook of Psychology.* Philadelphia: W. B. Saunders.
HEBB, D. O. (1968) Concerning imagery. *Psychol. Rev.* **75:** 466–477.
HEBB, D. O. (1974) What psychology is about. *Am. Psychol.* **29:** 71–79.
HELD, R., and A. HEIN (1963) Movement-produced stimulation in the development of visually guided behavior. *J. Comp. Physiol. Psychol.* **56:** 872–6.
HERRICK, C. J. (1949) A biological survey of integrative levels. In Sellars *et al.,* pp. 222–242.
HESS, W. R. (1968) *The Biology of Mind.* Chicago: University of Chicago Press.
HINDE, R. A. (1974) *Biological Bases of Human Social Behaviour.* New York: McGraw-Hill.
HIPPOCRATES (1948) Airs Waters Places. In *Hippocrates,* Vol. I, pp. 65–137. The Loeb Classical Library. Cambridge, Mass.: Harvard University Press.
HOBSON, J. A., and R. W. MCCARLEY (1977) The brain as a dream state generator. *Am. J. Psychiat.* **134:** 1335–1348.
HOOK, S. (ed.) (1960) *Dimensions of Mind.* New York: New York University Press.
HOYLE, G. (1976) Approaches to understanding the neurophysiological bases of behavior. In John C. Fentress (ed.), *Simpler Networks and Behavior,* pp. 21–38. Sunderland, Mass.: Sinauer Associates Inc.
HUBEL, D. H., and T. N. WIESEL (1962) Receptive fields, binocular interaction, and functional architecture in the cat's visual cortex. *J. Physiol.* **160:** 106–154.
HUBEL, D. H., and T. N. WIESEL (1963) Receptive fields and functional architecture of monkey striate cortex. *J. Physiol.* **165:** 559–568.
HULL, C. L. (1943) *Principles of Behavior.* New York: Appleton–Century–Crofts. .
HUME, D. (1739) *A Treatise of Human Nature* (Selby-Bigge, ed.). Oxford: Clarendon Press.
HUMPHREY, G. (1951) *Thinking.* London: Methuen.

JAMES, W. (1890) *Principles of Psychology.* Repr. New York: Dover, 2 vols. 1950.
JAMES, W. (1912) *Essays in Radical Empiricism.* New York: Longmans.
JAYNES, J. (1976a) *The Origin of Consciousness in the Breakdown of the Bicameral Mind.* Boston: Houghton Mifflin.
JAYNES, J. (1976b) The evolution of language in the late Pleistocene. *Ann. NY Acad. Sci.* **280:** 312–325.
JERISON, H. J. (1973) *Evolution of the Brain and Intelligence.* New York: Academic Press.
JOHN, E. R. (1972) Switchboard vs. statistical theories of learning and memory. *Science* **177:** 850–864.

JOHN, E. R., and D. KLEINMAN (1975) 'Stimulus generalization' between differentiated visual, auditory, and central stimuli. *J. Neurophysiol.* **38:** 1015–1034.

JOHN, E. R., F. BARTLETT, M. SHIMOKOCHI, and D. KLEINMAN (1973) Neural readout from memory. *J. Neurophysiol.* **36:** 893–924.

JONES, E. (1961) *The Life and Work of Sigmund Freud* (edited and abridged by L. Trilling and S. Marcus). New York: Basic Books.

KANDEL, E. R. (1976) *Cellular Basis of Behavior.* San Francisco: W. H. Freeman.

KATZ, J. J. (1976) A hypothesis about the uniqueness of natural language. *Ann. NY Acad. Sci.* **280:** 33–41.

KAWAI, M. (1965) Newly acquired pre-cultural behavior of the natural troop of Japanese monkeys on Koshime Islet. *Primates* **6:** 1–30.

KETY, S., and S. MATTHYSSE (1975) *Catecholamines and their Enzymes in the Neuropathology of Schizophrenia.* Oxford: Pergamon Press.

KEUTH, H. (1974) Objective knowledge out of ignorance: Popper on body, mind, and the third world. *Theory and Decision* **5:** 391–412.

KIM, J. (1971) Materialism and the criteria of the mental. *Synthese* **22:** 323–345.

KIM, J. (1972) Phenomenal properties, psychological laws, and the identity theory. *Monist* **56:** 117–192.

KNEALE, W. (1962) *On Having a Mind.* Cambridge: Cambridge University Press.

KONORSKI, J. (1967) *Integrative Activity of the Brain.* Chicago: University of Chicago Press.

KOOB, G. F., P. J. FRAY, and S. D. IVERSEN (1976) Tail-pinch stimulation: sufficient motivation for learning. *Science* **194:** 637–639.

KORTLAND, A. (1955) Aspects and prospects of the concept of instinct (vicissitudes of the hierarchy theory). *Arch. Néerland. Zool.* **11:** 155–284.

KOSHLAND, D. E., Jr. (1977) A response regulator model in a simple sensory system. *Science* **196:** 1055–1063.

KRIPKE, S. (1971) Identity and necessity. In M. K. Munitz (ed.), *Identity and Individuation*, pp. 135–164. New York: New York University Press.

KUPFERMANN, I. (1975) Neurophysiology of learning. *Ann. Rev. Psychol.* **26:** 367–391.

KUPFERMANN, I., and K. R. WEISS (1978) The command neuron concept. *Behav. Brain Sci.* **1:** 3–39.

LA METTRIE, J. O. (1745) *Histoire naturelle de l'âme.* In *Textes choisis.* Paris: Éditions Sociales, 1954.

LASHLEY, K. S. (1949) Persistent problems in the evolution of mind. *Q. Rev. Biol.* **24:** 28–42.

LAUGHLIN, C. D., and E. G. d'AQUILI (1974) *Biogenetic Structuralism.* New York: Columbia University Press.

LENNEBERG, E. H. (1967) *Biological Foundations of Language.* New York: Wiley.

LENNEBERG, E. H. (1970) Brain correlates of language. In F. O. Schmitt (ed.), *The Neurosciences: Second Study Program*, pp. 361–371. New York: Rockefeller University Press.

LETTVIN, J. Y., H. MATURANA, W. S. McCULLOCH, and W. H. PITTS (1959) What the frog's eye tells the frog's brain. *Proc. IRE*, Vol. 47, 1940–1959.

LEVINE, M. (1974) *A Cognitive Theory of Learning.* Hillside, NJ: Lawrence Erlbaum Associates.

LEVY, J. (1977) The mammalian brain and the adaptive advantage of cerebral asymmetry. *Ann. NY Acad. Sci.* **299**: 264–272.

LIEBERMAN, P., and E. S. CRELIN (1971) On the speech of Neanderthal man. *Linguistic Inquiry* **2**: 203–222.

LIEBERMAN, P. (1975) *On the Origins of Language: An Introduction to the Evolution of Human Speech.* New York: Macmillan.

LIEBERMAN, P. (1976) Interactive models for evolution: neural mechanisms, anatomy, and behavior. *Ann. NY Acad. Sci.* **280**: 660–672.

LIEBESKIND, J. C., and L. A. PAUL (1977) Psychological and physiological mechanisms of pain. *Ann. Rev. Psychol.* **28**: 41–60.

LLINÁS, R., and M. BUNGE (1978) Restricted applicability of the concept of command in neuroscience: dangers of metaphors. *Beh. and Brain Sci.* **1**: 30–31.

LOCKE, J. (1690). *An Essay Concerning Human Understanding.* London: George Routledge & Sons, s.d.

LORENZ, K. (1971) *Studies in Animal and Human Behaviour,* 2 vols. (R. Martin, transl.) Cambridge, Mass.: Harvard University Press.

LUDWIG, J. (1978) *Philosophy and Parapsychology.* Buffalo, NY: Prometheus Books.

LURIA, A. R. (1966) *Human Brain and Psychological Processes.* (Transl. B. Haigh.) New York: Harper & Row.

LURIA, A. R. (1969) Speech development and the formation of mental processes. In Cole and Maltzman, pp. 121–162.

LURIA, A. R. (1973) *The Working Brain. An Introduction to Neurophysiology.* Harmondsworth: Penguin.

LURIA, A. R. (1976) *Cognitive Development. Its Cultural and Social Foundations.* Cambridge, Mass.: Harvard University Press.

McCULLOCH, W. S. (1965) *Embodiments of Mind.* Cambridge, Mass.: MIT Press.

McDOUGALL, W. (1911) *Body and Mind: A History and a Defense of Animism.* London: Methuen.

MACGREGOR, R. J., and E. R. LEWIS (1977) *Neural Modeling.* New York and London: Plenum Press.

McGUIGAN, F. J., and R. A. SCHOONOVER (eds.) (1973) *The Psychophysiology of Thinking: Studies of Covert Processes.* New York: Academic Press.

MACKAY, D. M. (1978) Selves and brains. *Neuroscience* **3**: 599–606.

MACNAB, R. M., and D. E. KOSHLAND, Jr. (1972) The gradient-sensing mechanism in bacterial chemotaxis. *Proc. Natn. Acad. Sci. USA* **69**: 2509–2512.

MAGOUN, H. W. (1958) *The Waking Brain.* Springfield, Ill.: Charles C. Thomas.

MALCOLM, N. (1964) Scientific materialism and the identity theory. *Dialogue* **III**: 115–125.

MALCOLM, N. (1973) Thoughtless brutes. *Proc. Addresses of the Am. Phil. Ass.* **46**: 5–20.

MALSBURG, C. VON DER (1973) Self-organization of orientation sensitive cells in the striate cortex. *Kybernetik* **14**: 85–100.

MARGOLIS, J. (1978) *Persons and Minds.* Dordrecht and Boston: Reidel.

MARLER, P., and M. TAMURA (1964) Culturally transmitted patterns of vocal behavior in sparrows. *Science* **146**: 1483–1486.

MARR, D. (1970) A theory for cerebral cortex. *Proc. R. Soc. (London)* **B176**: 161–234.

MASTERTON, R. B., C. B. G. CAMPBELL, M. E. BITTERMAN, and N. HOTTON (eds.) (1976a) *Evolution of Brain and Behavior in Vertebrates.* Hillsdale, NJ: Erlbaum.

MASTERTON, R. B., W. HODOS, and H. JERISON (eds.) (1976b) *Evolution, Brain, and Behavior*. Hillsdale, NJ: Erlbaum.

MEEHL, P. (1966) The compleat autocerebroscopist: a thought experiment on Professor Feigl's mind/body identity thesis. In P. K. Feyerabend and G. Maxwell (eds.), *Mind, Matter and Method*, pp. 103–180. Minneapolis: University of Minnesota Press.

MENZEL, E. W., Jr., R. K. DAVENPORT, and C. M. ROGERS (1972) Protocultural aspects of chimpanzee's responsiveness to novel objects. *Folia primat.* **17**: 161–170.

METZLER, J. (1977) *Systems Neuroscience*. New York: Academic Press.

MEYER, D. R. (1971) The habits and concepts of monkeys. In Leonard E. Jarrard (ed.), *Cognitive Processes in Nonhuman Primates*, pp. 83–102. New York and London: Academic Press.

MILLER, G. A. (1964) *Mathematics and Psychology*. New York: Wiley.

MILLER, G. A., E. GALANTER, and K. H. PRIBRAM (1960) *Plans and the Structure of Behavior*. New York: Holt, Rinehart & Winston.

MILLER, N. E. (1969) Learning of visceral and glandular responses. *Science* **163**: 434–445.

MILNER, P. (1970) *Physiological Psychology*. New York: Holt, Rinehart & Winston.

MILNER, P. (1974) A model for visual shape recognition. *Psychol. Rev.* **81**: 521–535.

MILNER, P. (1977) A purposive behavior model. In William E. Hartnett (ed.), *Systems: Approaches, Theories, Applications*, pp. 159–168. Dordrecht and Boston: Reidel.

MOORE, R. Y. (1976) Synaptogenesis and the morphology of learning and memory. In Rosenzweig and Bennett, pp. 340–347.

MORRIS, C. W. (1938) *Foundations of the Theory of Signs. Encyclopedia of Unified Science*, Vol. I, pp. 77–137. Chicago: University of Chicago Press, 1955.

MOUNTCASTLE, V. B. (1957) Modality and topographic properties of single neurons of cat's somatic sensory cortex. *J. Neurophysiol.* **20**: 408–434.

MOUNTCASTLE, V. B. (1967) The problem of sensing and the neural coding of sensory events. In Quarton, Melnechuk, and Schmitt, pp. 393–408.

MOUNTCASTLE, V. B. (1975) The view from within: pathways to the study of perception. *The Johns Hopkins Med. J.* **136**: 109–131.

MOUNTCASTLE, V. B. (1978) Some neural mechanisms for directed attention. In Buser and Rougeul-Buser, pp. 37–51.

MOUNTCASTLE, V. B., and T. P. S. POWELL (1959) Central nervous mechanisms subserving position sense and kinesthesis. *Bull. Johns Hopkins Hosp.* **105**: 173–171.

MUNN, N. L. (1971) *The Evolution of the Human Mind*. Boston: Houghton Mifflin.

MYERS, R. D., and C. L. MELCHIOR (1977) Alcohol drinking: abnormal intake caused by tetrahydropapaveroline in brain. *Science* **196**: 554–556.

NAGEL, T. (1974) What is it like to be a bat? *Philosoph. Rev.* **83**: 435–450.

NASS, M. M., and L. N. COOPER (1975) A theory for the development of feature detecting cells in visual cortex. *Cybernetics* **19**: 1–18.

NEBYLITSYN, V. D., and J. A. GRAY (eds.) (1972) *Biological Basis of Individual Behavior*. New York: Academic Press.

NEISSER, U. (1963) The imitation of man by machine. *Science* **139**: 193–197.

NEISSER, U. (1967) *Cognitive Psychology*. New York: Appleton–Century–Crofts.

NEISSER, U. (1976) *Cognition and Reality*. San Francisco: Freeman.

O'CONNOR, J. (ed.) (1969) *Modern Materialism: Readings on Mind–Body Identity*. New York: Harcourt, Brace & World.

O'KEEFE, J., and L. NADEL (1978) *The Hippocampus as a Cognitive Map*. Oxford: Clarendon Press.

OLDS, J., and P. MILNER (1954) Positive reinforcement produced by electrical stimulation of septal area and other regions of rat brain. *J. Comp. Physiol. Psychol.*, 47: 419–427.

OMENN, G. S., and A. G. MOTULSKY (1972) Biochemical genetics and the evolution of human behavior. In L. Ehrman, G. S. Omenn, and E. Caspari (eds.), *Genetics, Environment and Behavior: Implications for Educational Policy*, pp. 129–172. New York: Academic Press.

OSTWALD, W. (1902) *Vorlesungen über Naturphilosophie*. Leipzig: Veit.

PAGANO, R. P., R. M. RÖSE, R. M. STIVERS, and S. WARRENBURG (1976) Sleep during transcendental meditation. *Science* 191: 308–310.

PAILLARD, J. (1976) Réflexions sur l'usage du concept de plasticité en neurobiologie. *J. psychologie* 73: 33–47.

PAIVIO, A. (1971) *Imagery and Verbal Processes*. New York: Holt, Rinehart & Winston.

PATTERSON, F. (1978) Conversations with a gorilla. *National Geographic* 154: 438–465.

PAVLOV, I. P. (1955) *Selected Works*. Moscow: Foreign Languages Publ. House.

PELLIONISZ, A., and R. LLINAS (1979) Brain modeling by tensor network theory and computer simulation. *Neuroscience* 4: 323–348.

PENFIELD, W. (1958) *The Excitable Cortex in Conscious Man*. Springfield, Ill.: C. C. Thomas.

PENFIELD, W. (1966) Speech, perception and the uncommitted cortex. In Eccles (1966), pp. 216–248.

PENFIELD, W. (1975) *The Mystery of the Mind: A Critical Study of Consciousness and the Human Brain*. Princeton: Princeton University Press.

PENFIELD, W., and T. RASMUSSEN (1950) *The Cerebral Cortex of Man*. New York: Macmillan.

PEPPER, S. (1960) A neural-identity theory of mind. In Hook, pp. 37–56.

PÉREZ, R., L. GLASS, and R. SHLAER (1975) Development of specificity in the cat visual cortex. *J. Math. Biol.* 1: 275–288.

PERKINS, M. (1971) Matter, sensation, and understanding. *Am. Phil. Qt.* 8: 1–12.

PIAGET, J. (1968) Explanation in psychology and psychophysiological parallelism. In P. Fraisse and J. Piaget (eds.), *Experimental Psychology*, Vol. I, pp. 153–191. London: Routledge & Kegan Paul.

PIAGET, J. (1971) *Biology and Knowledge*. Chicago: University of Chicago Press.

PIAGET, J. (1976) *Le comportement, moteur de l'évolution*. Paris: Gallimard.

PINCUS, J. H., and G. J. TUCKER (1974) *Behavioral Neurology*. New York: Oxford University Press.

PLACE, U. T. (1956) Is consciousness a brain process? *Br. J. Psychol.* XLVII: 44–51.

POLTEN, E. (1973) *Critique of the Psycho-Physical Identity Theory*. The Hague and Paris: Mouton.

POMERANZ, B., R. CHENG, and P. LAW (1977) Acupuncture reduces electrophysiological and behavioral responses to noxious stimuli: pituitary is implicated. *Exp. Neurol.* 54: 172–178.

POPPER, K. R. (1972) *Objective Knowledge*. Oxford: Clarendon Press.

POPPER, K. R. (1974) Autobiography. In P. A. Schilpp (ed.), *The Philosophy of Karl R. Popper*, Book I. La Salle, Ill.: Open Court.

POPPER, K. R., and J. C. ECCLES (1977) *The Self and Its Brain*. New York: Springer International.

POWELL, T. P. S., and V. B. MOUNTCASTLE (1959) Some aspects of the functional organization of the cortex of the postcentral gyrus of the monkey: a correlation of findings obtained in a single unit analysis with cytoarchitecture. *Bull. Johns Hopkins Hosp.* **105:** 133–162.

POWERS, W. T. (1973) *Behavior: The Control of Perception.* Chicago: Aldine.

PREMACK, D. (1971) Language in chimpanzee? *Science* **172:** 808–822.

PREMACK, D., and G. WOODRUFF (1978) Does the chimpanzee have a theory of mind? *Behav. Brain Sci.* **1:** 515–526.

PRIBRAM, K. (1960) The intrinsic systems of the forebrain. In J. Field, H. W. Magoum, and V. Hall (eds.), *Handbook of Physiology*, Vol. II. Washington, DC: Am. Physiol. Society.

PRIBRAM, K. H. (1971a) *Languages of the Brain.* Englewood Cliffs, NJ: Prentice-Hall.

PRIBRAM, K. H. (1971b) The realization of mind. *Synthese* **22:** 313–322.

PRICE, H. H. (1952) Survival and the idea of 'another world'. In Smythies (1965a), pp. 1–24.

PRIESTLEY, J. (1817–1832) *The Theological and Miscellaneous Works*, 25 vols. (J. T. Rutt, ed.). London: G. Smallfield. See in particular *Disquisitions Relating to Matter and Spirit.*

PRIESTLEY, J. (1962) *Selections from his Writings* (I. V. Brown, ed.). University Park, Pa.: The Pennsylvania State University Press.

PROVENCE, S., and R. LIPTON (1962) *Infants in Institutions.* New York: International Universities Press.

PUCCETTI, R. (1973) Brain bisection and personal identity. *Br. J. Phil. Sci.* **24:** 339–355.

PUCCETTI, R. (1974) Physicalism and the evolution of consciousness. *Can J. Phil.* Supplementary Vol. 1, Part **2:** 171–183.

PUCCETTI, R. (1977) Sperry on consciousness: a critical appreciation. *J. Med. Phil.* **2:** 127–144.

PUCCETTI, R., and R. W. DYKES (1978) Sensory cortex and the mind–body problem. *Behav. Brain Sci.* **1:** 337–346.

PUTNAM, H. (1960) Minds and machines. In Hook, pp. 148–179.

QUARTON, G. C., T. MELNECHUK, and F. O. SCHMITT (eds.) (1967) *The Neurosciences: A Study Program.* New York: Rockefeller University Press.

QUINE, W. VAN ORMAN (1953) On mental entities. *Proc. Am. Acad. Arts Sci.* **80:** 198–203.

QUINE, W. VAN ORMAN (1960) *Word and Object.* Cambridge, Mass.: MIT Press.

QUINTON, A. (1965) Mind and matter. In J. R. Smythies (1965a), pp. 201–233.

RAMÓN Y CAJAL, S. (1923) *Recuerdos de mi vida.* Madrid: Francisco Beltrán.

RASHEVSKY, N. (1972) Some remarks on the central nervous system. *Bull. Math. Biophys.* **34:** 231–242.

REDMOND, D. E., Jr., J. W. MASS, A. KLING, C. W. GRAHAM, and H. DEKIRMENJIAN (1971) Social behavior of monkeys selectively depleted of monoamines. *Science* **174:** 428–431.

RESTLE, F. (1971) *Mathematical Models in Psychology. An Introduction.* Harmondsworth: Penguin.

RITTER, W., R. SIMON, H. G. VAUGHAN, Jr, and D. FRIEDMAN (1979) A brain event related to the making of a sensory discrimination. *Science* **203:** 1358–1361.

ROBINSON, D. N. (1978) *The Mind Unfolded: Essays on Psychology's Historic Texts.* Washington, DC: University Publications of America.

ROE, A., and G. G. SIMPSON (eds.) (1958) *Behavior and Evolution.* New Haven: Yale University Press.

ROMANES, G. J. (1895) *Mind and Motion and Monism.* London: Longmans.

RORTY, R. (1965) Mind–body identity, privacy, and categories. *Rev. Metaphys.* **19**: 24–54.

ROSE, S. (1976) *The Conscious Brain,* updated edition. New York: Vintage Books.

ROSEN, R. (1974) Planning, management, policies and strategies. *Int. J. Gen. Systems* **1**: 245–252.

ROSENBLUETH, A. (1970) *Mind and Brain.* Cambridge, Mass.: MIT Press.

ROSENBLUETH, A., and N. WIENER (1950) Purposeful and non-purposeful behavior. *Phil. Sci.* **17**: 318–326.

ROSENBLUETH, A., N. WIENER, and J. BIGELOW (1943) Behavior, purpose and teleology. *Phil. Sci.* **10**: 18–24.

ROSENZWEIG, M. R., and E. L. BENNETT (eds.) (1976) *Neural Mechanisms of Learning and Memory.* Cambridge, Mass., and London: MIT Press.

ROTHERNBERG, A., and B. GREENBERG (1976) *The Index of Scientific Writings on Creativity, 1566–1974.* Hamden, Conn.: Archon Books.

RUMBAUGH, D. M., T. V. GILL, and E. VON GLASERSFELD (1973) Reading and sentence completion by a chimpanzee (*Pan*). *Science* **182**: 731–733.

RUSSELL, B. (1921) *The Analysis of Mind.* London: George Allen & Unwin.

RUSSELL, B. (1959) *My Philosophical Development,* Ch. 2. London: George Allen & Unwin.

RUTLEDGE, L. T. (1976) Synaptogenesis: effects of synaptic use. In Rosenzweig and Bennett, pp. 329–339.

RYLE, G. (1949) *The Concept of Mind.* London: Hutchinson.

RYLE, G. (1954) *Dilemmas.* Cambridge: Cambridge University Press.

SACKS, O. (1976) *Awakenings,* rev. edn. New York: Vintage Books.

SAVAGE-RUMBAUGH, E. S., D. M. RUMBAUGH, and S. BOYSEN (1978a) Symbolic communication between two chimpanzees (*Pan troglodytes*). *Science* **201**: 641–644.

SAVAGE-RUMBAUGH, E. S., D. M. RUMBAUGH, and S. BOYSEN (1978b) Linguistically mediated tool use and exchange by chimpanzees (*Pan troglodytes*), *Behav. Brain Sci.* **1**: 539–554.

SAYRE, K. (1976) *Cybernetics and the Philosophy of Mind.* Atlantic Highlands, NJ: Humanities Press.

SCHACHTER, S. (1964) The interaction of cognitive and physiological determinants of emotional states. In Berkovitz.

SCHACHTER, S., and J. E. SINGER (1962) Cognitive, social, and physiological determinants of emotional state. *Psychol. Rev.* **69**: 379–399.

SCHAPIRO, S., M. SALAS, and K. VUKOVICH (1970) Hormonal effects on ontogeny of swimming ability in the rat: assessment of central nervous system development. *Science* **168**: 147–151.

SCHARRER, E., and B. SCHARRER (1963) *Neuroendocrinology.* New York: Columbia University Press.

SCHLICK, M. (1925) *General Theory of Knowledge* (transl. A. E. Blumberg). Vienna and New York: Springer-Verlag, 1974.

SCHMITT, F. O. (1967) Molecular parameters in brain function. In J. D. Roslansky (ed.), *The Human Mind*, pp. 111–138. Amsterdam: North-Holland.

SCHMITT, F. O. (ed.) (1970) *The Neurosciences: Second Study Program*. New York: Rockefeller University Press.

SCHMITT, F. O., G. QUARTON, and T. MELNECHUK (eds.) (1967) *The Neurosciences: An Intensive Study Program*. New York: Rockefeller University Press.

SCHNEIRLA, T. C. (1949) Levels in the psychological capacities of animals. In Sellars *et al.*, pp. 243–286.

SCHWARTZ, E. L. (1977) Spatial mapping in the primate sensory projection: analytic structure and relevance to perception. *Biol. Cybernetics* **25:** 181–194.

SCOTT, T. R., and D. A. POWELL (1963) Measurement of a visual motion after-effect in the rhesus monkey. *Science* **140:** 57–59.

SEBEOK, T. A., (ed.) (1977) *How Animals Communicate*. Bloomington, Ind.: Indiana University Press.

SELLARS, R. W. (1922) *Evolutionary Naturalism*. Chicago: Open Court.

SELLARS, R. W., V. J. McGILL, and M. FARBER (eds.) (1949) *Philosophy for the Future: The Quest of Modern Materialism*. New York: Macmillan.

SELLARS, W. (1963) *Science, Perception and Reality*. London: Routledge & Kegan Paul.

SELLARS, W. (1965) The identity approach to the mind–body problem. *Rev. Metaphys.* **18:** 430–451.

SELLARS, W. (1975) The adverbial theory of the objects of sensations. *Metaphil.* **6:** 144–160.

SHAFFER, J. A. (1977) Personal identity: the implications of brain bisection and brain transplants. *J. Med. Phil.* **2:** 147–161.

SHALLICE, T. (1972) Dual functions of consciousness. *Psychol. Rev.* **79:** 383–393.

SHERRINGTON, C. (1906) *The Integrative Action of the Nervous System*. New York: Charles Scribner's Sons.

SIEGEL, R. K., and L. J. WEST (eds.) (1975) *Hallucinations: Behavior, Experience and Theory*. New York: Wiley.

SKINNER, B. F. (1953) *Science and Human Behavior*. New. York: Free Press.

SMART, J. J. C. (1959) Sensations and brain processes. *Phil. Rev.* **68:** 141–156.

SMART, J. J. C. (1963) *Philosophy and Scientific Realism*. London: Routledge & Kegan Paul.

SMITH, W. JOHN (1965) Message, meaning, and context in ethology. *Am. Nat.* **99:** 405–409.

SMYTHIES, J. R. (ed.) (1965a) *Brain and Mind*. London: Routledge & Kegan Paul.

SMYTHIES, J. R. (1965b) The representative theory of perception. In Smythies (1965a), pp. 241–264.

SNYDER, S. (1974) *Madness and the Brain*. New York: McGraw-Hill.

SOMMERHOFF, G. (1974) *Logic of the Living Brain*. New York: Wiley.

SOURKES, T. (1962) *Biochemistry of Mental Disease*. New York: Harper & Row.

SPERRY, R. W. (1964) Neurology and the mind–body problem. In R. Isaacson (ed.), *Basic Readings in Neuropsychology*, pp. 403–429. New York: Harper & Row.

SPERRY, R. W. (1966) Brain bisection and mechanisms of consciousness. In Eccles (1966), pp. 299–293.

SPERRY, R. W. (1969) A modified concept of consciousness. *Psychol. Rev.* **76:** 532–536.

SPERRY, R. W. (1970) An objective approach to subjective experience: further explanation of a hypothesis. *Psychol. Rev.* **77:** 585–590.

SPERRY, R. W. (1974) Lateral specialization in the surgically separated hemispheres. In F. O. Schmitt and F. G. Worden (eds.), *3rd Neurosciences Program*. Cambridge, Mass.: MIT Press.

SPERRY, R. W. (1976) Mental phenomena as causal determinants in brain function. In Globus *et al.*, pp. 163–177.

SPERRY, R. W. (1977a) Forebrain commisurotomy and conscious awareness. *J. Med. Phil.* **2**: 101–126.

SPERRY, R. W. (1977b) Reply to Professor Puccetti. *J. Med. Phil.* **2**: 145–146.

SPICKER, S. F., and H. T. ENGELHARDT, Jr. (eds.) (1976) *Philosophical Dimensions of the Neuro -medical Sciences*. Dordrecht and Boston: Reidel.

SPINELLI, D. N., and F. E. JENSEN (1978) Plasticity: the mirror of experience. *Science* **203**: 75–78.

STENT, G. S. (1973) A physiological mechanism for Hebb's postulate of learning. *Proc. Natn. Acad. Sci. USA* **70**: 997–1001.

SUTHERLAND, N. S. (1970) Is the brain a physical system? In R. Borger and F. Cioffi (eds.), *Explanation in the Behavioral Sciences*, pp. 97–122. Cambridge: Cambridge University Press.

SZENTÁGOTHAI, J., and M. A. ARBIB (1974) Conceptual models of neural organization. *Neurosci. Res. Program. Bull.* **12**: 307–510.

SZENTÁGOTHAI, J. (1978) The neuron network of the cerebral cortex. *Proc. Roy. Soc. London* **B 201**: 219–248.

TAYLOR, C. (1964) *The Explanation of Behaviour*. London: Routledge & Kegan Paul.

TAYLOR, J. (1976) The advantage of spacing-out. *J. Theoret. Biol.* **59**: 485–490.

TAYLOR, J. G., and E. BALANOVSKI (1979) Are there any scientific explanations of the paranormal? *Nature* **279**: 631–633.

THOM, R. (1972) *Stabilité structurelle et morphogenèse*. Reading, Mass.: W. A. Benjamin.

THOMPSON, R. F. (1975) *Introduction to Physiological Psychology*. New York: Harper & Row.

THORPE, W. H. (1966) Ethology and consciousness. In Eccles (1966), pp. 470–505.

TIBBETTS, P. (1972) Popper's critique of the instrumentalist account of theories and theoretical terms. *Southern J. Phil.* **10**: 57–70.

TINBERGEN, N. (1965) Behavior and natural selection. In J. A. Moore (ed.), *Ideas in Modern Biology*, pp. 521–545. Garden City, NY: Natural History Press.

TOULMIN, S. (1971) Brain and language: a commentary. *Synthese* **22**: 369–395.

TOULMIN, S. (1972a) *Human Understanding*. Princeton: Princeton University Press.

TOULMIN, S. (1972b) The mentality of man's brain. In A. G. Karczmar and J. C. Eccles (eds.), *Brain and Human Behavior*, pp. 409–422. New York, Heidelberg, and Berlin: Springer-Verlag.

TURING, A. M. (1950) Computing machinery and intelligence. *Mind* NS **59**: 433–460.

UTTAL, W. R. (1978) *The Psychobiology of Mind*. Hillsdale, NJ: Erlbaum.

VALDÉS, M. (1979) Sentidos del término 'conciencia'. In Fernández-Guardiola, 1979a, pp. 21–33.

VESEY, G. N. A. (ed.) (1964) *Body and Mind*. London: George Allen & Unwin.

VESEY, G. N. A. (1965) *The Embodied Mind*. London: George Allen & Unwin.

VIGOTSKII, L. S. (1962) *Thought and Language* (transl. E. Hanfman and G. Vakar). Cambridge, Mass.: MIT Press.

VINOGRADOVA, O. (1970) Registration of information and the limbic system. In G. Horn and R. A. Hinde (eds.), *Short Term Changes in Neural Activity and Behavior*, pp. 95–140. Cambridge: Cambridge University Press.

VON FOERSTER, H. (1965) Memory without record. In D. P. Kimble (ed.), *The Anatomy of Memory*, pp. 388–433. Palo Alto, Calif.: Science and Behavior Books.

WADE SAVAGE, C. (1976) An old ghost in a new body. In Globus *et al.*, pp. 125–153.

WALLEY, R. E., and T. D. WEIDEN (1973) Lateral inhibition and cognitive masking: a neuropsychological theory of attention. *Psychol. Rev.* **80:** 284–302.

WATANABE, S. (1975) Can the cognitive process be totally mechanized? In Cheng, pp. 182–199.

WEIZENBAUM, J. (1976) *Computer Power and Human Reason*. San Francisco: W. H. Freeman.

WELKER, W. (1976) Brain evolution in mammals. In Masterton *et al.* (1976a), pp. 251–343.

WERNER, G. (1970) The topology of the body representation in the somatic afferent pathway. In F. O. Schmitt (ed.), *The Neurosciences: Second Study Program*, pp. 605–616. New York: Rockefeller University Press.

WHITEHEAD, A. N. (1920) *The Concept of Nature*. Cambridge: Cambridge University Press.

WICKELGREN, W. A. (1974) Strength/resistance theory of the dynamics of memory storage. In D. H. Krantz *et al.*, *Contemporary Developments in Mathematical Psychology*, Vol. I: *Learning, Memory, and Thinking*, pp. 208–242. San Francisco: W. H. Freeman.

WIESEL, T. N., and D. H. HUBEL (1965) Comparison of the effects of unilateral and bilateral eye closure on cortical unit responses in kittens. *J. Neurophysiol.* **28:** 1029–1040.

WILSON, H. R. (1975) A synaptic model for spatial frequency adaptation. *J. Theoret. Biol.* **50:** 327–352.

WILSON, H. R., and J. D. COWAN (1973) A mathematical theory of the functional dynamics of cortical and thalamic nervous tissue. *Kybernetik* **13:** 55–80.

WITTGENSTEIN, L. (1967) *Zettel*. Ed. by G. E. M. Anscombe and G. H. von Wright. Oxford: Blackwell.

WOOLLACOTT, M., and G. HOYLE (1977) Neural events underlying learning in insects: changes in pacemaker. *Proc. R. Soc. Lond.* B **195:** 395–415.

WORDEN, F. G., J. P. SWAZEY, and G. ADELMAN (eds.) (1975) *The Neurosciences: Paths of Discovery*. Cambridge, Mass.: MIT Press.

WRIGHT, G. H. VON (1971) *Explanation and Understanding*. Ithaca, NY: Cornell University Press.

YOUNG, J. Z. (1965) The organization of a memory system. *Proc. R. Soc.* B **163:** 285–320.

YOUNG, J. Z. (1971) *An Introduction to the Study of Man*. Oxford: Clarendon Press.

YOUNG, J. Z. (1973) Memory as a selective process. In Australian Academy of Science, *Report: Symposium on Biological Memory*, pp. 25–45. Canberra.

YOUNG, J. Z. (1978) *Programs of the Brain*. Oxford: Oxford University Press.

ZANGWILL, O. L. (1976) Thought and the brain. *Brit. J. Psychol.* **67**: 301–314.

ZEEMAN, E. C. (1965) Topology of the Brain. In Medical Research Council, *Mathematics and Computer Science in Biology and Medicine*, pp. 277–292. London: Her Majesty's Stationery Office.

ZIEDINS, R. (1971) Identification of characteristics of mental events with characteristics of brain events. *Am Phil. Q.* **8**: 13–23.

Index of Names

Index of Subjects